For Kitty, Clay, Callie, and Careen

SALLY RAND

Sally Rand

American Sex Symbol

William Hazelgrove

LYONS
PRESS

Guilford, Connecticut

An imprint of The Rowman & Littlefield Publishing Group, Inc.
4501 Forbes Blvd., Ste. 200
Lanham, MD 20706
www.rowman.com

Distributed by NATIONAL BOOK NETWORK

British Library Cataloguing in Publication Information available

Library of Congress Cataloging-in-Publication Data

Names: Hazelgrove, William Elliott, 1959– author.
Title: Sally Rand : American sex symbol / William Hazelgrove.
Description: Guilford, Connecticut : Lyons Press, 2019. | Includes
  bibliographical references and index.
Identifiers: LCCN 2019006108 (print) | LCCN 2019008839 (ebook) | ISBN
  9781493038602 (e-book) | ISBN 9781493038596 (hardback : alk. paper)
Subjects: LCSH: Rand, Sally, 1904-1979. | Actors—United States—Biography. |
  Stripteasers—United States—Biography.
Classification: LCC PN2287.R243 (ebook) | LCC PN2287.R243 H39 2019 (print) |
  DDC 792.02/8092 [B] —dc23
LC record available at https://lccn.loc.gov/2019006108

CONTENTS

CONTENTS

I wish I'd lived a profound life, been able to produce great and wonderful things to advance the state of man. But I haven't. Not many people's lives are very profound. And perhaps those whose lives we look upon as profound don't realize it themselves.

—SALLY RAND

October 19, 2019

I FOLLOWED JOHN RUSSICK OF THE CHICAGO HISTORY MUSEUM DOWN into the basement of the building. I had been going upstairs to the archives for some time, poring over the sixty-one boxes of Sally Rand's papers. Like a coal miner trying to find a diamond in the dark, I had become fatigued with the letters, the articles, the suits, the divorces, the detritus of any life that has been lived fully. This would take me out of Western Union telegrams, cursive diatribes, and onionskin missives into something tangible. I was going to see Sally Rand's ostrich feather fans from the World's Fair of 1933.

They were in a deep freeze in the bowels of the Chicago History Museum, a department store–size refrigerator that kept the oxidation at bay and slowed chemical decomposition. John assured me the fans were still in good shape as we went down the polished steps and through several doors, walking down a long corridor past boxes and large plastic-sheeted, rolling closets full of clothes, costumes, uniforms from people who had lived a hundred years before. Down here in the basement of the Chicago History Museum, history had been frozen and the fight against time and circumstance was being waged.

Finally, we approached a large silver door not unlike that of a meat locker. John grabbed a handle and pulled back the door. We were now in the largest refrigerator I had ever seen. Hallways of items stretched down before me, all kept at low temperatures to freeze microbes in place. John, the curator of the museum, approached a long white box and pulled off the lid.

"Here they are," he announced.

I leaned over the seven-pound fans and took some photos with my phone. Then I just stared. They were still white but had curled inward and were fixed in place. The four-foot ostrich feathers that Sally Rand had waved at the World's Fair of 1933 after she crashed the opening night and become world famous now resembled giant moles of fluff. John moved the feathers and showed me the handles Sally would have grasped, moving the feathers fast enough to keep herself covered. The feathers were not impressive, really. The wingspan that had lifted a twenty-nine-year-old girl from the Ozarks into the bright light of world-wide fame was gone.

There was a slight whirring of the refrigeration pumps. The creak of time. John pointed out Nathan Leopold's glasses from the Leopold and Loeb murder case in Chicago, where Clarence Darrow defended the two murderers. The glasses had been left at the scene of the crime and sealed their fate. The tortoiseshell rims looked like something an accountant might wear. I took a few more pictures, and then John sealed the box and we went back out into the warmer air. We walked up the stairs back to the fast world of 2019. Ostrich feathers. Eyeglasses. It is the conundrum of history . . . how a butterfly's wing can create such a breeze.

The butterflies wing of Sally Rand's life is problematic. Her life was a frenetic arc that left behind the boxes of newspaper clippings, telegrams, letters, lawsuits, the detritus of a life lived. Somewhere in this intersection of newspaper articles, recollections, diaries, letters, interviews, is the life of one Sally Rand. The reason there are so literally different versions of the same event is that Sally Rand was a master of illusion. She made her living off a sleight of hand, luring people into another world for about eight minutes with lighting, giant ostrich feathers, and the lure of a body that might or might not be nude. So why should the records of her life be any less opaque? She habitually made up her own past as she was in show business from age fourteen.

So that leaves us with only the story. Facts will be a match of putting letters against recollections against official documents. He said. She said. But verisimilitude (that which is most true) is not established by finding a letter in a trunk in an attic. It is established by the life lived, and this we do know: there is a life here. A big life. The life of Sally Rand is large, and the big events match up and the arc is there. It is the journey and not the destination, for even her feathers in the basement of the Chicago History Museum are surrounded by doubt. The museum had supposedly turned her down decades before when she wanted to donate them. Another story is that her donation of the fans was part of a publicity stunt surrounding a show, and she bought new ones to donate. Frankly, who knows, and does it matter?

Sally Rand's life was wide and varied, and it would take a much larger book than this to catalog all her shows, all her lawsuits, depositions, business ventures, interviews, court proceedings, arrests, bankruptcies, accidents, and the very jazzed-up world that was her life in show business ever since she was fourteen. She lived to be seventy-five and so that would be sixty-one years on the road. So, really, I chose to focus on what turned Helen Beck into Sally Rand, and then how that life played out in the cultural zeitgeist of America in the twentieth century. Born in the year 1904, she came of age as did the country in that American Century.

What really matters is that Sally Rand is a rags-to-riches Prohibition-era story that transcended her time. She became a star in the worst year of the Great Depression by riding a white horse into the middle of the 1933 Chicago World's Fair. She lived large in the early and middle decades of the American Century and was one of the first to become famous for being famous. And in death she left us all wondering who exactly she was. Just as she did in her life. It is fitting for a woman who made her living off of an illusion that the story of her life will be a sleight of hand as well. The Rand may be quicker than the eye as she often said, but even a glimmer of stardust will come to earth eventually.

Let's go find her.

Prologue

1933

SALLY RAND STEPPED INTO THE SPEEDBOAT BUMPING THE DOCK OUT-
side the World's Fair of 1933 in Chicago. The Century of Progress had
ended for the year. The five-foot, 125-pound blond had single-handedly
made the fair profitable and now she had to get up to the north side of
Chicago, and the fastest way to do it was by boat. Lake Michigan was
calm, but it was dark, and fall was in the air. She stepped down into the
back of the boat, and it roared into the September night.

The country was in the fourth year of the Great Depression, and
some said it was the worst yet. A third of the banks in Chicago had
failed. People were starving and living in tents outside the city. The city
was broke. Al Capone had been hustled off to jail in 1931, but his soup
kitchens had fed many all over Chicago when the city didn't have a dime
to help people. But there had been the fair, and it had been a shining light
in a coal mine of darkness.

It was the second fair after the Columbian Exposition of 1893 and
could not have been more different. As I wrote in *Al Capone and the 1933
World's Fair*, "Forty years after the Columbian Exposition and Dr. H. H.
Holmes's macabre, psychopathic murders of many young women in 1893,
Chicago decided it was time to have another world's fair. The times and
the reasons differed, though. Orville and Wilber Wright had left the
earth for twelve seconds in Kitty Hawk, North Carolina, in 1903. The
Titanic had met black ice in the Atlantic and had already been resting on

the bottom of the ocean for two decades. The beaux arts tradition of 1893 had been left in the dust for a modernist vision of the world promoted by industry, architecture, and advertising."[1]

Sally Rand sat in the boat with the wind smoothing back her hair. She looked toward the city glittering in the third decade of the American Century and felt her pulse rise. The boat veered suddenly, and Sally was catapulted out of the back into the depths of Lake Michigan. She bobbed up and saw the boat still barreling toward the North Shore.

And now. Now the famous starlet of Cecil B. DeMille films, the trapeze artist, the David Sennett stuntwoman, the nationally famous fan dancer of the Chicago World's Fair found herself alone in the dark lake that was still warm from a hot summer. She stared at Chicago glittering along the lakefront. She could hear the bell from the lighthouse station but that was all. She was simply alone now, and for a girl who had come from nothing, a hillbilly from the Ozarks who had conquered the world and become famous, this was nothing short of amazing.

And what a perfect metaphor. Tossed out of a speeding boat after her triumphant run at the Chicago World's Fair, she could stare at the city that she had triumphed over. One cannot consider the life of Sally Rand without considering that other character of equal importance in her life, the Chicago World's Fair of 1933. It is the perfect storm of Sally Rand's intersection with this singular event that produced the synthesis of time, circumstance, place, and personality that created the iconic symbol of hope handed down to us as Sally Rand. It is the combustion of her interaction with the phenomenon that was the Chicago World's Fair of 1933 that made her a star and set the course of her life. The World's Fair years gave her a platform that would run for forty years, and one could make a case that the glimmer of the fair, the fairy dust sprinkled upon her began to slowly erode after she left Chicago, until eventually, it was all gone.

The *Chicago Daily News* on August 16, 1933, would later cover her rescue from the lake with an explanation of why she was leaving the fair. "Her descent into the waves came dramatically a few moments after Sally had left A Century of Progress Exposition following a farewell performance, having, it was reported, demanded a considerable raise in monetary emoluments for the dance. . . . having definitely concluded her appearances in the Streets of Paris, Sally dressed and boarded a speedboat for a hurried run to a north side night club."[2] The accompanying photo would show a waterlogged Sally wrapped in a blanket, looking like a wet teenager though she was touching thirty. The Columbian Exposition of 1893 had really set her up. As Cheryl Ganz wrote in *The 1933 Chicago World's Fair*, "The 1893 World's Columbian Exposition had served as one of Chicago's springboards for this transformation of public entertainment. Novelty ruled the day and the public loved it. Throngs packed the fair's beer gardens, thrilled to the Ferris Wheel, and gaped at the belly dancer Fahreda Mahzar—also known as Little Egypt, who gyrated in ways never witnessed by middle-class Americans."[3]

And so, the cooch dance was added to burlesque shows, and promoters learned from the 1893 fair that a good burlesque added to the coffers of any fair. Farm towns were deserted as old and young all over the Midwest went to see the "hoochie coochie," which often involved the dancer going topless. "The dancers appeared as part of the freak show attractions and in burlesque, providing an exhibition of direct, wordless, female eroticism and exoticism."[4]

But really, we have to go back further. To the evolving urban, commercial-driven consumer culture that would make a section of the fair known as the Midway phenomenally successful. Charles Dawes, who would finance the fair, reminded his brother Rufus, who was the president of the World's Fair Association, "What is going to draw your crowds is not museums or scientific charts or similar museum exhibits . . . people come to see a show, the great surviving memory of the Chicago World's Fair being the Midway."[5] People came to see the oddities, breathe the caramel popcorn–scented air, and duck into darkened tents to watch nude women dance or to watch a young blond dance behind two seven-foot ostrich feathers.

America was in transition. "The commercialization of popular amusements earlier in the century had signaled the rise of a new expressive urban culture . . . A Century of Progress opened during the peak of the Great Depression, and though expendable resources were few to none, many fairgoers still sought ways to satisfy their new taste for thrills."[6] The World's Fair of 1933 was a creature born in the worst times with many different purposes. It was to be a fair of science, of the future, a fair to jump-start the economy. "Not unlike Roosevelt's New Deal programs, a fair would, the planners predicted, counter the Depression's insidious economic and psychological impact by giving Chicago and its labor force a shot in the arm . . . the fair would be a privately organized New Deal."[7]

When twenty-eight-year-old Sally Rand is finally fished out of Lake Michigan, she is sitting in a Coast Guard station in a *Chicago Tribune* photo and we see the girl next door with stringy wet hair. Where did all that sex go? If you watch her comeback film, *The Sunset Murder Case*, you see the same daughter of America. There is a Judy Garland quality about her. She has that vulnerability. She is a bad actress in a very bad film. Her delivery is all wrong. The actors around her are B actors at best. The story is hackneyed, but there is something there that makes you root for Sally Rand if not fall in love with her. There is a determination, a spirit, a hope, an optimism, that transcends sex, that transcends the feather dance. Sally Rand is nothing short of the hope of the early twentieth century in the worst of times wrapped up in a five-foot bundle of energy that will not stop until she draws her last chain-smoking breath in 1979.

The sixty-one boxes at the Chicago History Museum of Sally Rand's papers are crumbling letters, yellowed newspaper articles, fragile Western Union telegrams, onionskin letters, faded cursive letters, long judgments, tax liens, car titles, brochures, baby manuals. One goes through these tan boxes looking for clues, and it can be frustrating for there is no hard answer as to why Sally Rand become famous when others did not. The dancer Faith Bacon had performed the fan dance years before Sally did. Others were better dancers, better strippers, actresses, more beautiful, more intelligent. But we don't know their names.

Who then is Sally Rand? She is like the changing, silky Lake Michigan water that she was floating around in, wondering if anyone would rescue her. This is where she marveled at her rise as she stared at those glittering buildings in the night. Maybe she could hear the traffic. Maybe an approaching boat, a seagull. She had been literally sleeping in alleys just a few years before, and now she was a star who could write her own ticket.

Like Sally Rand, the World's Fair of 1933 was a bet against logic. "When the Great Depression came crashing down, many thought people would never spend money on a fair in the bleakest times America had ever known. In 1933, when the fair opened, 15 million people were unemployed, and one-third of the banks had failed."[8] It was really based on hope. Hope that times will get better. Hope that the country will get through the Great Depression. Hope that a dream can become a reality. Hope that a hillbilly from the Ozarks could become rich and famous. And like any cultural force, we really can only define a person by their life. Anything else will be false.

So, the young girl in the water will wait to be rescued while we look for a life that began almost thirty years before. Helen Beck was all of three years old when Teddy Roosevelt held her in his lap and she looked up at the man who had charged up San Juan Hill. She remembered he smelled like a cigar. Like the audacious young country that would eventually rule the twentieth century, Sally Rand changed her life by sheer will, using the only assets she had: her body, a white horse, a boat, and sheer guts.

CHAPTER ONE

Crashing the Chicago World's Fair

May 27, 1933

SHE IS GLIDING TOWARD DESTINY. SHE IS GLIDING THROUGH THE COOL-ing night air toward a group of Chicago's well-to-do on the night before the opening of the World's Fair of 1933. Sally Rand's story begins here. Her life begins here. This is where Sally Rand will become the Sally Rand the world knows. On a boat on a white horse with nothing between her and the world except some flesh paint, a cape, an ankle bracelet, a wig. There is a scent of dead fish. The slightly swampy smell of Lake Michigan at night. The brooding lament of the lighthouse and a chiming from the halyards slapping the masts of moored sailboats along Chicago's lake-front. The music from the piece of land that would eventually be called Northerly Island reaches her ears faintly. The smell of the horse reminds her of her home in the Ozarks. That was a million years ago.

Now she is cold and goose bumped as the rumrunner makes its way toward the backside of the Chicago World's Fair. Sally Rand feels the blond wig ride up from her shoulders as she holds the horse's bridle. She has nothing on except a blond wig, body paint, and, we must assume, but maybe not, a G-string. Let's assume there is no G-string. Sally liked to wear nothing, and she did it often. The twenty-nine-year-old chugging toward the yacht landing of the fair was about to crash the biggest party in Chicago, riding a white horse with (maybe) nothing on except a cape and a blond wig.

Four decades after the Columbian Exposition of 1893, Chicago was doing it again with the 1933 World's Fair glibly named The Century of Progress. It was faintly comic coming during the worst year of the Great Depression, but fair president Rufus Dawes dedicated the moment: "We pledge ourselves to the use of this land for the enjoyment, education, and entertainment of the people of the world. The exposition will fittingly portray the history of Chicago and be worthy of the city's proud position among the cities of the world."[1]

Chicago had built a fair during the worst times in the history of the United States if not the world. Producer Herman Shumlin described a New York City scene for Studs Terkel's *Hard Times: An Oral History of the Great Depression*: "Two or three blocks along Times Square, you'd see these men, silent, shuffling along in line. Getting this handout of coffee and doughnuts, dealt out from great trucks, Hearst's *New York Evening Journal*, in large letters, painted on the sides. Shabby clothes, but you could see they had been pretty good clothes. Their faces, I'd stand and watch their faces and I'd see that flat, opaque, expressionless look which spelled for me human disaster."[2]

In Chicago 120,000 people were out of work. Churches ran soup kitchens, but they were small and ineffectual. Except for one thriving soup kitchen at 935 South State, which was feeding 2,200 men three times a day at a cost of $300 a day. Women in aprons served men at tables of eight. Soup and coffee and doughnuts were available around the clock, and the word was Al Capone was responsible. People would credit the gangster with saving their lives.

But tonight was a dinner for the top-drawer crowd of Chicagoans at a hundred dollars a plate held in the ballroom at the fair. "Inside the Streets of Paris concession, Chicago's elite enjoyed the fair's glitzy Parisian-themed opening extravaganza. It was quite a show. Everyone who mattered was there, laughing and dancing and enjoying lovely food at the Café de la Paix."[3] The star Arcturus, which forty years before had beamed its pinpoint of light at the earth, would open the World's Fair officially. Starlight striking a photoelectric cell would race through Western Union lines toward Chicago and then close a relay that would fire up a generator and light up the Chicago World's Fair of 1933. Of course, it didn't work, but they threw the switch anyway, and the fair was on.

Sally was heading for the Midway: the part of the fair where fairgoers could see bawdy acts and strange human oddities. "For those seeking an escape from the Depression's doldrums, the Midway was pure magic. Concessions included entertainment other than fan dancers and peep shows."[4] But it was May 27, 1933, and a respectable crowd of the upper crust of Chicago cheered and celebrated their own good fortune when many slept in tents outside the city limits.

The woman sitting astride the snow-white horse heard the cheer and watched the colored lights shoot up into the heavens. She pulled the white velvet cape around her and felt the wind pass over her loins and breasts. Sally Rand, aka Helen Gould Beck from Missouri, was staring at the dock coming closer. There were no fences walling off Lake Michigan, and so, like an army approaching by sea, she was floating directly toward the main fairgrounds that led to the Streets of Paris, where the party was taking place. Sally thought about the possibility of her falling off the horse, but now was not the time to worry. Now was the time to show the world who Sally Rand was.

Eddie, her boss at the Paramount Club, jumped out of the boat as the bow bumped the yacht landing. Then he snugged the boat close to the dock. A man on the dock stood openmouthed as Sally jammed her bare heels into the sides of the horse and galloped into the cooling night of the World's Fair.

Sally Rand could hear the commotion as she guided the horse through the Streets of Paris, instinctively homing in on the center of the celebration. This was her moment. She would either be thrown in jail or become famous. Maybe both. "The horse galloped through the warm night with the smell of rich food cooking and a soft breeze of perfume, cologne, and cigars. Her long blonde hair flew back as the white horse clattered down the cobblestone lanes of Paris."[5] Sally Rand's heart thumped in her chest as she heard people shouting. She saw a policeman raise his hand and shout, and then she hit the stage with the iron horseshoes on wood as the photographers' bulbs flashed her into infamy.

CHAPTER TWO

The Lap of Teddy Roosevelt

1904

A HILLBILLY HAD JUST TUMBLED INTO THE EARLY YEARS OF THE CENtury. The nineteenth century was still an echo in 1904, when Helen Gould Beck was born on Easter Sunday, April 4, at eleven a.m. in Elkton, Missouri, in the Ozark Mountains. The year she was born, Teddy Roosevelt won his first election after inheriting the presidency following William McKinley's assassination. She would later tell Studs Terkel, "I was born in the last naïve moment America was ever to enjoy, between the Spanish American War and the First World War."[1] Sally ended up in Roosevelt's lap at a social after a conference to which her father was invited due to his riding with the big man up San Juan Hill. It would seem fate had marked her for greatness. Her mother, Mary Annette Grove, was a teacher; her friends called her Nettie.

A Pennsylvania Dutch Quaker, Nettie had a lively mind and liked to discuss the politics of the day. She was pretty, with high cheekbones and blond hair. In later pictures with her famous daughter, they would mirror each other. She had met Corporal William Beck in Elkton, Missouri, and they had married. Beck, a West Point graduate and just back from the Spanish-American War, probably had the restlessness that Teddy Roosevelt demanded of his men. After riding up the hills of San Juan, settling down to family life was hard, and he didn't take the time to get to know his new daughter, Helen.

Her father had followed Teddy Roosevelt in Cuba and charged up San Juan Hill in 1898. He had been alongside Roosevelt and was close enough to inhale the reflected glory of the man who one day would be president. William Beck had been born in Illinois, and after a stint as a tailor he joined the army and shipped out for Cuba with the Rough Riders. He seemed to crave the discipline and order of army life. A pencil-thin scar slashed across his forehead and chin were testament to his years in Cuba. This was clearly the high point of William Beck's life. The dust and the blood, the heat, and, of course, the undaunted fearless man with thick glasses charging up San Juan Hill changed his life forever and gave the rest of it the patina of gentle rain after the fierce storm of TR's war. Like many men of his time, Beck, along with Roosevelt, believed a man lived large in battle, and when the young post office clerk met Mary Annette Grove at a party, he was still unsettled from the great adventure of his life.

Mary had just moved to Elkton from Kansas City to be a teacher. Seventeen and pretty, she was taken with square-jawed William Beck, who exuded military command even though at 5 foot 6 he was four inches shorter than Mary. They married in 1903. A violent temper showed the road not taken was eating up young William, and a strange religiosity combined with a hard-edged asceticism put the former cavalry man at odds with his more cultured wife, who bore him another child, a son, Harold Lawton, in 1908.

Helen and Harold would spend time swimming in a nearby river, Plumly Tar. A radio interview years later painted a picture of the farm years as idyllic. Sally "talked as tenderly and lyrically as any poet about the sudden pink of apple blossoms in the Missouri spring, summer nights in the country when you can hear a rhythmical insect chorus through the murmurous dark, the supper time fragrance of hickory smoked ham and browning potatoes."[2]

The family scrimped along, staying with Grandpa Beck on the family farm. Eventually, all the Becks would become dependent financially on the blond girl with blue eyes and curly golden hair who ran around barefoot. For now, they were a family in the lean years of the early century in the hardscrabble world of the Ozarks. Sally Rand's hickish accent combined with a lisp would betray her hillbilly roots and ruin her Hollywood career in later years, but for now she adored her father and mother.

In 1910 Colonel Beck moved his family to Kansas City. It would not last. Sally attended the Greenwood Grammar Russian Ballerina School while the family stayed temporarily at the Savoy Hotel. The same year Anna Pavlova started on her first tour of the United States, which would pass through Kansas City. The young Russian ballerina would put Helen Beck on a course that would take her to Hollywood, Chicago, and beyond. Sally Rand's feather dance is Anna Pavlova's *The Dying Swan*. The story conveyed by the Russian ballerina in four minutes tells the story of a swan's last moments; the struggle against death. Anna Pavlova would perform *The Dying Swan* four thousand times in her lifetime and on her deathbed would call for her *Swan* costume. Mikhail Fokine designed the dance when Pavlova wanted a solo for a 1905 concert. The young ballerina first presented it in St. Petersburg, Russia. She based her inspiration on swans she had seen in public parks and Lord Tennyson's poem "The Dying Swan."

Fokine gave her a dance that changed her life and the world. "It was revolutionary then and illustrated admirably the transition between the old and the new . . . it is a dance of the whole body and not of the limbs only; it appeals not merely to the eye but to the emotions and the imagination."[3] Pavlova then went on a tour of the United States, and in Missouri a ten-year-old saw her dance. The little girl fell in love with performing. Helen managed to see dancing, get books, watch nickelodeons . . . anything to glimpse the bigger world. Horatio Alger novels of the rags-to-riches variety were not known to her, but they had seeped into American culture, and if America grew anything in abundance during the early part of the twentieth century, big dreams were the mightiest crop.

What she saw in *The Dying Swan* was beauty, tragedy, the coming to life of the blue herons Helen had seen on the river close to her home. French critic Andre Levinson summed up the dance that Sally Rand would later emulate: "Arms folded, on tiptoe, she dreamily and slowly circles the stage. By even, gliding motions of the hands, returning to the background from whence she emerged, she seems to strive toward the horizon, as though a moment more and she will fly—exploring the confines of space with her soul. The tension gradually relaxes, and she sinks to the earth, arms waving faintly as in pain. Then tattering with irregular steps toward the edge of the stage—leg bones quiver like the strings of a harp—by one swift forward gliding motion of the right foot to earth, she sinks on her left knee—the aerial creature struggling against the earthly bonds, and there transfixed by pain, she dies."[4]

Sally Rand's ambition was to become a ballerina. She later told Studs Terkel, "I sat up and wept uncontrollably. At that moment, there was born this true knowledge: I was going to be a dancer, a ballerina."[5] Sally watched Pavlova's four-minute dance and cemented her soul to the freeing beauty of the dying swan taking final flight.

The family returned to Elkton. William Beck took a job at the post office and found himself restless. Maybe it was the domesticity that did not sit well with Beck. Trouble had found him early when at the age of sixteen a bully knocked him down in the street in 1890. "My head was swimming. I kept blacking out, my eyes wouldn't focus. I could only see him dimly. Just as he got hold of me, I went backwards, he on top of me and the gun went off."[6] The armed Beck had shot and killed Tommy Mashburn, a man twice his weight. He was tried and sent to prison before being let out a year later, pardoned after it was determined he was only acting in self-defense. The violence of the Ozarks would follow him into two major wars.

The last glorious war won by men on horseback must have haunted him at night while he was listening to his wife and children breathing in the Missouri night. Buried. All glory behind him, he needed to reconnect with the warrior heart or at least the wandering heart. A conference hosted by President Teddy Roosevelt rescued him from his angst-ridden soul. The man. Teddy Roosevelt was within his reach again, and he and Helen were heading to reaffirm that, yes, he had been part of something bigger than being a clerk or a tailor.

In 1910, Theodore Roosevelt had visited Kansas City to give a Memorial Day address, and 100,000 people crowded into Union Street Plaza to hear the popular ex-president. This was more than enough to get Beck on a train to the event, and maybe it was here he began to think that the military life might be a way out. Seeing the old comrades, smoking the cigars, the bigger world of Kansas City in a hotel where the world beyond called him. And then, of course, there was Roosevelt. Fresh out of the presidency after handing it over to his handpicked successor, William Taft, the man just radiated energy. Some would later call him *radioactive*, and to a man like Beck, saddled with a wife and children, this was a balm to his frustrated ambitions.

And then the little girl, his daughter, clung to him until there was a social after the conference. Beck probably felt restrained, in awe of the man whom he had seen charge up a hill under a hail of Mauser bullets and win the day while so many others died, and then had become president. Now Beck was sitting in front of Theodore Roosevelt with a cigar in hand with his portly stomach pushing out on his vest and Hattie was falling asleep, and Beck wasn't sure how the president came to be holding his daughter, who was suddenly sitting in the big man's lap, but Roosevelt was known to love children and promptly swept her up into his lap.

And there our future Sally Rand fell asleep in Teddy Roosevelt's lap. She looked much younger than six, small for her age, and would later say she recalled the scent of Roosevelt's cigar and a gray tweed coat. And then she just slept while the ex-president held court with that rapid-fast intellect firing out to his rapt audience transfixed by this human dynamo. He was a man who had built the Panama Canal, sent a White Fleet around the world, and set America on a course to become the superpower of the twentieth century.

Roosevelt was all action. William Beck could see that now. Action. It would become his daughter's credo. Do something. Make it happen. Charge the hill. Charge through the fair and take what is yours. This cross-pollination is a strange one. A president and a woman who would become famous though sheer will and ostrich feathers. But they were both products of an early century enthusiasm, a rush for glory, a rush toward the big American Century. How long Helen Beck slept in Roosevelt's lap is unknown, but we can imagine William Beck eventually taking her back to his hotel room and sitting up long after, smoking a last cigar, knowing then that his destiny lay elsewhere.

The marriage did not hold together. In 1912 Helen Beck's parents separated. Years later Sally told Lloyd Shearer, "When I was a child of eight my father, a colonel in the US Army, in the Cavalry no less, walked out on his family. He left me and mother and a brother—it was a simple case of desertion. I never thought Father rejected Mother. Never that. It was always, *Father has rejected me.* It left me with the idea that no man would ever want me."[7] If there is a clue to the way Sally Rand would conduct her own relationships, it begins here. Unrequited love is written all over her psychological DNA.

There was no divorce yet, but the guns of 1917 would give William Beck the release he so craved. Like many men who went to World War I, Beck saw it as a second chance. He might die but at the very least he was back in the place where the world made sense, the military. In 1917, America went to war and Beck joined the National Guard. The forty-three-year-old Beck would be given the commission of captain in the Quartermaster Corps immediately. His orders were to leave for France right away. As he said his good-byes to his family, Beck must have felt a great relief as his ship steamed out of New York Harbor bound for the Old World and the hell of trench warfare. It is hard to say how many men greeted this dance with death as freedom. William Beck had left behind his wife, son, and daughter and would never return. Helen was left with her mother and brother, and with the strict cavalry captain gone she began to see another world. Her nap in Teddy Roosevelt's lap would become part of family lore. The Rough Rider and the Feather Dancer could not have been more different and yet both characters would inflame the imaginations of millions.

Her mother struggled to find her dance lessons while Helen took out books on dance and watched nickelodeons in Kansas City. Helen Beck was determined to find the beauty of that four-minute dance in her own life . . . not knowing *The Dying Swan* would reappear in a very different way in Chicago twenty-one years later.

Sally's father wrote a letter home from France in 1918 the day after Christmas. "There is very little snow in this part of France and seldom any ice. It's mostly rain. The Seine River which flows through here and on through Paris is out of its banks and on the lowlands. I spent the day yesterday very quietly. . . . we had a nice dinner, not turkey but roast pork and apple sauce and many nice things including pumpkin pie."[8] Then another letter came in 1919. The war had ended, and her father was not coming back. William Beck filed for divorce and married Marie Louis Delamazure. Her mother cried. A divorce was granted June 16, 1922, with William Beck to pay fifty dollars per month for child support. To the children, their father had simply vanished.

Sally would later establish a relationship with her father and send him Christmas gifts in 1923, though he would return them with a letter saying, "I am sorry that I could not have anything to send you but a card, but that card bears a love message from all of us."[9] In 1925 he would write his daughter from New York explaining his situation and giving his show business daughter some advice. It is a strange and conniving letter of a father trying to justify his actions and at the same time complaining about the fifty-dollar child support. But he does give her credit for her early success with a pep talk of sorts. "If you win, it will be YOU WHO WON and no credit to anyone else."[10] He then complained to Sally about his financial situation and "that your mother had retained a lawyer to annoy and harass me with threatening letters . . . I know and a lot of others know that at a tender age both of you children were led to believe that your father was a very bad man . . . sometime you will both know differently."[11]

This was all in the future. But her mother managed to give her dancing lessons, and she performed in the chorus at the Empress Theatre in Kansas City. A reviewer from the *Kansas City Journal* mentioned her. Sally Rand would never finish high school. Her schooling in Kansas City was sporadic at best. She would later write, "The summer of 1919, after having spent my first year of high school at Central in Kansas City, Mama started talking to me about boarding school for my second year of High School."[12] Sally would eventually be enrolled at Georgia Brown's School of Drama and Dance and then the boarding school Christian College. Sally stayed there several years, running away to greet her father in New Orleans, who was returning from overseas. Sally would write later of her father coming down the gangplank, "he did notice me right away and looked utterly stunned . . . I told him how terrible it was for Mama and how sad she had been and how she had cried and cried and could never get over it and what were brother and I going to do without a father . . . he dried my eyes with his clean handkerchief and said things parents usually do—kids just don't understand parent's problems."[13]

Sally returned to high school and was almost expelled. She went home for Christmas and never returned. The family was now living on grandfather Beck's farm. Sally didn't forget her early theater performances. She would later say the applause was magical. She wanted the bright lights of the distant cities. Chicago, New York, Los Angeles. There was something out there and that was the bigger world. Like many young women of the twentieth century, she yearned for the bright lights that would lead to fame and fortune. Blind ambition was already pushing the young girl along, goading her, when a circus came to town. Sally Rand saw a way out as the tent poles broke the Missouri sky.

There is a part of American lore that entails a young person running away with the circus. "She ran away with the circus" is almost comical and conjures up someone with a weatherbeaten suitcase hitching a ride on the back of a circus wagon. But the circus gives the adventurer a mode of transportation, a way to escape the dreary confines of bourgeois middle-class life or working-class or farm life. This is part of the Horatio Alger ethos in America. That a person can leave her surroundings, remake herself, and escape to a faraway place where all is possible. The circus is a vagabond's trade of ne'er-do-wells who make their living off of entertaining the masses. The dusty tents and popcorn and hot dogs float in the twilight as Sally Rand, all of fifteen, makes her way toward the manager.

Escape. It is a theme of America. Escape from Europe. Escape from the Old World to the New World. Escape to the bright lights of fame and fortune, if not destiny. So, Helen Beck saw her escape during a warm summer when the circus came to town. A local paper described the arrival of the circus, which was a major event in early twentieth-century America. "A crowd of several thousand persons gathered yesterday afternoon at the circus grounds . . . to watch the unloading of the first of four trains of the Ringling Brothers Barnum and Bailey Circus."[14]

The carnival had set up among some birch trees outside of town. Helen had told no one of her mission and when she found the manager, she pled her case. We can imagine the man sitting in a chair outside a tent puffing on a cigar while this child, this fifteen-year-old, dances and sings. Small-town America lived for the circus pulling up outside of town to bring the exotic world to farm communities in the early twentieth century.

The circus could be dangerous as well, especially for a young girl. Were there lascivious designs at play as the manager asked her what she could do? Probably. The young girl then did some ballet steps she had learned. The circus manager was not impressed and quizzed her on her age. Sixteen, she proclaimed. So in in the year 1919, a young girl lies about her age and then creates a story saying she had to earn money because her father had left. The manager finally says she can come along and hoped she was a quick learner.

So, there it was. The girl who would be on the road into her seventies begins with a circus, and it is the beginning of the great climb for America. Women are on the move. The vote will arrive in a few years. But the girl knows none of this as she hurriedly packs the night before the carnival is leaving town. And then we have the heartbreaking scene of a young person leaving home, leaving her parent for the bigger world. Holly Knox, who interviewed Sally Rand, later paints the scene.

"Helen had supper with the family and went to the bedroom after the dishes were done. Her mother noticed a nervousness about her that was unusual. She dropped a frying pan and broke a glass while putting them in the cupboard." So, her mother checks up on her daughter and finds her packing with "clothes strewn on the bed and a large tailor's box opened on the floor. Helen was direct. 'I've got a job with the carnival, Mama, and I'm going with them tonight.'"[15]

Her mother was stunned. Her daughter was leaving with a carnival with all the danger that conjured up. Then her daughter positions it for her mother as she finishes packing a few pieces of clothing in a cardboard suitcase. This is a girl who has never left Missouri and now she was catapulting herself into the great unknown.

"It will be okay. The manager is a kindly person and I'll be alright. Don't worry about me. If I don't like it, I'll come back and go to school. And when we get to Kansas City, I'm going to get a job in the Ballet Company."[16]

It is the Wizard of Oz. Dorothy is telling Aunt Em she is leaving. She has a plan. And the first part of the plan is escape and then a ballet company or whatever will take her further. She hugs her mother. "Don't worry, I will be just fine. It's something I've got to do."[17]

And then out into the night, scampering down a road toward the carnival pulling up stakes. It is Americana. The rush for the developing urban culture that can hold people up to a bright light that transcends the thudding reality of middle-class life. Helen Beck would run all her life. Somewhere she left the circus and went back to Kansas City and ended up with a job in a German beer garden, the Green Mill. The amusement park called Electric Park would eventually be used as a model for Disney World. Here are the first shadows that would turn into the Century of Progress. "Electric Park was modeled on the 1893 Columbian Exposition . . . it was lively and well attended, noisy from the arcades and cafes. There was also a parade of young women 'living statuary' emerging from a fountain as part of the attractions. No doubt in some form of undress."[18]

Helen finagles her way back to dance and ends up under the tutelage of "Professor Peri and Georgia Brown," and makes appearances using a new name, Billy Beck, some sort of honoring the father who had left. She then joins the Bridge Stock Company before the long arm of Grandfather Beck pulls her back home. The truth was Helen was homesick by now and had probably had a few encounters where she had to fight off men. "I found many unscrupulous men in my path."[19] This is surely code for attempts to seduce or rape the unchaperoned fifteen-year-old. She was living in a hotel when Grandfather Beck found her. The old man who took a train to find his granddaughter had been pushed by her mother. They both returned on the train the next day to the Ozarks. She would tell her brother later she had been with the carnival and they were training her for a "wire act" or the trapeze. Her brother made her promise she would teach him the trapeze, something that would set a pattern between them as he eventually followed his famous sister to Hollywood.

Helen was enrolled in parochial school, the First Christian Church School, in Columbia, Missouri. She would eventually attend Central High in Kansas City for a few years. It is here she crosses paths with others destined for the greater world, fellow-dancer Lucille LeSueur, who would change her name to Joan Crawford, and even briefly dating a young man, Casey Stengel. Billie Beck, as she now called herself, would continue dancing and even toured with the "Al and Louie Bridge Troupe." But she was restless again and her salvation would once again be the world of elephants, peanuts, and high-flying trapeze artists. The circus was coming back to town.

CHAPTER THREE

Running Away with the Circus

1920

HELEN BECK BREATHED IN THE DUST UNDER THE MUSTY BIG TOP AND waited for the release. She looked down. The people and the dust were far below. She was at the very top and waiting to drop down into the darkness and swing up and grab onto the hands of the man swinging toward her through the lights and the shadows. Yes, she was now a trapeze artist. She would try anything, and this got her up to the platform after a five-minute climb up the center pole.

It was amazing two people could stand on the tiny platform, but of course she was small. At five foot and a hundred and five pounds, she was a perfect size to become a human cannonball. She held the bar between her hands, counted, and then released. She swung down through the air. She would try anything. She had no fear, and that allowed her to let go of the bar and grab the hands reaching out to her and then swing down though the darkness again and land on another tiny platform. Only in a circus.

Carnivals in America really began with the 1893 Columbian Exposition in Chicago. This would be serendipitous for the girl who would become famous in a fair held forty years later in the Windy City. The White City of 1893 was the first one to have a Midway. This is where Sally Rand would make thousands of dollars in the future. The Midway was where the real entertainment of a fair began. There were rides and different attractions and lots of bawdy sideshows.

For late-nineteenth-century America, the circus was the top of the mountain as far as entertainment went. Most people in the early 1900s had never been to a theater or even a zoo. The traveling circus was a connection to the bigger world of exotic animals, freak shows, and nudity. Burlesque attached itself to the circuses and carnivals, and there was more flexibility when it came to nudity. If the show brought in people, then nudity was just fine.

This is where Helen Beck would come of age. For a sixteen-year-old from Missouri, this was indeed an exotic world. At a time when homosexuality was illegal in America, this was a haven of liberality. This was the world of ne'er-do-wells, freaks, bohemians, and this would be a path that Sally Rand would follow if for nothing else than the money. Her life apart from the mainstream of society begins here.

So, the carnivals would head west or south and come into a town and people would flock to the big tents that held as many as ten thousand spectators. A headliner was always the main pull, and many times it was a burlesque dancer or a stripper. But carnival life could be brutal. Ten to fifteen shows a day. Living out of a trailer. Years later Sally Rand would proudly show off her trailer. An article in the *Post-Intelligencer* in 1953 has a photo of Sally cooking in her trailer and goes on to say, "it's a pretty good trailer too, as trailers go. Plenty of cupboards and closets, stove, refrigerator, and a nice big bed with inner spring mattress on which Sally rests when she isn't dancing with fans."[1]

But sleeping in a trailer, even a good one, was a hard life on the road. A different town every week, especially for the burlesque dancers. Candy Cotton, a stripper, recalled, "You were on your feet a lot, swollen feet and all. We used to soak them in tubs of ice."[2] Dixie Evans, another burlesque dancer, agreed. "Circus life and carnival life was lucrative but grueling. You do maybe ten to thirty shows a day. Whenever that weather is shining, and the sun is out there you do the shows . . . when you're through . . . you ride home, you just stop and get some Chinese and you soak in the bathtub, ya know. You don't go out. You don't smoke. You don't drink. You don't spend money."[3] This life was far in the future for Helen, but it is a world she would enter and leave several times and then finally become part of.

It is unclear if she ran away from home again or simply told her mother she was leaving when the circus came back to town. The image of a child with her pack over her shoulder on a stick is built into Americana, but the truth is that there just was no opportunity for anyone who wanted something beyond the local economies of small-town America. There were no Walmarts or Kmarts or shopping malls to sample the outside world. The microcosmic economies that died in the late twentieth century were in their heyday in the early years of that same incredible century.

This was self-limiting for anyone who aspired to something beyond the teacher, drugstore clerk, hardware store employee, farm hand variety. Someone who wanted to be a dancer or craved the thunderous applause of an adoring audience need not apply. You simply left. And transportation was limited. Most people did not own a car. Only 10 percent of Americans owned a car in 1931. So that left the train, a passing ship, horses, or a carnival coming through town. And so, Helen Beck with her new name, Billie Beck, hitched another circus and found herself in Chicago.

She joined the Adolph Bohm Chicago Ballet Company in the slaughterhouse that was Chicago during this time and toured with the dance company. As if all things led back to *The Dying Swan*, Bohm was at one time Anna Pavlova's dance partner before an injury had put him into the role of teacher. It is amazing how deftly Billie jumped from the circus to further her training with an almost intuitive sense of what would move her along to her goal of fame and fortune. She stayed with the dance company until it closed, and then joined the Ringling Brothers Circus.

Now she was working as a net girl for the trapeze. She had reached her full height of five feet. Billie Beck was compact and strong, with athletic thighs and a full figure. She was perfect for the trapeze, and more than all that, she had no fear. This is often overlooked with Sally Rand. The ability to risk her personal safety without thinking twice would make her a star and later put her into bankruptcy. She later claimed she joined the Wards Trapeze act as a flyer. This would seem perfect. We can see the sixteen-year-old flying into the darkness and reaching out for the next hands that would save her.

In the sawdust and dust of carnival life in America, Billie Beck was flipping through the twilight, wondering how far a life as a trapeze artist would take her. The truth is we don't know exactly what she did with the great trapeze artists, the Flying Wards, except what she said later. Eddie and Jenny Ward had taught themselves the art of the trapeze in their backyard in Bloomfield, Illinois. They opened a trapeze school sometime after 1900 and taught girls and boys how to fly. The Wards usually performed without a safety net on their most ambitious tricks, and we can imagine Sally Rand following their lead. But it was not the trapeze that would kill Jenny Ward but a train crash in Indiana when a second train plowed into their twenty-six cars of circus animals and circus performers. So, it was Eddie who would train the young girl from the Ozarks.

Hard to say what really happened under the musty big tops where Sally spun through the darkness with audiences staring up openmouthed. It took at least five years to become a proficient flyer, so did Billie Beck really fly? She might have shown the strength and the judgment to grab a human being in midflight. We can see her climbing up a tent pole ladder in her sequins, reaching the top and looking down, and then grabbing the bar and flying down through the smoky ether and then releasing and *reaching reaching reaching* for that next hand to take her along. Was there any better metaphor for a teenager wandering the United States in the 1920s?

Billie stayed with the circus world until 1925; she left the circus again at age twenty-one in New York City. Then it gets fuzzy until she surfaces in a list of child dancers at the Riverview Country Club put on by "the studio of Mildred Haggerty of Green Bay." There is no social safety net in America at this time. When people ran out of money, they starved, and the twenty-one-year-old did go hungry. "I did go broke, but I didn't care," she would say later. "I did go hungry and I didn't mind. I was put out of my little $4 a week room and had to sleep in Central Park, but it didn't matter."[4] No education beyond the tenth grade in high school, no lineage, no money, and really no family, she had only a conviction that she was destined for something greater. The great party of the 1920s was gearing up, and Helen Beck or Billie Beck was going to be part of it.

She just didn't know how. And then she pops up in New York City. This is at a time when people hitched rides, rode in boxcars, or walked. It was also a time when people simply disappeared and were never heard from again. Billie Beck was in the school of hard knocks and class was now in session as a beauty contestant for Ziegfeld's Follies of 1922 on Broadway. She is now twenty-two and her name does not appear among the cast, but who knows she might have been part of it. Sally Rand would use this as part of her pedigree, as Ziegfeld was a god in the dance world of his time.

"The Ziegfeld Follies was a magnet for an ambitious dancer like Billie and his Midnight Frolics, which performed on the rooftops of the New Amsterdam Theatre, included acrobats from Ringling Brothers. The rose and green colored rooftop nightclub was lush, tropical, and popular during the summer months in pre-air-conditioned times."[5] If she was there, we can only marvel again at her ability to drop herself into the center of the world. Like being at the World's Fair of 1933, she had a nose for what could be life changing, where the hub of the world was turning, and then inserting herself right in the center of it. One has to be very young, very cunning, and very bold to pull this off time and again without it devolving into disaster.

Ziegfeld was simply the top of the pyramid for a young dancer. How did Sally Rand move about with no money and no means of transportation? It was a time when people hitched rides and lived off the generosity of others. And she probably did not eat for extended periods of time. Sleeping in alleys, fields, vacant rooms, abandoned houses, this was her way. There was no mass culture instructing people on how to live beyond the newspapers, and Americans simply made it up as they went along. Much as Charles Lindbergh would do when the twenty-two-year-old Billie Beck bumped into the young flyer after meeting him through a wealthy Texas boyfriend, Houston Allread.

This becomes even more fantastic. She learns how to fly planes and dates Lindbergh. By 1923 she is flying alone, but we must remember this is at a time when people would buy planes and just start flying with very little training. A pilot's license was not required in most states, and planes belonged to the world of daredevils and trapeze artists. Lindbergh would parachute out of his own plane many times before crossing the Atlantic, and Sally Rand would later boast she flew herself to many gigs. But it gets better. She receives her transport pilot's license, which was a high designation at the time for a pilot. A quote stands out here. "It's the quickest and cleanest and most comfortable mode to travel."[6] This sounds a little off, as she was flying biplanes that tended to coat the pilot with engine oil, hence the scarf to wipe off the goggles.

But Sally Rand would use planes extensively her whole life to make an impossible schedule run on time. She did believe in air travel at a time when most Americans had never flown. It is incredible she is dating the man who would become a world celebrity in a few years for being the first human to cross the Atlantic Ocean solo in a plane nonstop. How did she find the divining rod of the people who would change the world? But she did it over and over and crossed paths continually with other nascent stars. From William Powell, who attended her high school, to Joan Crawford to Humphrey Bogart, whom she would act with, she had a knack for hooking her wires to the sparks of future fame.

We would call it destiny today. But is it self-generated or is it an anointment from beyond? The teenager knocking around New York City dancing supposedly on the rooftops of Ziegfeld Follies on a "large stage with a proscenium stretched thirty-four feet in width,"[7] in the warm rising air of New York City must have marveled at different moments how far she had come and still how far she had to go. She had blond hair, baby curls, luminous blue eyes, and a figure that could stop a man cold. These were givens, but she was surrounded by beautiful women. There had to be more.

Then she ends up modeling in a swimsuit for the Gus Edwards Revue. His vaudeville company made regular stops at the Orpheum Theatre in Kansas City, where he saw Helen Beck in a chorus line. Edwards had formed the touring company "School Boys and Girls" and would end up developing actors ranging from Walter Winchell to Ray Bolger to the Marx Brothers. He was an accomplished songwriter beginning with "By the Light of the Silvery Moon," and continuing with many hits. Not bad for a German-born young man who at one time sang from burlesque house balconies. Eventually Hollywood would award Edwards a Bing Crosby vehicle, the movie *The Star Maker* based on Edwards' life of creating stars out of young hopefuls, aspiring starlets from Kansas City. Starlets like Billie Beck. After a tryout she was offered a job with Edwards School Days Revue to perform a ballet act. Billie Beck accepted.

Chapter Four

Hollywood Bound

1925

SHE ALWAYS WANTED TO BE A HOLLYWOOD STAR. WHEN SHE FIRST RAN away with the circus, Helen Beck had her sights set on the coast. She would never give up the idea of herself as a Hollywood star who happened to do a fan dance for money. It was part of her armor. She demanded respect, the respect of a serious actress who had made it in Hollywood. And now she was there. It had been a crazy circuitous route, but she had made it to the city where dreams were made. She had made it to La La Land. But first let's back up.

Who knows what happened with the show producer Gus Edwards, but Billie Beck's time with his touring company ended. The sixty-one boxes of the Sally Rand papers at the Chicago History Museum hold bits and pieces of a life lived, but it is not chronological. Telegrams are mixed up with letters mixed up with car titles mixed up with drawings mixed up with newspaper articles. The article showing a soaked Sally Rand in 1934 is next to a letter to her mother in 1921. The frustration of any biographer is that of looking for chronology when it simply doesn't exist. But this is a good metaphor for the life of Billie Beck or Sally Rand or Helen Beck. Her life is literally mixed up mirroring the high-flying times of the 1920s and the lows of the Great Depression's unofficial school of survival.

But taking what we do know, Sally Rand left Gus Edwards' show and ended up back in Chicago. She goes to the Art Institute and drops her clothes for a few bucks, posing nude for would-be artists, and this presages what will be her famous quote, "I haven't been out of work since the day I took off my pants."[1] We can imagine the 105-pound Sally Rand standing on a pedestal while gawky art students with Van Dyke beards painted, sketched, sculpted her nude body. And there are reports she danced almost nude at a beer garden, Ernie Young's Marigold Garden.

Hot Chicago nights found her outside maybe topless in a revue of girls high kicking or soft-shoeing their way through those years of the roaring twenties. Prohibition had come to America and everyone was drinking more than ever before in speakeasies with beer provided by Al Capone. Breaking the law was in the air and so was jazz and interracial mixing. So, nudity was just one more convention punctured by a nation trying to come of age in a corset.

Sally Rand was in training. Learning to dance. To be an acrobat. To model. To talk. To get where she wanted to be. And then in the sixty-one boxes there are clues to a return to New York City to the Gus Edwards company and then the company falls apart and Billie Beck is walking the streets. How many young girls who ran way with circuses from America's rural landscape were walking in the hot dust-filled days of America in the second decade of the new century? Probably thousands. Mass media is cranking up. Movies are cranking up. Radio. And yet there is no clear path. This new urban life is in its infancy . . . it is a roller coaster just built, and many will fall off and many will simply fade into obscurity.

She loses her four-dollars-a-week room and is now sleeping in Central Park with the hobos, and then she is staring at people eating food in restaurants through glass windows. When they finish the young woman bolts in and grabs leftover food from their plates. She would perfect this art of stealing food over the years when times get rough. But the Gods throw her a bone, and she ends up with Lew Leslie and the Blackbirds, an African American company with two nascent stars, "Bojangles" Robinson and Cab Calloway. Sally hits the road again and meets Ethel Waters in the cast and finds herself in California. She leaves the show, but she and Robinson remain friends.

She's now back in New York City, where she joins Will Seabury's Repertory Company. Billie Beck has now locked onto a profession. She likes the greasepaint, the heavy body paint, the hurried dressing, the curtain calls, the bohemian world of actors, and more than all that she loves the applause. It fills her soul. Like a shot of cocaine. She rides high for a day after each performance and only slowly comes down. Fame is a drug when it is all said and done.

Seabury was no Ziegfeld but was adept at vaudeville lined with young girls. In a strange interlude during her tryout, Billie Beck has to show her feet to the producer, who was looking for a certain look, "long narrow feet." Who knows, but she gets the part and then she is on a train headed for Los Angeles, headed for Hollywood. She plays opposite an unknown Humphrey Bogart in the play *Rain*. The year is 1925 and Billie feels she is on her way again. She loves the partying crew of Seabury's ensemble. This is all a training ground for a life on the road that the twenty-something loves. Why not? No kids. No husband. If there was ever a time to be a gypsy in the headlong pursuit of her destiny it was now. It was only later that the road would become a grind, slowly wearing her down over the years.

Seabury was a philanderer who ran through wives and showgirls and took Billie Beck under his wing until he fell ill in Los Angeles. Some say he was her mentor, but Seabury probably "mentored" many young girls and got not a few of them pregnant. A strange article in the *Los Angeles Times* features Billie Beck as an "aviation fannette"[2] who flew herself to gigs in her own plane. Where did she get the plane? Who knows? Seabury's illness eventually causes the dissolution of the company, and Billie is once again out on the street. But this time she is close to Hollywood. She can see the green hills and feels the breeze off the Pacific Ocean. This time she is not going back to New York City or Chicago. She is staying where they manufacture stars every week. She is staying where the name Sally Rand will be born and come into the world.

This was the beginning. The hot empty spaces of the desert that would become Hollywood. The back lots where early films were shot. The young starlets pouring into California to latch onto the new medium. Movies would change the world, and Billie Beck as she called herself now had a knack for being in the right place at the right time.

The letters in the boxes at the Chicago History Museum tell a story of a young twenty-something asking her mother to follow her to a place called Glendora, California. She had been stranded again and like many actors of her time had taken a room with a family. But this family lived in Glendora and the young woman from the Ozarks fell in love. Glendora was close to Azusa, where a lot of movies were shot on location. The topography was wide open and only thirty-five miles from Hollywood. To the girl from the Ozarks, the town located at the foot of the San Gabriel Mountains was paradise.

In this silent movie mecca, Billie Beck began her career as did others. In the sandy dusty loam of California, the movie industry was just beginning. Part of Sally Rand's success would be due to the fact that as she matured so did the entertainment business in America. Silent movies were in full swing when she met Nils T. Granlund. He was a promoter, producer, and showman who helped showgirls, and he gave the girl with only a winter outfit a new set of clothes. Then Harry Richmond, who would have lasting fame singing "Putting on the Ritz" and who helped many young starlets including Joan Crawford, took pity on her and gave her name to his associate Joseph Schenck. Schenck would later run 20th Century Fox.

Billie Beck was now knocking on the doors of Hollywood Boulevard trying to get anything. She ended up as an extra in several films. Her dance instructor Ernest Belcher would work with many nascent stars, with Shirley Temple and Betty Grable heading the list. Billie adopted a formula that would work for her very well throughout her career; she would do anything to get noticed and better anything to get paid. She even put on boxing gloves and boxed in high heels for photographers.

This was when she had a bit part in Harry Carroll's *Pickings*, performing at the Orange Grove Theatre. Then a Canadian-born director and producer looking for a girl who could dive into a tank from a fifteen-foot ladder noticed her. His name was Mack Sennett, and that name would become synonymous with Keystone Cop movies, pie throwing, and early stunts performed in silent movies that were not stunts at all but people risking their lives. The old-time car chases would forever be associated with Sennett films but at the time they were cutting edge.

Sennett saw Sally doing some stunts off a diving board and hired her to do a thirty-foot dive for which she received her first check, fifteen dollars. It is during this time also that she had an appendectomy in

Sacramento and had just recovered when she hooked up with Sennett. With some financial backing, Sennett had founded Keystone Studios in Edendale, California, which had plenty of room for car chases and was the first totally enclosed film stage and studio built in America.

The list of actors who would pass through the Sennett orbit is staggering. Marie Dressler, Mabel Normand, Charles Chaplin, Harry Langdon, Gloria Swanson, Bing Crosby, W. C. Fields, Polly Moran, Mabel Normand. The Keystone Cops series would make his name, but he also would develop kid comedies that would eventually turn into the *Our Gang* films. Sennett would become synonymous with short comedies called "flickers."

This was the baby steps of an industry that would take over the world, and Billie Beck was there to be swept up along with it. Sennett hired her and paid the young starlet fifteen dollars to make the dive into the tank. The money was needed as she was literally starving between gigs and constantly moving from one room to the next. Many hotels posted signs "No Actors." The profession was just a few steps up from being in a burlesque show. Sally would later write a different version of how she got the job with Sennett. She had been posing nude for an artist and living in the back room of his studio. The artist assisted her in getting a job, and later Sally would say he got her the job to free up the back room for girls he brought home at night.

Then came a few Hal Roach films in Culver City that gave Billie some money but not much else. But the Mack Sennett connection had led to a man who was a former actor turned director who was forming a stock company. Cecil B. DeMille. The Canadian-born filmmaker would produce over seventy films between 1914 and 1958. He would form the "contract player system" or "star system" where studios owned actors and used them in whatever films they chose. *The Squaw Man*, an interracial love story, was the first feature film shot in Hollywood and would designate Hollywood as the land of films. DeMille would go on to form Paramount Pictures.

Cecil Blount DeMille was born to theatrical parents in Ashfield, Massachusetts. His father, Henry DeMille, wrote his first play at age fifteen and was a natural-born dramatist. His mother, Beatrice DeMille, was also a playwright and scriptwriter. The DeMille household in Brooklyn was ablaze with creativity. After the death of Cecil's father from typhoid fever, Beatrice opened an acting workshop in her home. This was all early training for young Cecil, who went on to attend the American Academy of Dramatic Arts. He then went to Broadway as an aspiring actor but soon found himself producing and directing plays. In July 1913 he and Jesse Lasky and Samuel Goldwyn formed a film company, the Jesse Lasky Feature Play Company, and headed for Arizona to shoot a film.

It is here that providence takes a hand. When the light proved unsatisfactory in Flagstaff, the company continued to Los Angeles on the Southern Pacific and picked a place called Hollywood to make the movie. The movie was *The Squaw Man*, and it ran an astounding sixty minutes. DeMille never looked back and never left Hollywood. Five years and thirty hit films later, he was known for trademark scenes involving Roman orgies, lion attacks, and bathtubs. He experimented with color early on and developed dramatic lighting techniques and pioneered the microphone boom and the camera blimp. He became Hollywood.

DeMille was busily making silent films and had just discovered "the most beautiful woman in the world." Billie Beck. Sally wrote of her first encounter with the famous director. "I learned the ropes and crashed DeMille's office, pushing his secretary out of the way. I got by his desk spotlight without tripping over his trick rug, and showed him my stills, all kinds of poses. He said, 'Okay.' And I got bits right away."[3]

DeMille saw the twenty-something as America's next sweetheart. He was an autocrat with his jodhpurs and a microphone in hand, demanding absolute control over cast and crew. He would become legendary in a town that produced legends every week. And now another legend was born: Sally Rand. How she got her name is open for some debate, but it was a christening of sorts. Holly Knox, a fellow dancer, describes the iconic moment this way:

> *They were shooting a film on a Paramount movie set when he called her over to him, asking what her name was. She replied, "Billie Beck," which she thought was a shade more chic than "Helen Beck." DeMille frowned his famous scowl and pronounced, "I see you as Sally." Helen*

was compromising. "Oh," she said. "Sally Beck?" DeMille was not listening. His eyes were darting around the set for a name idea. He spotted a Rand McNally World Atlas. *"That's it," he proclaimed. Helen and the others on the set were speechless, waiting to see what would come next from the great man. Helen could not contain herself. "My God," she said, "not Sally McNally!"[4]*

DeMille smiled a rare smile and said, "No Goose, Sally Rand."[5]

A 1976 interview gives a different story. "One day I was in his office . . . and Mr. DeMille said he thought Billie Beck was too girly. 'You're going to be doing more dignified parts now and I think you ought to have a new name . . .' There was a Rand-McNally atlas on his desk, and I said, 'What about Rand?' And that's how it came about."[6]

It doesn't matter how it happened; Sally Rand now had arrived. Gone were Billie Beck and Helen Beck. The names reflected her transition from hillbilly to circus girl to an unknown actress and finally to a budding starlet under the direction of a man who created an industry that would rule the world. Los Angeles was booming as a million people crowded into the city in 1925. What an amazing time to be in Hollywood. Sally Rand was in on the very beginning of movies, mass entertainment, a beautiful, fit, twenty-one, poised for stardom. The warm breezes off the Pacific fluffed her hair as she drove down the boulevards and continued to lobby her mother and brother to come from Kansas City to Hollywood to join her.

DeMille proclaimed, "Sally Rand is the most beautiful girl in America . . . she is young, piquant, athletic and intelligent—possessed of a trim type of film fascination which should make her a star of the first magnitude."[7] In a sense Sally Rand was born from DeMille's vision for her. She would never give up the idea of being a Hollywood star even when she was at the height of her fan dancing. She had been anointed by the God of Hollywood. Her fantasy life had begun.

Sally recognized the competition and did everything she could to improve her hand, from winning Charleston dance contests to getting any type of publicity for anything. DeMille cast her in twenty silent films between 1925 and 1928, including in *King of Kings* as a handmaiden. She began to have an affair with H. B. Warner, who was playing the role of

Jesus Christ. The English actor was an alcoholic and a good twenty-five years older than Sally Rand. When they came late to the set, DeMille boomed over his megaphone. "Miss. Rand leave my Jesus Christ alone. If you must screw someone, screw Pontius Pilot!"[8] It was the story of Jesus of Nazareth and the film would reach eighty million viewers.

Then she was cast in *The Fighting Eagle* as a Fifth Avenue model and in *The Dressmaker* directed by Paul Bern, where she would sing and dance. One week before the release on March 15, 1925, Sally was featured in a full-page promotion, "Beauty Secrets of Some of the Beauty Stars." She and Bern would have a quick affair as Bern added her to his long list of actresses he had slept with, including Joan Crawford. Sally Rand had crossed into the world of dreams. "Sally spent her time as many starlets of her day did, posing for ads like canned milk or the Bootery . . . in September she appeared in the Southern California Forward beauty pageant . . . While not making movies, there were concerts to attend at the four-year-old Hollywood Bowl under twinkling stars or loud and raucous nightly boxing matches, or perhaps a twisting drive in the hills along Mulholland Highway."[9]

In her first movie magazine interview, Sally shocked Hal K. Wells with her intelligence. "I knew that Sally was very young and very attractive to the eye . . . instead before I had time to catch my breath, I found myself involved in a discussion of psychoanalysis that left me feeling about as intelligent as a Fiji Islander who had unwittingly opened a book on differential calculus . . . Sally Rand has an eight cylinder brain and she knows how to use it."[10]

This will come up again in interviews throughout her life. Because Sally Rand took off her clothes behind ostrich feathers and made her living in show business, the assumption was that she was not intelligent. This simply was not true. She was self-taught to a large degree, but she had read deeply, and she had a high degree of emotional intelligence that would burst forth in letters and interviews. This does not match with the blond-haired bimbo behind ostrich feathers, but one could make a case that only a very intelligent person could figure out how to make the equivalent of a million dollars in Depression-era America.

But for now, Sally Rand had arrived. The name would create the persona. The publicity photos of her show a classic star of the silent movie era. She was headed for stardom in an industry just warming up. There was a casting couch culture in Hollywood at this time, and how much Sally Rand had to deal with this is not known. She was promiscuous. A *Chicago Daily News* article claimed that DeMille had propositioned her. Sally herself recalled, "there was Erwin Gelsey, that brilliant young redhead assistant to Walter Wanger, just coming on the scene and fun to be with. And Abe Lipsey, my oldest boyfriend in LA and a darling going to USC and slated to be Hollywood's largest seller of mink coats." In an interview in 1925 she was asked what kind of boy appeals to her. "I'd like a Pan boy . . . slim and brown with long slim brown fingers, creative fingers. Hands mean such a lot."[11]

There was a Johnny mentioned in a letter to her mother on January 22, 1926. It is here that a mysterious trip to Mexico was necessitated. "We had a wonderful trip to Tijuana. I think the first time I have ever seen a real bar and gambling and that sort of thing. It is the first time I ever saw a horse race too . . . I also attended some urgent business which you know about, and it turned out very happy for me."[12] The urgent business was probably the reason she would never have a child of her own. Abortions were crude at this time, and many ended with the mother unable to have a baby after the procedure.

In an early draft of an unfinished autobiography, Sally writes, "There was Johnny Maschio for whom I had wrangled a position of Asst to Mitch Leisen, DeMille's head set designer and set dresser. We did a lot of sailing together and a lot of happy lovemaking . . ."[13] Johnny Maschio would later go on to become a major agent representing Humphrey Bogart, Henry Fonda, Jean Harlow, Gregory Peck, and John Wayne.

A boyfriend named Carl Schalet would later encourage her "to get more details from Dr. Hart" concerning "the question of whether any part of the tubes were left."[14] Carl and Sally apparently had plans to marry, but Carl wanted to get everything settled before they wed. In 1927 he wrote, "Meanwhile, we have several important things to consider. Most important of all is your divorce. That, of course, must be completed, and you must have the final papers before we can marry. Please look into it and let me know how it stands. I think you'll agree that it would be best for us to get the license in your real name—Helen Beck . . . If you are quite certain that the fact of your former marriage will never come out, I can see no reason for it being mentioned, even to my Mom and Dad."[15]

Carl closed with a cryptic note "better to burn this."[16] Carl and Sally would never marry, soon after his letter she cut off communication. There obviously was a marriage and an abortion but to whom Sally Rand was married has never been revealed. Carl's insistence to bring this into the light of the day cost him his own marriage to Sally Rand. Sally would operate her entire life in two worlds. One was the public media-driven world of the celebrity, the other was the upside-down world of the poor girl from the Ozarks with the tenth-grade education whose life was one crisis after another where she would make up her own rules and this would cost her money, litigation, and even jail time. The hillbilly with the father who murdered a man when he was sixteen was always one step away from the glare of the spotlight.

Carl was tossed to the side and the party continued. Sally wrote another letter to her mother describing a party for Mary Pickford. "There were many notables there, among whom were Mr. and Mrs. Charlie Chaplin . . . Donald Ogden Stuart, Mary Pickford and Douglas Fairbanks, Jack Gilbert, King Vidor . . . Sam Goldwyn, Jesse Lanske, Joseph Schenck . . . I don't think I have ever been in a more celebrated, witty and intelligent crowd than that. Mary Pickford was charming and so sweet. I am very thrilled because it was the first time, I had ever seen she or Douglas Fairbanks, and I was not disappointed at all."[17]

Top of the mountain. The girl from the Ozarks, the hillbilly, was now going to pool parties with the cream of Hollywood. The Tijuana visit would affect Sally Rand for the rest of her life, but for now she was young and beautiful and had a Hollywood career. Her mother, Nettie, and brother, Harold, moved to Glendora to be close to their successful movie star. The studio had publicity photos of Sally Rand posing with Babe Ruth. She filmed the movie *Heroes in Blue* in 1927 where real flames burned behind her, and she jumped from a building into a net below held by firemen. She drove large fire trucks through the streets of Los Angeles for another scene. There was nothing she would not do. Sally was headed for the top after years of a hand-to-mouth existence. Dream was meeting reality . . . what could possibly go wrong?

CHAPTER FIVE

WAMPAS Baby Star

1927

SALLY RAND WAS TWENTY-THREE AND HAD ENOUGH MONEY TO BRING her mother, Annette, and her nineteen-year-old brother, Harold, to California. Harold was handsome and saw his sister's success as an entry point for him into show business. Women got the vote in 1920. *The Great Gatsby* had come out in 1925. Lindbergh flew across the Atlantic the same year. By 1927 the movie business of Hollywood was established, and silent movies ruled. Sally Rand had hit her stride and was in *Man Bait* for PDC Productions, a DeMille company . . . *Night Love* for Goldwyn, United Artists, *His Dog* for Pathé, *Getting Gertie's Garters* for PDC. These would be followed in 1928 with *Crashing Through*, *Girl in Every Port*, *Women Against the World*, *Nameless Men*, *Golf Widows*, and *Black Feather*. In short, Sally Rand was close to becoming a star and was christened a WAMPAS Baby Star in 1927.

The Western Associated Motion Pictures Advertisers (WAMPAS) had touched her on the forehead, and she joined the ranks of other WAMPAS baby stars, Bessie Love, Colleen Moore, Mary Astor, Mary Brian, Dolores Costello, Janet Gaynor, and Fay Wray. Loretta Young, Ginger Rogers, Gloria Stewart, and Joan Crawford would later join the elite group of young actresses destined for stardom. A letter from her father, William Beck, in 1926 is revealing. Sally had apparently written him and suggested he and his new wife and two sons come to California. This would be the beginning of a process of bringing her entire family to join her. Her father was still in the service and expressed doubt about getting to California. "I do not quite see how it is to be accomplished. I know of no one in the service out there who wished to come to New York on an exchange transfer." Her father also told Sally he had not seen her picture in the movie magazines. "I went to the newsstands to see what I could find and was told that the February issues of the magazines were all sold."

What is interesting is that Sally wants her father to come live by her after his desertion and that her newfound movie fame is still on a level where people generally don't know who she is. She was in films, but she was not yet a star, although her father does mention he has seen pictures of her in the "New York papers."[1]

The United States was undergoing change. At a time when Prohibition was in full swing, the stock market was roaring, credit was cheap, the middle class had claimed its rightful place as the main engine of consumerism, and women were becoming empowered. Hollywood held up a mirror to the times and pumped out movie after movie reflecting back an urban culture sweeping the country. Speakeasies had become chic, gangsters were in, and men and women now drank together in dark places as sexual taboos were broken along with the laws of the Volstead Act. Prohibition made middle-class people outlaws, and prosperity and Hollywood elevated the flapper to an iconic standing pushed on by F. Scott Fitzgerald. The Charleston was in full swing and Sally performed the dance with others at clubs and for the movies. She would later say in an interview, "You have to be happy to do the Charleston. It is a dance that is full of the joy of living."[2]

It was an amazing time to be young, beautiful, and in Hollywood.

And Sally Rand was there right in the nexus of this rapidly developing industry. The thirteen starlets selected that year included the twenty-three-year-old girl from the Ozarks now promised publicity and a three-year contract in vaudeville. The christening took place at the Ambassador Hotel on Wilshire Boulevard. Arc lights shot into the night sky as movie stars went into the Cocoanut Grove nightclub decorated with fake palm trees and floating stars that hung from the ceiling for the thirteen starlets. All of Hollywood was there, and this was the inauguration for getting into the most exclusive club in the world, that of Hollywood Stardom.

Columnist Dan Campbell described the event. "The sixth annual frolic and ball drew the elite of the artistic and social world to the Ambassador hotel where for hours before the stars began to arrive, thousands of curious screen fans lined the corridors, waiting for some glimpse of some favorite player . . . the baby stars of 1927 were presented to the vast audience of more than 3,000 in a dazzling array of stunning gowns in a brilliant setting."[3]

Gloria Swanson, Mary Pickford, and Douglas Fairbanks rubbed shoulders with others who paid the ten-dollar admission. A disco ball turned and shot beams of light around the room as Babe Ruth strolled in while Joan Crawford led a dance contest. Hollywood royalty. Top of the mountain. And now came the big moment. "One by one the girls stepped on stage through a silver star-shaped frame where a tiny pink and gold fairy held a wand. Niblo gave each girl a bouquet of flowers and the audience scrutinized and cheered. It was an auspicious presentation for the young, gorgeous beauties filled with dreams of mansions and movie premiers."[4]

Then it was over, and Sally Rand went back to being the starlet trying to find the elusive combinations of roles and publicity that would put her over the top. But a film released on October 6, 1927, changed the industry and altered Sally Rand's life forever. The Warner Brothers film premiered in New York City. The stakes couldn't have been higher. The brothers had spent $420,000 to make the musical film with a synchronized recorded score backed up by a Vitaphone sound on disc system. Al Jolson's *The Jazz Singer* would be the torpedo into the side of the good ship Silent Movie and eventually would lead to Gloria Swanson's famous line in *Sunset Boulevard* as the faded silent movie star, "So they opened their big mouths and out came talk! Talk! Talk!"[5]

When the movie opened, Warner Brothers knew they were rolling the dice. The film was pushing known recording technology of the time. The success or failure of the film hinged on the prowess of the projectionist. Fifteen reels had to be switched out along with fifteen discs and the Vitaphone records had to match perfectly with the film. If the projectionist got it wrong, the film would be a disaster. The audience in the New York Theater was astounded when Al Jolson's face appeared on the screen and he said directly to the people sitting in the darkness, "Wait a minute, wait a minute, you ain't heard nothing yet!"[6] People were amazed that the person on the screen was speaking to them.

After every Al Jolson song there was applause. The fact it was a film was lost on the audience that had only heard live performances up to that moment. During several dialogue scenes the audience became hysterical. Drama had never been played this way before. After the show the audience turned into a milling, battling mob, chanting "Jolson Jolson Jolson." *Life* magazine journalist Robert E. Sherwood watched the film that night and wrote, "I for one suddenly realized that the end of the silent drama was in sight."[7]

Indeed, it was. The first full-length talkies showed that people loved the new medium and would flock to see more. The coffin nails of silent movie stars all over America were pounded in for those who could not make the transition to speaking on celluloid. Many actors hired vocal coaches. Sally Rand might have been able to hire a coach to help her, but two things occurred that would foreshadow a strange way of life that would haunt her. A warrant was issued for her arrest over a nonappearance for driving without a license or operator card and a suit was brought for nonpayment of a bill to a dressmaker. The legal troubles of Sally Rand were just beginning and would eventually engulf her. A strange tendency to not pay what she owed would trip her up over and over.

By 1928 the movie industry was in full-swing conversion to the new medium. Broadway actors flooded Hollywood well versed in the ability to speak on stage and project. Humphrey Bogart was among the new crop of actors who would become famous for their speech patterns as well as their acting. Sally Rand would have to take a sound test and let the chips fall.

What happened next was a disaster. A movie made ten years later, *The Sunset Murder Case*, illustrated why Sally Rand didn't make it in the movies. The lore is that after Al Jolson's *The Jazz Singer* brought talkies to the forefront, Sally Rand had to try out and have her voice recorded, and a lisp along with an Ozark accent undid her. This could well be the case. But in the movie *The Sunset Murder Case*, a Sally Rand film, there are other problems as well. This was to be a Sally Rand vehicle produced in the late 1930s. It is awful. Bad acting. Bad script. And Sally Rand's voice is that of a child. At times it is soft and other times it sounds as if it might just blow away. There is no projection. There is no assertion in her voice. She sounds like an amateur, a young girl from a small town who found herself in a movie.

Silent movies served Sally well. She photographed well. She was beautiful. Her face was expressive. But in the movie *The Sunset Murder Case*, she delivers her lines with the same aplomb as if in a high school theater production. There is no emoting. There is simply a girl producing what she thinks are expressions and emotions that match with the dialogue, but a true understanding of the lines seems absent. Now saying that, there is something else that comes through on the screen. A naivete, a hopeful yearning that things will work out. She is of her time and carries the hometown girl in her pocket as she smiles for the camera. This effervescence will serve her well in a different medium where Sally Rand will become *Sally Rand*, the star of the 1933 World's Fair. But in 1930s Hollywood, it was death.

An interview with Sally Rand by Studs Terkel is recorded in the 1960s, and now her voice belongs in the Eleanor Roosevelt category. Her voice is high, delicate, and cultivated, thanks to years of study with Margaret Prendergast McLean. Many hopeful actresses and actors found their way to McLean's studio to learn how to speak for the new medium of "talkies." Sally learned a careful refined erudition that sounds labored, but she successfully buried her twang and her lisp, but of course this would all be too late for the girl whom movies and Cecil B. DeMille had given her walking papers.

Sally immediately returned to a vaudeville circuit and hired a brother and sister, Fanchon and Marco, to perform with her. She created her own show, *Sally from Hollywood*, and with no fewer than ten men on stage she danced for the crowds. Her dance partners were Jack Crosby and Harvey Karels. Sally danced and sang and did comedy routines. A review in Ogden, Utah, was positive. "Sally Rand with her wonderful personality and gorgeous costumes, won the heart of Paramount theatre goers . . ."[8]

Other reviews damned with faint praise. *Variety* threw her a bone, saying she had a "good singing voice" but "for all of her shapeliness and pulchritude, although she is too much legs on the personality business, has not enough of the real variety entertainment to register indelibly."[9] In other words, she is a mediocre dancer with neither the deep well of talent or originality to stand out.

At this time, she had a relationship with a man named Jack in Chicago who wrote her long love letters in 1929. He apparently was an actor or dancer, but he was smitten with Sally Rand. "I sure did miss you. First time I have felt sick when you weren't around to help me feel better. It is six below tonight, but it would take much colder weather than that to cool my ardor for you. . . . I love you. I loved, I love you. I do I do I do I do I do I do I do I do. And how and how and how and how. I crave to have your arms bout me and to kiss your sweet face. Lordy Lordy. I miss you."[10]

But Sally Rand could not think of having a relationship. Her career was in trouble. She had to be in shock to have her Hollywood career vanish over the next hill and leave her in dusty theaters on a vaudeville circuit. Her mother and Harold joined her on the road. Her mother Annette was now being courted by Ernest Kisling, who was living at the family home in Glendora. Annette wrote him a letter describing New York City and running into her ex-husband, William Beck. "I can't say I like NY so far. I haven't had a single thrill since I came here not even when I shook hands with my ex . . . Sally said it burnt him up when he saw how young and beautiful I was. He is bald and what little hair he has is white. He has four little boys under six years of age and is living in this city on P.O. clerk's salary."[11] Annette returned to Glendora with Harold while Sally stayed in New York City. On March 10, 1929, Annette Rand Beck married Ernest Gordon Kissling in Glendora.

Sally briefly played in George White's *Scandals* in the chorus and then 1929 arrived and destroyed the lingering good times of her heady Hollywood days. The stock market crash eviscerated the entertainment industry, and Sally was broke and borrowing from fellow actors to survive. She went back to vaudeville for any work she could find and did a brief stint in musical comedy with *Variety* shooting a few more arrows into her bruised ego, "a very young girl, pretty both in face and figure . . . showed little talent."[12] She created another show of her own with the Crosby Brothers, but again the reviews were awful.

In a letter to her mother, she paints a grim picture of Depression-era New York City:

"The work here is so hard and confining . . . When I get home I am so exhausted and sleepy I can't take a bath, just fall in bed and take a bath at dinner hour at the theatre and run across the street for something to eat real quick and all for 50 a week . . . I spent a miserable Xmas, just the same work and rehearsal and no one here I know . . . locked the keys to my apartment in the apartment and had to climb through snow and slush over back fences to get in. . . ."

She told her mother of going to see her father and trimming a Christmas tree, but she "felt so terribly blue."[13] First Hollywood and now vaudeville has collapsed. Then a story surfaces that years later people could point to and say, you see, she was a nudist all along. Her dance partner Bob Crosby walked into her dressing room and there was Sally Rand nude as the day she was born, cutting her toenails. The story is she continued talking to Crosby as if there was nothing strange about a young woman sitting around naked.

The Depression had decimated America with bank closures and a quarter of the population out of work, but this would set the stage for what would happen next. Then there is another glimmer of things to come. Sally Rand would be arrested many times in her life, mostly, of course, for obscenity. But she also had a bad temper that would get her dragged into court for assault. It would happen more than once. In this early incident she and brother Harold, who was an aspiring actor, were set to play in the musical comedy *Luana* at the Hammerstein Theatre. It happened during rehearsal when Harold was tap-dancing and the dance director Jack Haskell told him to stop and blew smoke into his face. Things degenerated from there.

He then called Sally a prima donna and Sally scratched the dance director with her nails, whereupon he told the director, Arthur Hammerstein, who fired them on the spot. Harold then punched Haskell and Sally bit his elbow and they all ended up in court. The charges were dismissed but it showed a certain ferocity that would surface when Sally was cornered or challenged. Biting people would be a form of aggressiveness that would come up more than once. It also shows how desperate she is becoming.

Hollywood had shifted gears and started looking for vehicles to get audiences to forget their troubles. Fred Astaire and Ginger Rogers danced in tuxedos and long dresses and everyone sipped champagne. In a strange turnabout, Hollywood seemed to be going into the fantasy business of telling Americans the good times would return while at the same time putting out Busby Berkeley productions and, of course, Ziegfeld Follies. Girls could get Americans out of their funk, and no one had more of an American Girl look than Sally Rand.

It was as if the rags-to-riches Horatio Alger character had been melted into her smile and her hopeful blue eyes. She was from rags and was now in danger of being a footnote to the evolution of the studio system. Could this really be it? One would think so. The hallmark of many artists was the quick rise and the equally quick descent. It is a fuse that burns brightly and then suddenly burns out before reaching the main power, the combustion that produces stardom. Sally Rand had ridden the Hollywood Ferris wheel, then vaudeville, and now she was reduced to playing in skits in high school auditoriums in Minnesota. The film roles were that of an extra soon forgotten after the film was shown.

The summer of 1931 Sally went to Chicago to star in the play *The World Between* at the Adelphi Theatre. This gave twenty-seven-year-old Sally Rand a legitimate role on the stage that might be able to restart her career. The show opened on September 17 and closed four weeks later. She finally scored a dancing role in *Sweethearts on Parade*, which was a burlesque show that left her in Chicago. The show had either disbanded, run out of money, or fired Sally Rand. Now she was broke in a city devastated by the Great Depression and with a third of the banks closed. Fifty percent unemployment plagued the city.

Sally Rand was now part of that 50 percent and was sleeping in alleys, back rooms, anywhere she could find. She would later recall, "It was the worst of the Great Depression. I thought that if things got tough, I'd just pick up my toe slippers and go back into the ballet. But there wasn't a working ballet in America. No theatres had openings because of the Depression. There were no nightclubs because of Prohibition. Getting laid was easier than getting drunk. There were more whorehouses than speakeasies. So, what does a ballerina do? You do the best you can with what you've got . . . and I did."[14]

In eight months, *A Century of Progress* will open in Chicago. The World's Fair of 1933 is a bet against the darkest times America had ever seen. Many people thought the city was insane to have a fair when no one had any money to spend. Chicago shrugged. It was just the time to have a fair and show the world it was time to fight back. The girl sleeping under cardboard in the alleys of the city would have understood that. She was down but she was not out. It is here in Chicago she goes to find some ostrich feathers for a tryout at the Paramount Club. It is here where she hatches a plan. And it is here that the Chicago World's Fair will change her life.

CHAPTER SIX

Down and Out in Chicago

1931

TWELVE YEARS AFTER HELEN BECK HAD RUN OFF WITH THE CIRCUS, Sally Rand is walking down State Street in Chicago. The Model Ts are snugged to the curbs, and people are huddled in long coats with hats pulled low. Bad times. The Depression has clapped down like a lid on a box with the crash of 1929, and Chicago had been hit harder than other cities. Newspapers blow along the sidewalk, and Sally catches one with her hand. She is freezing after sleeping in an alley all night. The garbage man had lifted the box she was under and jumped straight back. Her coat she had worn in Hollywood was too thin for Chicago winters. She was so hungry she stared in windows at people eating in restaurants.

Sally Rand had been stranded in Chicago when *Sweethearts on Parade* folded. She had been to Chicago before for a publicity stunt with the Polar Club. The group that plunged into Lake Michigan in the dead of winter usually picked a day where the ice was thawing, but Sally Rand plunged into the icy waters and literally felt her breath leave. She would do anything for some press, but that was years ago and now she was desperate enough to jump into Lake Michigan again if someone would give her some money.

The Depression had people out on the street corners selling apples. Homes were foreclosed, and families lived in alleys or under bridges or disbanded. Many sold their children to other families in desperation. A reporter for the *New Republic* described a scene in New York City in

1931: "There is a line of men three or sometimes four abreast and a block long and wedged so tightly no passerby can break through. The reason for this is those at the head of line will eat tonight."[1] Fifty-four men arrested in Times Square considered themselves lucky because they would be fed. President Herbert Hoover believed in laissez-faire and that the American people just had to wait for the economy to right itself. He did not put stock in government intervention or stimulus programs. He served as the poster boy in 2008 for what not to do when the economy crashes. Americans began to starve. A 1932 *New York Times* article read, "Found starving under a rude canvas shelter in a patch of woods on Flatboard Ridge, where they had lived for five days on wild berries and apples, a woman and her sixteen-year-old daughter were fed and clothed today by the police and placed in the city almshouse."[2]

The paper blared the bad news of the Great Depression. A third of the banks had failed. Twenty-five percent unemployment. Franklin Delano Roosevelt would tell Americans that the only thing to fear was fear itself. Thousands of Americans were sleeping under bridges or going through the scraps of food in the alleys. Sally Rand had become one of those thousands.

She was just about to let the paper go when she saw an advertisement for the Paramount Club. They were having tryouts for dancers. Sally felt her pulse rise. It was the first bit of good news she had since Hollywood gave her the boot. The talkies had come. She had been in over twenty silent movies and now she was sleeping under boxes in alleys. The twenty-seven-year-old was down but not out. She would be at that tryout. Sally held the paper, her eyes watering, and saw another article. Chicago was having a World's Fair in 1933 and they were calling it *A Century of Progress*. It was to be built on the lakefront and rival the 1893 Columbian Exposition.

Sally stared down State Street. Men were sleeping in doorways and alleys. Who were they kidding? People were sleeping in tents outside of Chicago and starving. Chicago itself was bankrupt. How were they going to pay for a World's Fair? The article said the fair would cost twenty-seven million dollars and would celebrate the one-hundred-year anniversary of the incorporation of Chicago. It would be a technology fair. A fair of the future. Chicago just had a fair back in 1893 and it had barely broken even, and that fair was publicly funded. Then there was a smaller one in 1921 on Navy Pier. The 1933 World's Fair was to be a one-season, one-shot affair. Sally's fingers ached from the cold. She shook her head. Who would have money to spend at the fair? Maybe the gangsters. They were the only people with money now. Maybe Al Capone.

They said the fair would have a Skyride and a Midway. There would be lots of concessions with lots of shows. Sally Rand felt her heart quicken. She wanted to get back to Hollywood. She didn't believe that a speech impediment could derail her career. She had already decided to find a voice coach, someone who could get rid of her lisp and her Missouri accent. She wanted to get back into the light and this World's Fair could do it for her. But first she needed a job. And that meant she had to wow them at the Paramount Club.

Sally turned the paper over and read that Adolf Hitler was consolidating power in Germany and Benito Mussolini had risen to power in Italy. The paper said Chicago saw the 1933 World's Fair as a way to rehabilitate its sagging reputation as a Wild West town of gangsters. Later, a book published to promote the 1933 World's Fair gave a snapshot of the best statistics the organizers could offer up: "3.475 million people lived in Chicago in some 400,000 dwellings; they drove 396,533 automobiles along 226 miles of parklike boulevards; they attended 1,800 churches and sent their children to 360 public schools. Only 11 percent of the population owned a car in 1933. Horses delivered milk, blacksmiths dotted city blocks, and carriages competed for space."[3]

Sally let the paper go and watched the wind take it away. She had to get that job at the Paramount. She needed something that would set her apart from everyone else. She still had her biggest asset, her body. She was five-foot-tall, athletic, and had a figure that could still stop men in their tracks. She didn't mind being nude and was not self-conscious at all. She had to shock people. She had to get back to Hollywood, where she could take her rightful place once again among the rising starlets. She saw a secondhand store and peered inside. A man leaning against the wall outside in a slouched hat smiled at her. Sally did a quick soft shoe and he clapped.

"You know you should be in show business," the man rasped.

"I am, honey."

Sally went inside the gloomy store full of clothes people had pawned so they could get something to eat. That's what people did in the Great Depression. They sold everything just for some bread to eat. Sally grabbed up a chemise. She could do something with that. She walked along the rows with the woman at the counter watching her. She saw two four-foot ostrich feathers near some discarded Navy coats. Sally picked up the two feathers and swept them over her body. They weighed about seven pounds. She waved them back and forth and saw the swans at her farm in the Ozarks again in the ponds and the swamps. The feathers reminded her of Pavlova's *Dying Swan* she had seen in Kansas with her mother. She kept moving the feathers back and forth. Maybe she could just fly right out of the store and leave Chicago. They whooshed through the air and now she was moving back and forth swishing the fans one in front and one in back. People wanted something sexy now. That's what men wanted, they wanted to see the clothes come off, but slowly. You always held something back.

But there was art in her vision. There was something else. Something that could transport people to another place away from the bad times. Sally could feel it as she moved in the dim light, her blond hair shining, her dancing shoes sanding the wood floor. The woman behind the counter watched her lift one fan over her chest and one behind her rear. Dancing to the right music it might just work. Something that went beyond the strippers and the burlesque dancers. Something that would evoke the ethereal beauty of *The Dying Swan*. She pivoted and did a kick and then turned around and faced the woman with her arms folded.

"How much for these?"

Up to now Sally had never taken her clothes off for anyone on stage, but the ad she saw in the newspaper on State Street gave her hope. "Wanted—Exotic Acts and Dancers. Apply Paramount Club." The other dancers form *Sweethearts on Parade* showed up, too. Sally was so broke, she was later quoted as saying it was either this or "prostitution."[4] It is hard to know if she was serious, but she was desperate.

The red-light district of Chicago on South State Street was a short distance from the fair. The burlesque theaters featured "programs of comic skits, films, strip acts, singing, and dancing."[5] Surprisingly, both men and women went to these shows and paid from "ten to twenty-five cents at the seamier sites and 1.75 at the classier venues."[6] Women often made up one-third of the audience, but both sexes wanted to escape the grinding reality of the Great Depression into some sort of fantasy.

The Chicago police looked the other way and allowed the striptease to make its appearance. At bottom the burlesque was a way for women to make money. And this was what Sally Rand had in mind as she stood in the back of the Paramount. She had no way of knowing it, but the times had changed, and the fact that she had no costume and only two ostrich-feather fans worked in her favor. "The shift in attitudes toward drinking, smoking, wearing makeup and experiencing premarital sex culminated in heightened emphasis on eroticism."[7]

Some would say Sally's decision to go out and dance nude behind two four-foot fans had roots far back in her own psychological makeup—that she had no alternative at that point and literally nothing to lose. A dozen other chorus girls in the same predicament were looking for a spot at the Paramount. She saw two other dancers from Sweethearts, and they had all lined up on the stage and did a walk across earlier in the day. Big Ed Callahan, the owner, shook his head.

"Girls. Business here in the Loop is taking a nosedive. We have to come up with something to get the customers in. . . . [W]e've all got to eat this year. If you want the job, come in with your costume at ten o'clock tonight. That's all."[8] The two dancers before her had asked Sally what she was going to wear, and Sally confessed she didn't know. The two ostrich feather fans were her only chance. When Sally arrived, the Paramount was deserted. She went into a dressing room and saw five girls getting ready. As Holly Knox writes in *Sally Rand: From Film to Fans*, "A woman putting on fake eyelashes patted the dressing table next to her. 'This one is yours honey and I hope you're ready cause curtain is in ten.'"[9]

"My wardrobe isn't ready. I'm new here. It's my first night."

The brunette shrugged. "Callahan said you're first. That's the rule here, honey; the newest girl goes on first. Isadora over there has been here over a week. She goes last."[10]

Another girl dressed as a harem dancer planted the seed and suggested she go on nude: "You'll never get the gown done in time. I saw someone dance with only the fans once."[11] Sally sat down and began to apply makeup and wondered if things could get any worse. "I hope they have a phonograph here." The woman shrugged. "Sorry, no phonograph. All we have is Hector. He's Callahan's nephew. He plays the piano."[12]

Sally groaned. Holly Knox, who worked with Sally Rand in later years, claimed to have interviewed the star and built her scenes from Sally's recollections. The small book is lightly researched, but it does have the ring of someone who took notes while interviewing her subject. This is Knox's version of the tryout at the Paramount on that cold Depression-era night.

"The lights were bright on the tiny stage of the Paramount Club and the piano player was not sober, but the essence of Sally's future was established that night. She manipulated the huge ostrich fans slowly and gracefully to the strains of 'Clair de Lune.' She artfully showed only teasing glimpses of her body, caressing the fans as she pirouetted on the small stage. A unity evolved with the fans and the woman. At times the fans assumed a lifelike amorosity. Her dance was eight breathtaking minutes long. At the end of it, when she threw up her fans like the Winged Victory statue, even the dancers who were watching backstage applauded loudly."[13]

Sally Rand would years later offer this version of that night. "I finally convinced one club owner that if my costume was small enough and the fans big enough, the audience would love it. . . . Suddenly it was time to go on and I didn't have time to go back to the hotel to get the little nightgown I was going to cut down and use for the costume . . . so I reasoned that if I kept the fans moving fast enough no one would know if I had on a costume or not."[14]

In this version Sally said she had the pianist play "Moonlight Sonata" and had blue gels put in the spotlights. This sounds like something she would have done later, as now she was just another chorus girl trying out for a spot. From then on, her fan dance would be to "Moonlight Sonata," Frederic Chopin's Waltz in C Sharp Minor, or Claude Debussy's 1890 composition "Clair de Lune," which meant "the light of the moon" in French.[15] Sally later reflected, "I've never been quite sure if the audience was stunned by the beauty of the dance or by the uneasy feeling that they had just seen a naked lady dancing before them for five minutes."[16]

Sally was hired. But what did Eddie Callahan see that night? He saw what John Van Guilder, a businessman from Knoxville, Tennessee, would see when he would go to Chicago and buy a ticket on the Midway to Sally Rand's show at the World's Fair.

The lights dimmed as he settled into the theater, and then something happened. The world of failed banks and soup lines faded away. By now Sally was using a large plastic bubble to hide behind, and as the music flowed out from the darkness, Van Guilder saw a nymph from another world. A single blue spotlight illuminated her painted white body, and Van Guilder later recalled, "With all the grace of a woodland nymph, she toyed and danced around and played with and tossed into the air her transparent soap bubble. Somehow, one felt as though secretly watching some little woodland creature at play in the moonlight." Van Guilder was so taken with Sally Rand's dance that he arranged to meet her backstage and offered to buy the bubble from her. She could not part with it but gave the businessman from Tennessee an autographed picture and a kiss. Van Guilder sent her roses with a note expressing his belief that she had made the world a better place. Certainly, for John Van Guilder, she had.[17]

Eddie Callahan saw sex when Sally Rand danced, but also "a vision that would transport people from the grim realities of the early Depression years and give them a glimmer of hope that at least, for a little while, they could see something beautiful . . ."[18] Sally Rand was a poor girl from the Ozarks who had run away with the circus and then gone to Hollywood and was now living on the streets and eating hand to mouth to survive. She was living what people all over the country also were going through. The unrelenting hard times gave no quarter, it gave no escape. She had unknowingly danced in the Paramount Club in a way that channeled the ballet dance she loved, *The Dying Swan*, and a yearning for something beyond the cold wind of bad fortune blowing down State Street. By taking two ostrich feathers and dancing for her next meal, Sally Rand had inadvertently found the theme of the 1933 Chicago World's Fair . . . hope.

CHAPTER SEVEN

The Paramount

1932

It was rough. One show after another. Gangsters coming in and propositioning her. Smoke-filled nights and long hours. She slept during the day and returned to the Paramount in the evening. Men grabbed at her, they threw things, they wanted sex after the show. This was not Hollywood. Not even close. But it was work when most people had no work.

The antihero arrived in Hollywood in 1931. *The Public Enemy* with James Cagney hit the big screen. Humphrey Bogart and Edward G. Robinson would cue up their own films as gangsters and give Al Capone a run for his money with flashy suits, fast cars, and lots of violence and, to some degree, sex. Because she was working in a world on the fringes of society, Sally Rand encountered gangsters at the Paramount Club. She claimed to have met Al Capone, who offered her a job, but there is no evidence of this.

Still, the Chicago winters were brutal and dark and walking down State Street under a low ominous sky, Sally felt if she didn't get back to California soon, she never would. The burlesque world just didn't have enough for her hopes and dreams. But there was a World's Fair coming that promised a brighter future. Sally Rand still was bitter over her Hollywood failure and, worse, that she had her family move there when her Hollywood fame seemed assured.

The truth is it was an amazing piece of serendipitous luck that put Sally in proximity to the 1933 Chicago World's Fair. If she had stayed in Hollywood, the chances are she would have remained a B actress and faded into obscurity. She did not have the overwhelming talent required to break out of the pack. Her fame would have never approached what would happen at the Chicago World's Fair. There was danger though in the path she had chosen. One night men came into the club and talked to the owner, Ed Callahan. Holly Knox describes the scene.

> *The first summer after she had begun performing at The Paramount, she saw Big Ed talking to two men in long coats and bowlers. One of them poked Big Ed in the chest, and Sally could see her boss turning red. The men left, and he came over to the bar where Sally was sitting. "Not only are we getting the shaft from the Government, they give gooks like that the right to push people around." Ed turned to the bartender. "Give me a Scotch . . . the good stuff."[1]*
>
> *Sally looked at her boss.*
>
> *"They want you to change booze dealers?"*
>
> *In Chicago everyone knew where the booze came from. The gangsters supplied the beer and whiskey and inevitably wanted the clubs to buy from them exclusively. Most people didn't see the cost of their booze firsthand. Ed stared down at his drink and nodded slowly.*
>
> *"They're coming back tonight with the regional boss. Said something about wanting to catch your act, Sal. That must be why I'm rating a visit from the number two boy."[2]*

Then Sally found herself attracting the attention of a very dangerous gangster. One night during a performance, she noticed the atmosphere in the club was very tense with only one table applauding loudly. After the show there was a knock on her dressing room door. "Another dancer, Isadora, stood there with a dozen red roses. She was chewing gum and gushing. 'This guy says he'll see you in front after the show.'"[3]

Sally took the roses and knew who they were from. Isadora went on, "Boy, this guy must be some big shot. He gave me ten bucks to tell you he'll be waiting."[4]

Sally picked up the card from the rose petals and saw two initials, V.G. The would-be suitor was Vito Genovese, a notorious gangster from

New Jersey who would eventually lead the Genovese crime family. At this point Vito is an enforcer who is out for a night on the town and has his sights set on Sally Rand. Vito would have been in conflict with Al Capone if he was moving in on the Paramount, but he also had ties with Lucky Luciano. He was known for his viciousness and had worked for Joe Masseria in Manhattan, a powerful gang boss. Sally Knox then describes what happened when Sally Rand went out into the club and saw Vito surrounded by gangsters. We must assume this was told to Knox when she met Sally Rand in the 1950s.

She held her hand out in greeting. Vito Genovese stood up and took her hand and held it a moment too long. The other men remained seated.

"Your dance is exciting, Miss Rand ... or should I call you Sally?"

She looked squarely into his dark eyes. "All my friends call me Sally. Pick what category you fit in and take your choice."

Vito laughed. "Sit down with us and we'll decide that." He called the waiter. "Drinks here, please."

Sally looked up.

"My usual ginger ale."

"So, Sally. Afraid to touch Ed's stuff?"

"Certainly not! I never drink when I'm working and only when I celebrate something."

Vito moved closer to her.

"Then why don't we celebrate your quitting this joint and coming to work for me at the shore?"

"I never make spur of the moment decisions."

Vito's voice became cold. "I'll give you till tomorrow night to make up your mind. You're too good for this dump."

"Mr. Genovese ... Ed Callahan is a good friend of mine. We have an agreement. When my contract is completed, I'll leave."

"I think he'll agree, baby." The icy voice went on. "He'll agree to anything."

Sally got up.

"If you'll excuse me, Mr. Genovese, I must get ready for the next show."

She turned her back and left.[5]

53

A week later Vito was back with more roses, ominously red and white with a card that read Red for Life White for Death. According to Sally her boss, Eddie Callahan, had been walking her home since Vito's visit. It is hard to know how much of this was about Sally and how much was about whose booze Eddie Callahan was using for his club. It is plausible Vito was using Sally to get to Ed. In a year her boss would be found shot dead. The assumption was he didn't comply with the demands of Vito or whoever wanted to muscle in.

Sally would later say a hit was put on her by Vito but that she was too big and that kept her alive. This might have been true, but it does have the ring of Sally Rand hyperbole. One thing was for sure, the seediness of the Chicago nightclub scene was a long way from Hollywood and Sally wanted desperately to get back to the land of dreams that had tossed her out. And that path led through the Chicago World's Fair of 1933.

The burlesque world Sally Rand joined almost by accident began in the early twentieth century and then died in the middle. Her timing could not have been more perfect because by 1960 it would be all over. In Europe around 1811, a burlesque made fun of the legitimate plays of the time. There were no chorus lines, comedians, or exotic dancers. By 1840 it was comic plays or entertainment for the working classes in Great Britain. America would add to this as the new century began, burlesque evolved, "into grand productions performed by scantily clad women."

In 1869 a fusion between minstrel shows in America and the burlesque occurred and set a standard framework: "This new show followed a three-act formula that was to become the signature burlesque show we know today—an opening with a lavish song and dance number, a second act of variety performers, a third act or skit or send up of popular play, and finally a grand finale by the entire company."[6]

This vaudevillian fare lasted into the 1920s when the striptease elbowed its way in as radio and film destroyed vaudeville and the Great Depression demanded entertainment that would take people away from their troubles. Stripper Dixie Evans recalled that "people in that era were so depressed and there was no hope. The masses were just out of work and out of money, but for those small pennies, it was worth it to see one of those great shows. They were mostly for the American public that had nothing."[7] Dixie was talking about the burlesque, but by the 1960s hard-core pornography would finish off the burlesque and its upstart cousin the striptease. But Sally Rand was in the middle of a time when America wanted escapism and along came a new variation on the old theme of burlesque.

People in 1932 on State Street in Chicago could forget their cares and duck into the Paramount Club and watch a young woman dance behind feathers for a few cents. The woman appeared to have nothing on except for some body makeup. And when she finished and raised her feathers, people were sure she had nothing on. This type of nudity slipped by the cops and occasionally landed Sally Rand in court, but at this point the fix was in and Eddie Callahan's Paramount Club was able to have the kind of entertainment people wanted.

In 1932, the year Sally Rand began her fan dance at the Paramount, veterans marched on Washington demanding payment for bonus certificates they had received for service in World War I. The Bonus Army marched on Washington and camped around the capitol, with 17,000 veterans and their families living in tents and pledging not to leave until Congress paid them their promised money. President Hoover dispatched the US Army under General Douglas MacArthur and General Patton with six tanks to drive out the marchers. Tear gas was used, and two Bonus Army veterans were shot and killed in skirmishes. Jim Sheridan, a veteran who marched on Washington, later recalled, "The picture I'll always remember is MacArthur coming down Pennsylvania Avenue. And believe me, ladies and gentlemen, he came on a white horse. He was riding a white horse. Behind him were tanks, troops of the regular army . . . the soldiers through tear gas and vomiting gas . . . they were younger than the marchers. It was like sons attacking their fathers."[8]

The shanties and tent city were burned. Some believed this was the beginning of a revolution with soldiers firing on other soldiers. But this was the times, and we cannot separate Sally Rand from the Great Depression. Her decision to do anything from 1929 on was dictated by a need to eat. The feather dancing was in one sense just another gig to survive. But Sally had stumbled into something that she didn't even understand.

Nudity. Sally Rand became a pioneer in nudity. She wore panties on her first show but nothing up top. In the following shows she wore nothing at all and then she began to mix it up. Sometimes she wore a sheer stocking, sometimes nude, sometimes just some pasties. Depending on who recalls the shows the answers vary. At the Paramount Club, even though she was partially covered at the beginning, it was rumored she was nude most of the time. Sally Rand would also begin using a body paint and eventually a sheer leotard. The Paramount began to do a booming business. Two weeks after Sally was hired, she had a line out the door. The girl from Missouri had thought she was going to be a star once before in Hollywood, and now it looked like she might get a second chance at stardom in a very different world. Chicago's World's Fair was right around the corner, and Sally saw a ticket back to the land of milk and honey that had rudely sent her packing. Hollywood, she had learned, was a fickle bride, but there was always the comeback.

The 1933 World's Fair would give her a platform. They would hire twenty thousand people to run the fair. Why shouldn't she be one of them? She had gone down to the lakefront several times and watched the cranes and the endless boxcars snaking to the lakefront. They had built special tracks that went right up to the lake. Here they unloaded a small city. Sally watched the men swinging around on the girders of the Skyride 625 feet up. The World's Fair appealed to her. It was new and young and looked to the future. A Century of Progress. Science would point the way to the future, and the bright colors of the buildings reminded her of sets in Hollywood. It was the biggest set in the world, complete with streets that resembled Paris. Sally often watched the construction until the evening, when she had to go back to the club. Lake Michigan caught the last light of the day, and many times she walked along the lake pretending it was the Pacific Ocean. She had been to Hollywood once and she would return. It was still hard to believe she had been thrown out.

CHAPTER EIGHT

A Century of Progress

1933

SO NOW WE ARE BACK TO SALLY RAND WHO IS STILL FLOATING AROUND in Lake Michigan after falling out of the boat. Chicago preened in front of her, a glittering metropolis strutting its stuff. She is still waiting to be rescued and considers swimming toward the lights of the city. She wonders about Chicago now. She had always taken the city for granted but it is where she became a star. To hell with it. That is what Chicago said when people said no one could have a World's Fair during times when people did not know where their next meal was coming from.

Sally spit out some water. She was getting cold. She looked at the city again. Times were tough. Chicago said it was going to have a fair celebrating its incorporation of one hundred years. But then it changed, and it became a fair of the future, *A Century of Progress*. "Fair organizers sought to generate optimism in a city beaten down by economic woes, but they also sought to redeem Chicago's unsavory reputation, drilled into imaginations worldwide by events such as the St. Valentine's Day Massacre. . . . Chicago reform politicians saw an opportunity to re-create the city's image in the proposed exposition."[1] The old model of the civic-minded and -funded fair was gone, replaced by a fair that would generate income from the fruits of capitalism.

Sally saw a break wall that ringed the outer harbor. Might as well swim toward it. She began a slow chop. The water wasn't that cold and besides she had swum in lakes in the Ozarks ever since she was a little girl. She swam toward the city that had ignored the world and put itself out there and said not only would it build a World's Fair, but that fair would point the way to better times. In short, the fair would remedy the Great Depression. "Fair organizers' futuristic plans for what came to be called A Century of Progress championed corporate capitalism, the very culprit that many Americans blamed for their economic woes . . . a fair would, the planners predicted, counter the Depression's insidious economic and psychological impact by giving Chicago and its labor force a shot in the arm."[2]

Sally used a light chop as the seawall came closer. She could now hear the water slopping up against the cement. She rested and saw the lights of the Skyride. Six hundred and twenty-five feet tall, it was to rival the Ferris wheel of the 1893 fair. People could see the city from the air. Technology. Science. They had remolded the fair and told everyone that science and consumerism would solve their problems and the future was indeed bright. But they were broke.

The fair was not pulling in what it needed. That is until Sally Rand came along. They were supposed to come for big spectacular things like the Skyride or the Zephyr, the train that set a new speed record from Denver to Chicago. Or the television that showed a faint image or to watch a car get assembled or to call anywhere in the United States while eating microwave popcorn and sitting in the air-conditioning of a futuristic home. But what they came to see was not the lights or the fireworks or the man who could turn his head all the way around or the preemie babies in incubators . . . they came to see Sally Rand.

It surprised her. She had slept in alleys, been threatened by gangsters, been broke, hungry, sick . . . but never did she think a random event, an inspiration, *a stunt*, would lead to the kind of money she saw appear in her hands. Thousands a week. They had to hire extra accountants. People just had to see her. She literally pulled the fair from the red into the black. Yes, this little woman of just five foot and 105 pounds was responsible for the profitability of this glittering city they had built on the lakefront. The Rainbow City. It had its own police department, fire department, hospital, and it needed twenty thousand people to run it and one Sally Rand to turn it around.

A Century of Progress had smashed the records. Privately funded. Built in record time. Using as much power as Madison, Wisconsin, the fair had made her a star and she had bailed out the investors. No wonder they paid her so well. It was nothing compared to what she had brought in. And they had gotten rid of Al Capone just a few short years before. Chicago had looked down the barrel of the gun and not blinked and neither had she. It was a hell of a run. People from all over the world came to the fair. Over thirty-nine million in all, and Sally Rand had become nationally famous for a dance she did on a whim. And now . . . now she was in Lake Michigan, swimming toward a cement retaining wall.

What was it they came to see? In 1952 she would give an interview to a Chicago newspaper and was asked where the idea for the fan dance came from. "White birds flying in the moonlight on my grandfather's farm . . . the farm was a swampy place and the big herons migrating South always stopped there. And the moon comes out real early out there, an enormous big Harvest moon."[3]

Sally stared at the city. Sure, she was naked behind her feathers but there was something else. They saw *The Dying Swan*. It was all about life to her. Death came eventually but you had to fight against it. That is what Anna Pavlova had been able to communicate through her ballet. That is what Sally communicated with her feathers. What was the Great Depression anyway but a fight against the darkness? They saw her as The Swan. She was the light in the dark. She showed them a moment of beauty in what had become an awful world. Then another thought occurred to her; maybe they just came to see a hillbilly from the Ozarks who had managed to go from rags to riches, even if she wasn't rich, yet. Either way she was alright with it. You didn't look a gift horse in the mouth.

Sally had been swimming for a half hour. A short, neat freestyle. She kept swimming and then heard a motor rumble across the water. She stopped and saw a light sweep toward her. She held up her hand and shouted. The Coast Guard boat paused, then a light blinded her. The boat began a steady chop toward her.

"It's about goddam time," she muttered.

Sally waited and then turned back to the glittering Skyride and the lights of the World's Fair buildings along the lakefront. It would all soon be torn down. Just a memory. She would remember her time there forever. It was where she had become Sally Rand. And to think she had almost not been able to dance at all at the fair. In fact, they wouldn't even let her in.

CHAPTER NINE

Lady Godiva

1933

AFTER SALLY WAS FISHED OUT OF LAKE MICHIGAN, THE PICTURE IN THE
Chicago newspaper showed Sally Rand sipping from a large mug of coffee
in a flannel nightie from Capt. John O. Anderson of the Coast Guard. Her
hair is braided and flat from the lake. She is wearing the captain's bathrobe
and handing her the steaming coffee is George Arnold, who pulled her
out of the lake. George has a captain's hat on the back of his head and
is smiling as the photographer takes the picture. Sally Rand looks like a
little girl with her feet pointed inward. She had bested the fair and bested
the world, but you have to wonder if she knew she was on the pivot of
her career. She was between fame and fortune and yet she had it before.

Sally didn't want the picture. It was bad for her brand. She was an
American sex symbol. A star. How did that happen? Opening night of
the fair then with fireworks from barges in Lake Michigan while the
National Anthem blasted out of the loudspeakers. May 27, 1933. Flags
waving along the promenade while bathing beauties posed on the running boards of Chryslers and Studebakers. The Queen of the Fair looks
like a prettier Statue of Liberty in her costume while Mayor Kelly opens
the fair that will run for five months. Fake steamship funnels beckoned
people to travel to the Streets of Paris. This would be where Sally would
make her mark.

But that opening night with cigarette girls giving out cigarettes to
children on the bawdy streets was amazing. You could sketch a naked

woman and drink beer and wine now that Franklin Roosevelt had said it was alright. This phantasmagoria of pleasures was the citadel where Sally Rand would launch her fan dance. There was a merry-go-round bar and artists sketching people on sidewalks outside of cafes. It was Paris, New York, and Chicago.

One could see microwave popcorn and television, buy a box of Cracker Jacks, eat a bowl of Shredded Wheat, see Judy Garland sing, watch the Zephyr make a Denver to Chicago record-setting run, watch cars get assembled and then drive off an assembly line, see peas get canned, see babies in incubators, see Eleanor Roosevelt make a long-distance call to anywhere in the world, see a modern home with air-conditioning, a plane port, and a dishwasher, ride in a dirigible, ride in the Skyride 625 feet up in the air, take a seaplane ride, or just simply marvel at the fantastic light shows and the buildings painted with all the colors of the rainbow.

Chicago was going to kick off its bad reputation and break into the light with a fair that would bring money and jobs to the masses. But the one thing the World's Fair of 1933 did not have on its opening day was Sally Rand. How the girl now sitting in a Coast Guard station in an oversized robe with a cup of coffee in her hand had come back from absolute obscurity is almost too impossible to believe. Almost as impossible to believe as the disaster of her Hollywood career.

It all really started with the Beaux Arts Ball in Chicago in which costumed students every year partied all night to raise funds for a worthy cause. Sally would later sum it up this way years later to Studs Terkel, "There were bread lines and people were starving. Yet, women in Chicago had the bad taste to have themselves photographed in gowns, they were going to wear at the ball."[1] By 1927 it was a staple of the Chicago social calendar, but they felt they needed something to spice things up. Committee members Benjamin Marshall and Andrew Rebori suggested an appearance by Lady Godiva to boost ticket sales. Marshall would later write, "Certainly we should have a Lady Godiva. The legend about her is beautiful. Her appearance on a horse, provided it isn't too cold, will be an artistic achievement such as Chicago has never seen."[2]

The story of Lady Godiva had to be in Sally's mind when she made her ride into the World's Fair in 1933. She would later tell Studs Terkel the original idea of crashing the ball came from a friend. "A friend was doing press work for me. We were socially conscious. She said, 'Why don't you have your picture taken in the costume you're going to wear at the Beaux Arts Ball?' I didn't have a costume. She said, 'How about Lady Godiva?'"

Lady Godiva was a woman who rode naked through the streets of Coventry in the eleventh century to protest her husband's taxation of his tenants. The legend has come down through time in the image of a nude woman on a horse, long hair covering her loins, with the townspeople ordered to shutter their homes. A man named Tom violated the order, and "Peeping Tom" would forever be used to describe voyeurs.

But Sally Rand's income would depend on the Peeping Toms of the world.

Dancing in Chicago at the Paramount during the Great Depression beat starving, but, like every person who has tasted quicksilver fame, Sally wanted it back. As her friend Holly Knox would later write, "She was more than a little bitter with Hollywood because she had expected great things for herself there. Her family had moved out to be with her in her success and she was the one who had to leave them there because of lack of work."[3]

We can imagine her frustration. The biggest show in the world and she was not part of it. Sally Rand had left Hollywood when her voice proved she was not to be part of the future of the motion picture industry. Now she was stuck at a strip club on State Street in Chicago. And right next door on the lakefront they were building the largest fair in the world.

The fair cost thirty-seven million dollars. The Streets of Paris were full of open-air cafes with the smell of fried food, popcorn, cigarette smoke floating up into the summer night. Barges full of fireworks had blasted over Lake Michigan with whistles from steamships adding to the cacophony of the opening of a World's Fair in the year 1933. A faux ocean liner with real gangplanks and towering smokestacks over seventy feet in the air attracted people who felt like they had truly entered another land, another country. People could now drink. And the people wanted to see sex. There were peep shows and burlesques shows, and if you wanted to draw a picture of naked women, there were plenty of those, too. Fortune-tellers, palm readers, cigarette girls, barkers, clowns, strange human oddities, and if you wanted to you could take a ride on a roller coaster or go fly away in a blimp or ride 625 feet up in the Skyride. The Skyride was supposed to be the kicker, what everyone would remember, but the kicker was a 105-pound blond who was gearing up for her show on the Streets of Paris.

She had ridden a white horse into a hundred-dollar-a-plate dinner with nothing on but body paint, a blond wig, and sheer guts. And now she would perform for seventy thousand people in the first month alone as a master of ceremony announced her fan dance. The revenues from Sally Rand's act would require the fair owners to hire extra accountants. This stripper at the Paramount Club was now responsible for the Chicago World's Fair of 1933 becoming profitable . . . how did this happen?

We have lots of different takes on the Sally Rand ride into history. The supercharged version is she crashed the fair with her white horse and was immediately arrested and immediately hired. This did happen in a sense. But let's dissect it a bit. Sally had tried unsuccessfully to get into the fair, and she was frustrated and ended up hatching her plan with her boss, Eddie Callahan. But before that she had been a thorn in the side of one Charles Weber, who ran the beer concessions on the Streets of Paris.

Sally would later say Weber gave her the idea to crash the party. "I'm harassing Charlie Weber for that job at the World's Fair, and he's not coming up with it. Because the Streets of Paris was sponsored by the high and mighty of this town, the social set . . . he suggested I crash the prevue, the night before it opens."[4] There were some mob connections rumored that tied Weber to Al Capone, but the stripper at the night club on State Street got nowhere.

Sally was not going to be invited in. The opening party took place the night before the fair officially opened. A Mrs. William Hearst put on the hundred-dollar-a-plate dinner, and this was the dinner that Sally and Ed Callahan crashed with their stunt of a naked woman sitting sidesaddle on a white horse. Local Chicago papers described the party of three thousand notables: "The cream of Chicago glided through the party in formal evening clothes or in clever costumes that sometimes aped their social inferiors—cavemen, Native Americans, peasants, and French maids . . ."[5] Sally would later cite a woman with thousand-dollar bills composing her dress.

The precedent was Sally trying the same stunt the December before at the Chicago Artists Ball in 1932 where they had a "Lady Godiva" appear. An article in the *Chicago Tribune* sheds light on how this unfolded. "Miss. Rand not yet come into the full flush of her fame appeared at the hotel wearing a blond wig and a large white horse. The horse turned out to be temporary. Worried hotel minions took one cautious look and decided Dobbin was wearing the wrong shoes." Sally was freezing on the horse that she had ridden down a wintery Michigan Avenue. The horse stayed outside while Sally threw herself onto "a snowy dining table . . . four smirking porters picked up the table, the wig, and Sally, and bore them across the ballroom floor."[6] Sally was paid twenty-five dollars and called reporters to take a picture of her on her horse.

These ended up in the *Chicago Tribune* and ultimately in the Papers of Sally Rand in the sixty-one boxes in the Chicago History Museum. The picture shows Sally Rand barefoot and apparently naked on the horse with long hair covering her breasts. The caption reads, "Sally Rand. Beautiful Former Los Angeles Dancer and Film Actress is chosen as Lady Godiva at the Artist Martian Ball to be held in Chicago."[7]

Sally was not allowed to take the horse in, but this was a dry run for when she hired a boat to take her around to a yacht landing just off the Streets of Paris. Well, not exactly. Sally would tell Studs Terkel thirty years later how she solved the problem of crashing the party.

I hired the horse again, but the gates of the fair were closed . . . We go up to the Wrigley docks. The Streets of Paris had a yacht landing there . . . So I paid $8 for the tickets to the boat. He said, "Who's going with you?" I said, "Just a friend." So, I brought the horse on the boat and the man demurred. I said, "What do you care if it is a horse or a human?" At the yacht landing of the Streets of Paris, there was this little Frenchman who spoke no English. He figured that a broad that *arrives in a boat with a horse is supposed to be there. So, he opened the gate.*[8]

Sally then began her charge through the fair and ended up in the opening ceremonies. "Up to this time the party been pretty dull. They had two bands . . . The fanfare sounded, and the MC announced, 'Now Lady Godiva will take her famous ride!' Music played. Every photographer in the business, especially the Hearst ones, were there. Flashlight went off and the music played, and everybody was happy. They said, 'Do it again.' So, I did it again."[9]

The guests were shocked, but this was a World's Fair after all, and this was Chicago, and if there was a nude woman on a white horse, well then this must be part of the show. They applauded like mad. It was the Chicago World's Fair with a Lady Godiva. Sally Rand was then arrested by the police, but an attorney facilitated her release while photographers rained down with flashbulbs and questions. By the time Sally Rand returned to her flat just off Division Street, she had no idea if any of it had worked. She was still just working at the Paramount Club, but in the morning, walking blearily down Rush Street, she saw the newspapers and the pictures of herself perched on the white horse. She had become famous overnight and was national news. Lady Godiva had crashed the World's Fair; a naked woman on a white horse. Sally would later attribute a social consciousness to the motivation for her ride. "The ride, she recalled, did indeed secure for her a lucrative niche in the fair's activities. More than that, it made a social statement. She had felt a sense of satisfaction at having exposed herself to the elite women who were wearing expensive gowns. Rand claimed that riding naked was like saying, 'How dare you have a dress of thousand-dollar bills when people are hungry?'"[10]

Maybe. But it was a publicity stunt to get herself into the biggest show in the world at that moment. Sally Rand had a knack for sniffing out power and publicity and putting herself in the center of that vortex. She had done it very well in Hollywood and would have stayed there if she could have delivered a line without a lisp. She was intuitive with her career as any aspiring star must be. She felt where she should be and then did anything to make it happen. The dry run at the Artists Ball had stuck with her and she saw the way photographers swarmed her then. Something about a naked woman on a white horse or, simply put, sex sells.

And so now she is scurrying back to the World's Fair after seeing her photo on the front pages of the *Chicago Tribune*, the *Chicago Sun Times*, and the *Chicago Defender*. She rode the trolley back to the fairgrounds, where apparently there were people searching for the woman in the papers, Lady Godiva. As she later recalled, "I couldn't get in. There was a riot. All the people were waiting to tell them when Sally Rand was going to appear. You see, the fair had opened. To hell with cutting the ribbon. Every newspaper in America came up that morning with Lady Godiva opening the fair. The place was jammed. When does she go on? Nobody knew. A poor soul was walking the floor. 'Nobody's gonna come in unless Sally Rand's gonna be here.' I said, '*I'm Sally Rand*' . . . they hired me at 90 a week."[11]

She borrowed taxi fare back to Division Street to get her fans, and from that moment on, she would never get off the road. Another *Tribune* article attributes her fame to the fact she was arrested four times in one day. One of these arrests resulted in a jury trial. "Sally was pinched. She was pinched four shows in a row by a policewoman named McShane. At a jury trial . . . Sally testified with dignity and she did her dance for the jury with aplomb and the usual two fans. The jury found her guilty of exposing Sally too much and too often. After that Sally was famous."[12]

It would seem Sally herself backed up this view in a later interview. "This enormous policewoman . . . comes crashing through the scrim curtain. I thought she was a sex maniac . . . the police sirens are going and the whole detective squad is out there . . . I'm arrested. By this time, it's all over the radio . . . I went down to the police station, signed the necessary papers, came back, did my show, I was arrested again. Four times that day . . . the lines queued up for eleven solid weeks. I was doing seven shows a day at the Chicago Theater and seven shows a day at the Streets of Paris. I got my first 1,000 a week that week."[13]

Sally was eventually sentenced to one year in county jail until the policewoman Bessie McShane decided to come clean and admitted, in fact, Sally was not nude. "The fact is that Sally pays $42 a week for the pants she wears, a new pair for every performance. They are made of maline, which is a net. They are sewed on tight and pasted down. Over her breasts she wears a similar material, pasted on so no strap shows when she turns around. She spends more time dressing than she does in dancing. It hurts when she takes off the costume because it's stuck to her . . . that's all. As for the people who stand in line to see her, they're suckers."[14]

The sentence was reduced to just ten days and a two-hundred-dollar fine. Sally would not serve a single day. She would be arrested again and again for indecency. In a letter from her father to Sally's brother, William Beck cites a newspaper article of her arrest in Chicago in 1933. "It would appear at the end of her season in Chicago, Helen must have cut off the police graft allowance, so that in retaliation they closed in on her and then got the case before another judge. The statement of that juror showing that they convicted Helen because all the members of the jury were married men is unsettling to say the least. She may be able to pay the 200. Fine but the costs may be a lot more than that . . . she will have to appear in Chicago at the end of sixty days . . . but the sentence of one year in prison would still stand against her in Chicago."[15]

This was not all fun and games as Sally liked to frame it. Her legal problems took her income and time. Sally would view the resulting publicity as ultimately a good thing, but this would turn against her eventually. When it was all said and done, the result of her ride into the Chicago World's Fair of 1933 was that Sally Rand the actress, the stripper, had become for all time, *Sally Rand the Fan Dancer, The Star of the 1933 World's Fair*. The *Chicago Tribune* was right. She was famous, and she would have to stay famous.

Sally's definition of her dance as being inspired by the herons who flew over her grandfather's farm would be questioned by many. "My interpretation of a white bird flying in the moonlight at dusk . . . it flies up into the moonlight. It is dusk. It flies low. It flutters. Then it begins to climb into the moonlight."[16] But Sally also said of her dance, "I searched my mind for something that would hit the public fancy enough to make large financial returns."[17] An even more mercenary statement was attributed to her later, "I have done this dance to get money to get back to Hollywood."[18]

The truth is probably between the lines of all these statements. Sally did want to get back to Hollywood, she did observe the herons on her grandfather's farm, and she desperately needed money. These were desperate times, and Sally Rand was dancing in the South Loop among the shady elements of society. Other gangsters came into the Paramount and Sally came to know "Machine Gun Jack" McGurn, who was a hit man for Capone, and of course she later claimed Capone offered her a job in New York City. There were rides on rumrunners at night on Lake Michigan where Sally rubbed shoulders with mobsters who worked for Capone or other gangs on the rise.

Some would say it was luck that she became forever associated with the fair and essentially world famous. But several things were in her favor. A scandal involving Mayor Kelly threatened to dominate the headlines, so the city decided it was time to get tough on vice. The ensuing campaign against nudity at the fair created headlines for dancers like Sally Rand that made people flock to see her. Every time she was arrested her notoriety increased, and she was always arrested.

She began working at the Chicago Theatre as well as performing at the fair. Her dance only lasted eight minutes, so she could give as many as sixteen performances a day. A newspaper critic of the day, Mae Tinee, loved Sally's dance. "Perfectly beautiful—as presented and lighted. Airy, exquisite, artistic! So, adept is Miss. Rand with her fans, so cunning the hand at the colored light switch, that you're good if you can tell where the body starts, and the fans stop. . . . is there anything indecent about the fan dance I couldn't see it."[19]

There are many stories of her arrests during this time, but one is that a policewoman after her performance at the Chicago Theatre met her and handed her "gauze, tape, and pins" and instructed her to put it on or she would be arrested. The question that has come up time and again is what Sally Rand was wearing behind those ostrich feathers. The answers are as varied as her career. "My technique . . . is to manipulate the fans so the audience will think they are seeing things they are not."[20] There were rumors of a body stocking and body paint but, "unless forced to put something on, Sally was nude, verified by photos and eyewitness accounts, including from her own son."[21]

This would be contradicted by a letter dated 1933 from a police-woman in Indianapolis who described exactly what Sally was wearing. "Witnessed Miss Rand put her makeup on which consisted of a foundation of greasepaint after which a thick coating of powder was applied, then she used a saline covering for her breasts which was either pasted or glued on and across her hips and abdomen was about four to six thickness of silk and maline. On leaving her dressing room she wore a silk robe which she used during most of her act, also used two large fans and at no time was her body exposed."[22] Obviously, this letter would back up Sally's assertion there was nothing "indecent" about her act.

Sally herself said that clothes inhibited her movements as judges admonished her to put something on at the same time commending her as a "beautiful artistic dancer." The five-foot shapely young woman batted her eyes and returned to the Paramount or the World's Fair only to be arrested again. And the papers loved it. The papers loved Sally Rand. When looking at the boxes of papers in the Chicago History Museum, one is struck by the sheer publicity she generated. Sex. Nudity. Beauty. Indecency. Public Morality. The Depression. Hope. Hollywood. Burlesque. Vaudeville. The World's Fair. She was a reporter's dream, and they had a myriad of angles to pursue when writing a Sally Rand story.

Sally at the same time was beginning to rake it in. Estimates of her weekly pay range from $100 to $1,000 to $5,000 . . . in cash during the Great Depression. Audiences got what they paid for when Sally Rand's signature moment came at the end of her dance and she lowered her fans and revealed all.

The zircon, the beacon of hope, became this small blond woman with blue eyes who looked like someone's sister but could produce a fantasy that transported men and women from the grim realities of the Great Depression. It doesn't really matter what Sally Rand's motivations were; the phenomenon of Sally Rand is she was caught up in a developing culture that needed a symbol to divert people away from the hard times. In this way the perfect storm of Sally Rand's fame had her stumbling into the spotlight at precisely the right moment with a publicity machine to hold her up over and over. That publicity machine was the World's Fair of 1933 that needed revenue badly and a confluence of luck, circumstance, destiny, a national crisis, and an evolving culture pushing the boundaries of sex that put Sally Rand front and center. And then kept her there.

It was soon after this amazing turnaround of her career that Sally bought a fifteen-acre orange orchard in Glendora, California, for her mother and gave it to her as a gift at Christmas. She had more money than she knew what to do with. At a time when sex and escapism were at a premium, Sally Rand was the hottest thing going. And people were willing to pay.

Chapter Ten

Gold Diggers

1933

THERE WAS A MODEL FOR THE NEW WORKING-CLASS SEX SYMBOL CALLED Sally Rand. The movies had found it and made very good money on their new women characters. Not exactly flappers though they did smoke and drink and were sexually liberated, a more working-class version of flappers was put forth in Busby Berkeley's film *Gold Diggers of 1933*. At a time when only 2 percent of the population went to college in the 1920s and women were severely limited in their career choices, one thing they could do was snare a rich husband. Busby Berkeley, a director in Hollywood, made hay with this when he produced the movie *Gold Diggers*.

The plotline was simple, with all the money around in the 1920s, young women could do well to snare a rich man and the best way to do this was through sex. Berkley took this notion out of the closet and put it front and center and made it respectable in his musical. It was a way to climb up for young independent women who didn't want to be a teacher, a nurse, or a secretary.

As Cheryl Ganz writes in *The 1933 Chicago World's Fair*, "As the showgirl who achieved rare individual recognition, Rand's own life story paralleled the storyline in the Busby Berkeley's film *Gold Diggers of 1933*."[1] The film used the themes of race, class, and the commodification of sex that had been popularized during the century's early decades. "[I]ts gold-digger chorus girls portrayed modern, aggressive women, always native-born whites, whose professional misfortune might push them into prostitution. Seeking security and upward mobility, these attractive characters contrived traps for wealthy men."[2]

The truth was Sally Rand did not seek a sugar daddy. In an interview in 1932, Sally had given her view on life. "Work and accomplishment in your work, that's the best happiness you can get out of life. I don't care whether your work is just winding string on a spool . . . idle persons are the unhappy ones. But they who have work to do and are busy at it, occupying their minds and hands and bodies with it, filling their lives with the joy of accomplishing something, they're the ones who get the most out of life."[3] The columnist Edgar Hay noted that "there is that wholesome quality about this unusual young woman. She stems from the good, clean soil. From the earth she learns her wisdom, from books her amazing knowledge."[4]

Isadora Duncan was probably a closer model for Sally Rand. Rand would often point to the Paris dancer as her model. The truth was she had many models. Faith Bacon, Lady Godiva, Isadora Duncan, and the Little Egypt dancer of the 1893 fair. But then she added her own spin to the fan dance that had been around for a while.

Duncan performed during good times for socialites. Rand's audience was more proletarian; the working class hit by the hard times of the Great Depression. The truth was Sally had to do something bold like Berkeley's *Gold Diggers*. There were not enough jobs to go around and she had no real chance of becoming a dancer for the Century of Progress. She was just another dancer in a seedy theater on State Street in Chicago. The fair was less than two years away when "she sat down on a black leather stool at the end of the bar and ordered a ginger ale." Big Ed smiled. Holly Knox, in *Sally Rand: From Film to Fans*, paints the picture. This is yet another version of the genesis of the Lady Godiva charge into the opening ceremony.

> *"Sally, I'll buy a real drink. We got the good stuff today."*
> *"I'm not ready for that right now, Ed. I need all my faculties and a sympathetic ear, please."*
> *"What's troubling you honey?"*

"It's the goddamned world's fair commissioners! These idiots won't even let me talk to them. I've tried every avenue I can think of to get in to see them. I've used up every friend and connection I've got in Chicago, but they refuse to see me. Hell! Lady Godiva couldn't even get in to see those bluenoses."

"Who?"

Sally's eyes widened, and she pounded her fist on the bar excitedly.

"That's it, Ed! Lady Godiva!"

Big Ed looked at her.

"Sally, you haven't had some of our bad scotch, have you?"

Sally clutched his hand.

"No, Ed. I've just come up with an idea. One that will make those SOBs sit up and take notice. Will you help me? It's something that I know will work!"

"You know I will, Sal."⁵

Another version of Sally Rand's plan to crash the fair. Still, it would take luck and skill and amazing hubris to pull off her plan. But exotic sexy women were in vogue in the 1930s and hubris was their hallmark. Esther Williams was famous for her swimming musicals and Carmen Miranda in her midriff gave sex a Latin spin. Sally Rand had a hunch her feather dance was just different enough to give her an angle, but she had to get in front of the people. The Streets of Paris or the Midway of the fair was tailor-made for Sally Rand's fan dance. Sexy, new, exotic, and strangely mesmerizing at a time when people desperately needed escapism.

Even Sally's plan fit in with *Gold Diggers'* plotline. She would crash the party of "bluenoses," the working-class girl with an accent bashing up against privileged society with beauty, youth, and sex. This is a standard plotline in the *Gold Diggers*. The brash girls shocking the more educated women and men who secretly admire their verve and sexuality. Audiences rooted for Berkeley's girls the way they would root for Sally Rand. She was a sexed-up Horatio Alger story who had come from the Ozarks to find fame on the world stage. And like in the *Gold Diggers*, a conventional approach to her problem would not suffice. We could even see the *Gold*

Diggers girls pulling a Sally Rand and riding in on a white horse to crash the World's Fair.

The difference of course is that the *Gold Diggers* is a fantasy and Sally Rand really did smash convention, and though she did not find a rich husband, she found something more coveted, more elusive . . . she found—fame. In the same interview with columnist Edgar Hay, Sally reflected on her time in Hollywood. "I was in Hollywood. I was quite young and successful, too young to appreciate my success rightly. I was commencing to 'Go Hollywood,' thinking I was the most important actress in the world."[6]

Sally Rand's problem would actually be her series of husbands. The gold digger's end goal was to get a husband who would take her out of a bleak future of working for pennies or being on the showgirl circuit. Heaven was the man who takes her away and allows her to live in a palatial home with money to burn. The truth was this did not happen for most women. Sally Rand would have three husbands, and each would prove worse than the one before. Her problem *was* her husbands and the hard-economic truth is a reverse of the gold digger's motif. She would have been better off with without them. The gold diggers were much more mercenary than Sally Rand. They did not look for anything beyond money and in that way their expectations were probably more in line with reality. Sally Rand would marry for romantic love three times, but later she wished she had found someone rich or at least with the same earning power she had. Neither would be the case.

Chapter Eleven

Indecency

1933

THE POLICE ARRESTED SALLY RAND UP TO FOUR TIMES IN ONE DAY AT the Chicago Theatre for indecency. The biggest draw of the Chicago 1933 World's Fair would not keep her clothes on for anybody. She would finish her show and then follow a policeman to the precinct. Judge Erwin J. Hasten faced down the young beauty in court and had to decide what to do about the fan dancer. She took the stand and said in a soft sibilant voice with a lisp, "My dance is art . . . my public wants me. There is nothing vulgar, lewd, or obscene about my dancing."[1]

Besides, she did have something on. Thick white cream. Judge Hasten then asked if her breasts and loins were covered. They were she replied, looking at the judge with green eyes, "except in the middle of the dance, without ostentation, my gown is removed at the side of the stage. After that I open my fans."[2] The judge banged his gavel. Twenty-five dollars for indecent exhibition. The Chicago papers said the judge saw the dance as art and everyone had their picture taken with Sally Rand. She then went back to work. No one was going to stop her from dancing now. Money talked at a time when there was none. "Chicago theatre admission fees topped 79,000 in one week, at the fair revenues soared and Rand's salary climbed to 1,000 a week during the worst year of the Great Depression . . . the Streets of Paris took in so much cash that A Century of Progress had to establish a separate banking operation."[3] The Streets of Paris was taking in a hundred thousand dollars a day. The reality was clothes would not work in the bawdy Midway. Another dancer, Faith Bacon, said any type of clothing took away from the performance. "Long legs, long hair, a small waist, full breasts, and two fans were required to create this ethereal art."[4] Bacon added that getting arrested was key, because that brought publicity, which brought people. "Be sure you spell your name right to the reporters,"[5] she admonished.

Sally Rand stole the headlines, but there was plenty of sex to go around. For a dime or a quarter, people could go to the peep shows, which might be a clown or a woman or a man on the other side of the wall. The seediness of the fair came through all around the famous fan dancer. "In Life Class, people paid a quarter for a crayon and a piece of paper and sketched a mostly naked woman sitting on a chair. In Visions of Light, three topless women danced to flashing lights and music. In another show, three baseballs thrown at a target might bring a mostly naked woman rolling out of a bed. The fair allowed nudity but balked at prostitution. At *The Dance Ship* a man could dance with a woman who 'wiggled her body up and down,' and then a date was arranged for a price in an annexed room. Sex was rampant."[6]

People were drinking again in public. Inhibitions were abandoned. And then there were people who had a problem with sex in general. A lawyer, Mary Belle Spencer, filed a suit citing the nudity of the Streets of Paris. The suit contended that nudity "represented a cesspool of iniquity, a condition of depravity and total disregard of purity and display of the most disgraceful lewdness and abandon ever publicly shown in any institution of the character such as this Century of Progress purports to represent."[7] Spencer claimed that Sally Rand and her like would harm property values, as families would not want to come to Chicago after going to the fair and "businesses were less likely to settle in a town that promoted such lewd displays."[8]

Superior Court judge Joseph H. David would become famous after hearing the suit for his pronouncement, "They are just a lot of boobs to come to see a woman wiggle with a fan or without fig leaves. But we have the boobs and we have a right to cater to them."[9] Attorney Jay McCarthy fought an uphill battle to show that nudity corrupted the public. Judge David dismissed his argument, saying, "Some people want to put pants on a horse. . . . If a woman wiggles about with a fan, it is not the business of the court. . . . I would be the last person to cast a blotch upon A Century of Progress."[10]

The case was dismissed. But the fair did get heat for the nudity, and Rufus Dawes, the president of the World's Fair Association, directed concessionaries to modify nudity in their shows. Women had to at least wear something over their loins and breasts. Mayor Edward Kelly went to the show and said some of the shows were cheap, tawdry, and downright suggestive. The new rules said that all dancers had to wear bras and panties. Sally put on a piece of gauze and assumed the heavy body cream she used would be enough. "Several dancers began to wear 'invisible clothing.'"[11] With the use of special lighting that masked the invisible clothing, police couldn't be sure what the dancers had on. "In frustration a policewoman named Hazel Ward forced Sally Rand to dance in a long nightgown one night."[12]

Sally Rand was at the cutting edge of the early twentieth-century sexual revolution because her livelihood depended on people thinking she was naked behind the fans. She reasoned that if word got out she had on clothes, then people would stop coming. But she was blazing a trail as a working single woman at a time when women were expected to marry and depend on their husbands. "Singled out by the media as the fan dancer extraordinaire, Sally Rand became the popular heroine of sexual service work. . . . Rand defied those who would define public morality by banning nude dancing, and in doing so she represented those who enjoyed a bit of sex and vice in films, tabloids, magazines and on stage."[13]

Sally Rand was ahead of her time, but the fair was A Century of Progress after all. She pushed the boundaries that brought public consternation, and that brought in more people, which brought in dollars. The wink by the police and the judges at a time when morals were the last thing anybody minded allowed Sally Rand to stretch the boundaries of moral codes regarding sex to places they had never been. The Great Depression put survival over morality, and if Sally Rand was making the Chicago's World's Fair profitable, then no one was going to stop her. Essentially, in 1933, Sally Rand could do anything she wanted. It was the privilege of celebrity and, more importantly, money.

Comic George Burns played the World's Fair at the same time Sally Rand was there. "I remember playing the Chicago World's Fair in the 1930s. I was on the same bill as Sally Rand. She did her famous fan dance and it was supposed to be very very naughty, but it was nothing. She came out on the stage wearing flesh-colored leotards and the lights on the stage were dark blue, you could hardly see her. And when she did her fan dance, her fans were so big they mostly covered her . . . she got sick one night. So, I took her place, and nobody knew the difference."[14]

So, it was in the eye of the beholder. The stress of her schedule and the court appearances took a toll, and one night Sally collapsed in her dressing room. She was rushed to St. Luke's Hospital, where it was concluded she had a nervous breakdown from the strain of going to court and performing. Add to this that she got into a salary dispute with the management of A Century of Progress and you have a very sick fan dancer. Sally decided to concentrate on her acting career and would leave the fair on August 18, 1933. She jumped into a boat at midnight to take her to the north side of the city for another engagement. The speedboat took off, and near the mouth of the Chicago River the boat took a turn just as Sally Rand stood up. She flipped overboard into the darkness of the lake.

Chapter Twelve

The 1934 World's Fair and the Balloon Dance

The plane was going down. Sally Rand, her personal assistant Ralph Hobart, her Japanese maid Stella Onizuka, her two Pekingese dogs, Snootie and China Boy, all were headed for a farm field. The plane swerved, leveled out, then made an emergency landing right into a haystack. Sally was supposed to perform in Nebraska and flew out of St. Louis in a chartered plane on February 22, 1934. The flight did not go well, as Sally later recalled. "The dead of winter, me in my mink, Stella in her kimono, Ralphie and Pekes. How would we know there was no heat in the plane? We were numb with cold and miserable. Just as we got over Council Bluffs the oil line broke and we made a forced landing in a meadow."[1]

Sally and her entourage then trudged to a farmer's house to use the phone. "The farmer drove us into Omaha and to the theatre . . . my feet were frostbitten and so were Ralphie's ears. We were never able to get the black oil off my mink coat or Stella's kimono. We could have been killed or burned to death."[2]

This event never made it into the newspapers. Which is amazing considering that in 1934 Sally Rand was one of the most famous women in America. It would be another episode of a life spent on the road that was just beginning. The surprising thing here is that Sally Rand was not to be part of the 1934 World's Fair in Chicago. In fact, there should have never been a 1934 fair. The fair was originally going to be a one-year event, but when Franklin Delano Roosevelt attended, he saw an engine to jump-start the economy. People were buying again. The fair had started out as celebrating the incorporation of Chicago. The one-hundred-year anniversary was to produce a history fair, but fair planners quickly gave this up in favor or a more modern fair based on science and technology. The Century of Progress was now taking on another mission and that was to rescue the American economy from the Great Depression.

The *Chicago Tribune* announced in an article one week before the 1934 fair, "Chicago Fair Opens in a Week Shy Fan Dance." The article then went on to say that "informative and educational" exhibits would be given precedence, explaining, "directors have put the ban on fan dancing because the average American is more interested in exhibits of an informative and educational nature."[3] President Roosevelt would appear on a screen and throw a switch to open the fair while Eleanor Roosevelt would also throw a switch to turn on the lights of the fair. The article had a large picture of Sally Rand with her feathers with NO FAIR! across the top.

The reality was Sally Rand had decided to leave the fair in 1933 after asking for more money. Her ill-fated boat ride was the beginning of her new life. She declared she was going to concentrate on being an actress. The truth here is murky. Sally wanted more money, and fair management felt she was well paid. Also, there was her collapse earlier in 1933 that came from exhaustion. Sally Rand would have a love-hate relationship with the fans that brought her fame her entire life. She would have gladly walked away from being a fan dancer if other opportunities opened up. Sally always saw herself as a Hollywood star, and fan dancing was simply a means to an end.

So, the second year began without Sally Rand. There was an effort to clean up the fair and the Worlds Fair of 1934 would be a more wholesome family-friendly event. A new corporation was taking over and decided to do away with all the vulgarity on the Midway. That summer when the fair opened the fair planners must have realized the folly of what they had done. Sally had made the fair profitable in 1933, and now they were going to turn their back on her and the allure of lascivious acts on the Streets of Paris. Sally Rand had taken the fair from the red into the black, and now they saw their revenue streams plummet.

When attendance fell, the fair dropped any pretense of taking sex out of the fair and quickly brought back the erotic acts that brought in so much money. Sally received a telegram from Joseph Imburgio, the impresario of Italian Village at The Century of Progress. "Cancel all engagements. We must have you here by Monday."[4] Whatever happened, Chicago realized once again that money trumped morality. "By the summer of 1934 nudity returned to the fair concessions because fair officials again refused to enforce obscenity regulations. Topless dancers, nude dancers covered with grease, or dancers covered only with flower petals, tape, or transparent gauze could be found in concession entertainment, peep shows, and dinner floor shows."[5]

The police and fair officials had to walk a fine line. They needed the income from the shows that Sally Rand had pioneered and yet they had to be mindful of the amount of negative publicity the shows generated. Nude shows were added along with more peep shows. There was "Mona Leslie, a 'Dancing Venus in platinum colored paint who dove into a pool only to rise, a harrowing ten minutes later, on a pedestal from the water' . . . there were nudes and semi-nudes in practically every café, beer garden, or racy concession at the fair."[6] And there was Faith Bacon. She would later claim she had originated the fan dance before Sally Rand. She danced at the Hawaiian Gardens and was quickly arrested for nudity.

"I'm not nude. I've got tape,"[7] she protested.

Lenox Lohr was a military man tasked with building the Chicago World's Fair of 1933. He would later write a book on the fair and addressed the dilemma of shows like Sally Rand's fan dance this way: "Fan dancers and oriental dancers presented a serious dilemma." He reported, "they violated the law, sought notoriety, and were disappointed if not arrested and taken to court."[8] Clearly, Lohr understood the method to their madness and he knew where the money had come from that had made the 1933 World's Fair a financial success. But he would never publicly acknowledge what journalists wrote and confronted him with and assistants knew was true. They "refused to cooperate with journalists who credited Rand as crucial to the fair's turnout and financial success. Lohr and his assistant McGrew preferred to promote the fair as a successful exposition that promoted science and education."[9]

Of course, Lohr could not verify what the press and everyone already knew, that people would rather watch a woman behind ostrich feathers who was naked than go on the Skyride or watch a car being assembled. Sex sells even though no one could publicly admit it. The police and even the judges understood that to shut down these shows would shut down the revenue stream badly needed by the city in 1934. There was no money around except for the money being generated by the Chicago World's Fair and that led directly to the coffers of the city of Chicago.

So, what was good for Sally Rand became good for Chicago, and so every bit of publicity that spread her name, her notoriety, her fame, generated more money for the bankrupt city. In this way Chicago and Sally Rand became one and "the actions and inactions of the fair officials were surpassed only by those of law enforcement and the courts in their inability to behave decisively regarding public nudity. The judges ignored the state and municipal laws that clearly designated many of the displays at the fair as illegal."[10]

So, the fix was in. The police would drag Sally Rand to court, but there a sympathetic judge would slap a light fine on her and send her back to do her dance. Sally Rand's feather dance had some cover as being "art," but many of the shows of the Midway were simply just sex. Fan dancing as a craze swept across the country. Many women saw Sally Rand's success and wanted to emulate it. What they didn't understand was that the combustion of Sally Rand's fame was generated by a confluence of being at the exact right spot at the right time. The fame machine of the 1933 World's Fair in Chicago had pushed her up as a symbol of hope and escapism just as people were desperate for anything to turn them away from the Great Depression.

For the 1934 fair, Sally came up with a different act without the ostrich feathers.

Sally would later claim she invented the balloon dance because of the problems of dancing outside with her feathers. Maybe. The Firestone Tire and Rubber Company did have an exhibition at the fair and maybe that gave her the idea. Sally had come up with a giant rubber ball, spending eleven thousand dollars to have one produced by the Defense Department. "After I spent 11,000, they finally developed one that I could use," she would later tell a reporter. "But I didn't have to fill it with helium. I found out that when you spin the bubble around, it created air currents and floated upward."[11] This produced the iconic photographs of a nude Sally Rand kicking or tossing this giant sepia-colored ball into the air. She was milking her moment of fame for all it was worth.

A Chicago newspaper covering her balloon dance proclaimed Sally Rand and the US government were in business together. "It's a strange but true fact that the huge five-foot balloons which serve as the costume for Miss. Rand's famous dance are her private property and are not available to anyone else except the United States government."[12] Sally wanted a large lightweight balloon that was essentially what the government was using for weather balloons. Sally found no manufacturer could give her what she wanted, a large balloon that could rise on its own. "The government had long been anxious to buy larger balloons but would not pay for the expensive aluminum forms which larger balloons required [. . .] an expense of several thousand dollars was required."[13]

Sally agreed to pay the expense, signing an agreement that the balloons could only be used for weather balloons or target practice by the US government.

A witness to the dance in 1934 described it this way. "With all the grace of a woodland nymph, she toyed and danced around and played with and tossed into the air her transparent soap bubble. Somehow, one felt as though secretly watching some little woodland creature at play in the moonlight. The audience seemed hardly able to breathe!"[14] Watching this balloon dance today is surprising. Sally hides nothing. She dances to the same classical music, but she is wearing a diaphanous slip essentially and it is quickly apparent there is nothing on under the slip. She starts out behind the balloon and then elevates it to the sky. She moves like a young nymph, kicking the balloon, bending back toward it, laying down and kicking the balloon up. At the end she tosses the balloon up and drops her light slip and she gives the audience a full-frontal nude. It is in a half light but there is no mistaking, Sally Rand is totally nude.

The amazing thing is that it works. There is the same mesmerizing moment watching this young beautiful woman essentially dancing a ballet with this giant transparent balloon. Where the feather dance left more to the imagination, the balloon dance is more of a declaration; here is my body, and Sally celebrates it by bending to the balloon, toying with the balloon, then finally tossing the balloon away as if she is a young woman succumbing to sex.

The low spotlight in the opening made it look like she was inside the balloon when she was standing behind it. When she tossed it up into the darkness it seemed as if she was emerging from the balloon. She usually played Brahms and her movements are that of the ballerina who is moving in slowed time. This too is like the fan dance, where her movements seem to be of another dimension. This slowed time allowed audiences to be transfixed, to stare at some moment between moments. In this way Sally Rand was an artist, as she understood the impact of illusion and imagery. *The Dying Swan* seems to be evident here, too.

As Brahms played, she would twirl around holding a piece of the rubberized balloon and then she would lie down and kick the balloon, slowly extending her leg. Finally, at the end of the eight-minute dance, came the payoff, she would throw the balloon up and reveal herself. The new dance was popular, with Sally performing extra shows that sometimes ran up to thirteen a day.

Apparently, critics were not as enthralled with the balloon dance as the fans. A point might be made that it was too slow. It was too revealing. Chicago columnist Hob Steely wrote, "They may call it art but to us this nudity is nothing short of barbaric paganism and exploitation of the form divine . . ."[15] Steel then interviewed Sally Rand about her arrests for indecency. "When I started the fan dance my father, a staid, old fashioned army officer was shocked. No girl of his was going to peel off her clothes and gyrate in front of the public but after he saw me his opinion was completely changed. So was my mother's view altered. So you see this nudism should not offend even our grandmothers."[16]

Sally was certainly more revealing in the bubble dance. The fan dance generated energy because each movement was fast and depended on choreography to keep her body hidden. The balloon dance revealed her body the whole way through and then finally gave the audience a full frontal. The anticipation was simply not the same. But it was a variation on a central theme and probably more enjoyable for Sally Rand. And it was the first attempt to get away from the fan dance that she was shackled to from the opening night of the Chicago World's Fair. The people wanted what they wanted. And they wanted Sally Rand, the feather dancer. It was a blessing and a curse, but many times it was the only way for Sally Rand to generate income. The question of course was what would happen when the World's Fair closed its doors for good in 1934. Her career had vanished over the next hill in Hollywood when she thought she had made it. It could well happen again when the lights of the Rainbow City went out forever.

Chapter Thirteen

The Other Fan Dancer

1934

IF FAITH BACON PROVED ONE THING IT WAS THAT SALLY RAND'S success went beyond holding up some moldy ostrich feathers and dancing
around in the semidarkness of a stage to classical music. If Sally was
nothing more than a stripper who found success at the World's Fair, then
she would have flamed out the way Faith Bacon did. Or to put it another
way, Faith Bacon would have enjoyed the same success as Sally Rand, but
sadly she did not.

They were both beautiful young women who were willing to show
their bodies in novel ways that the public had not seen before. They were
both ambitious self-taught young women who came of age with the new
century and an entertainment industry of mass media, movies, music, and
eventually television that would give them access to a much wider audience.
And they both used ostrich feathers to tantalize and created an illusion of
sexual intrigue, but Sally Rand became world famous and a cultural icon
where Faith Bacon slipped down into obscurity, drugs, then finally, suicide.

Faith would come to the World's Fair in Chicago in 1933 and try
to emulate the success of Sally Rand. She was born in Los Angeles,
California, and started in burlesque in the 1920s after meeting Maurice
Chevalier and appearing in his revue. She, too, would use bubbles, flow-
ers, and fans in her dance. When Faith Bacon launched a lawsuit against
Sally Rand, it was to claim that the fan dance was hers alone and Sally
Rand had cut into her earnings and that was why she was due $375,000.

This was based on her work with a producer named Earl Carroll, who produced a show on Broadway called *Earl Carroll's Vanities*. Faith was all of eighteen when she had a part as a nude dancer in his show.

Faith's role in Carroll's show was to be one of the thirty beauties in one-piece bathing suits. Rehearsals were long, some sixteen hours, but Carroll paid well. The basis of her claim to be the original fan dancer came during a rehearsal. "Faith had an idea, stepping up from the chorus line during a rehearsal she spoke up, 'Mr. Carroll, why can't we do a number where I'm covered when I move, and undraped when I stop? For example, let us say the orchestra plays a waltz, I dance around, but on every third note the music stops and I stand still and uncover.'"[1]

A law on nudity at the time forbade dancing while naked. "As long as she held still when the music stopped, it would be within the limits of the law."[2] Faith then went further and explained the routine. "I'd cover myself with fans while dancing and as soon as I'd reached the proper position I'd stop and hold them over my head."[3] It does sound like Sally Rand's routine right down to the feathers up over her head, revealing all. Faith had considered fans made of different materials but eventually settled on the ostrich feathers. This again would be the same type of fans Sally Rand would use at the Paramount Club.

Carroll's Vanities opened at the New Amsterdam Theatre and was an immediate hit. Faith appeared in several different scenes during the show with her fans. Leslie Zemeckis describes her dance. "She dances to Bolero, a piece that had only just premiered in 1928 . . . and a gorgeous shimmering Faith was enchanting. She masterfully fluttered the giant white feathers in front and behind her pale slim figure, smiling as she lifted one heavy fan behind her head while the other rippled under her chin. Her movements were fluid and minimal. Barefoot and dancing on her toes as she dipped and swayed her body with the fanning of the feathers. The audience leaned forward, glimpsing her lean arm, petite ankle, keeping eyes trained for more . . . provocative, it was a small dance, intimate, achingly beautiful and private."[4]

It does sound like Sally Rand's dance at the Chicago World's Fair performed three years later in 1933. Then why did Faith Bacon not enjoy the same success as Sally Rand in all parts of her career? Faith, like Sally

Rand, was arrested for "giving an indecent performance." Like Sally she was bailed out and continued performing, also understanding the value of publicity with every arrest. After Carroll's show closed, she was a dancer in the Ziegfeld Follies in 1931, and then she headed to Chicago to claim her title as the inventor of the fan dance.

It didn't work out. She and Sally went head to head with dueling shows, but the people flocked to see Sally Rand. Faith Bacon never stuck to the fame machine of the World's Fair where reporters pumped out one story after another on the girl who had crashed the fair. Sally Rand was rumored to be in the audience when Faith first came to Chicago, and she changed her own routine to be more daring and show more than ever before.

There was a "dueling quality" to the fan dancers at the Chicago World's Fair, but Faith never came close to the screaming celebrity of Sally Rand. This is curious as there should have been plenty of room for two fan dancers for Depression-era audiences who wanted to lose themselves in the dim woodland world of nymphs dancing to enchanting music. Their routines were very similar, but the difference between Faith Bacon and Sally Rand came down to how people responded to them.

For good or for bad, Sally Rand had a girl-next-door quality that Cecil B. DeMille had recognized and that had landed her in twenty films. She was not a good actress, but she had a vulnerability, an extra bit of wholesomeness that allowed people to see her as a sister or a daughter. A very sexy sister or daughter, but this played into it as well. And Sally Rand had come up through the hard knocks of Hollywood and she had been battle-tested and she had a nose for what would create publicity and where she should be for maximum exposure. Would Faith Bacon have ridden a white horse into the opening ceremonies of the World's Fair after hiring a boat to take her to a landing and sneaking into the fairgrounds? Maybe, but the truth is she probably wouldn't have thought of it.

Sally Rand took her talent and her verve and combined it into a projection of a young woman dancing in a very choreographed moment that she duplicated over and over. In this way Sally Rand approached her career as a job. She saw the monetary value of an act and monetized it to a high degree, and then she negotiated deals to maximize her income.

She had a hard-nosed approach to her career, where Faith Bacon was a burlesque dancer who didn't have the hard-boiled emotional makeup that allows people to survive in show business.

Faith had a reputation as being difficult to work with, while Sally Rand, for all her explosive moments, never was tagged that way. Faith went on after the World's Fair to appear at the Lake Theatre in Chicago in 1936 and fell through a glass drum she was standing on, severely cutting her legs. She sued the theater and settled for five thousand dollars. She would then appear in her only movie, *Prison Train*. Here is where Faith tried to pull a Sally Rand with the 1939 New York World's Fair. Taking a page from Sally's success in Chicago, she came up with an idea for publicity that might have rivaled Sally Rand's legendary ride.

She was booked in the fair to do a "Fawn Dance," and so the week before she paraded down Fifth Avenue with a fawn on a leash dressed in a wispy revealing chiffon ensemble complete with maple leaves over her privates. Faith was arrested for disorderly conduct and fined five hundred dollars. She danced at the fair to terrible reviews citing the fan dance as dated and old. What happened? It did seem a setup, and why did the same accolades and fame not come Faith's way that had rained down on Sally Rand?

The times had changed. There was a World War in Europe. The novelty of the fan dance had been made famous by Sally Rand, and for six years she had kept the publicity machine humming along and had appeared in movies and shows, and more than all that, she was a fixture in the press. Sally Rand had become a star not *because* of ostrich feathers but *with her ostrich feathers*. The ineffable quality that is mostly undefinable that had worked so well for Sally Rand had to do with timing, force of personality, and a public that reflected their own hopes and dreams on the smiling five-foot blonde from the Ozarks.

Faith simply could not tap into that well. Even though she had a similar dance and even tried to position herself as the new Sally Rand in New York, there was only one *Sally Rand*, and therefore her suit was bound to fail. It was based almost on a trademark concept that the fans were invented by her and she was entitled to missed royalties. She estimated that Sally Rand had made a million dollars from her fans, and along with the suit she filed an injunction demanding Sally be stopped from performing her feather dance.

Sally Rand's response to the suit was, "The fan ideas are as old as Cleopatra . . . she can't sue me for that."[5] It wound up in a court in Hollywood, where Faith made her case that she was the inventor of the fan dance and that Sally be barred from using fans again. The suit got as far as a deposition where Faith claimed she had shown Sally the fan dance during a vaudeville routine. There was some back-and-forth during the deposition where Sally admitted to meeting Faith in 1929. Faith had tried to make a case she couldn't get bookings because of Sally Rand. Then the suit was dropped. The fact is Faith Bacon did not have the money for the lawyers a suit like this would require, and Sally Rand in 1939 was still financially very solvent and could afford to defend herself. The difference between the two women is very plain in Sally's statement, "when you get something that's economically successful you grab the bull by the horns and ride it to the bitter end."[6]

Sally Rand viewed her career as a business, and it didn't matter where the idea of fan dancing came from, it was really who used the product in a more profitable way. Sally stayed on the road using the fan dance for every nickel it would produce. Faith hit hard times and though the 1940s appeared in different clubs, ultimately suing a carnival promoter for $55,444 and losing the case. Her downward spiral came quickly in the 1950s after a failed attempt to open a dance school and a suicide attempt with sleeping pills.

Broke, she was living on the streets in Seattle, Washington, when an old friend and dancer, Elaine Stuart, came upon her after leaving a theater. Faith was in an alley begging for handouts. She headed for Chicago in 1956. Faith could not find work, and on September 26, 1956, she jumped out of a hotel room after her roommate Ruth Bishop tried to stop her. She died at Grand Hospital that night. She had been estranged from her husband, Sanford Hunt Dickinson, and had eighty-five cents to her name. Her story is tragic, but Faith never found the fame that allowed Sally to smooth over the rough spots. Fame would fade for Sally Rand as well eventually, but it was the great fire burning down while Faith became lost trying to ignite the coals of a career that never flamed up.

Chapter Fourteen

Last Days of the Fair

1934

IT'S HARD FOR US TO FATHOM HOW FAMOUS SALLY RAND BECAME WHEN she danced at the World's Fair. She was famous enough to be making four thousand dollars a week and up. The World's Fair publicity machine had produced a star. Reporters from all over the world covered the fair, and they turned this unknown fallen starlet from the Ozarks into a household name. It was amazing. It was as if she was continually riding that white horse into the opening night of the fair and the photographers and reporters were just as amazed, and the flashbulbs never stopped popping. The Papers of Sally Rand have articles that range from the silly to the absurd to the more serious coverage when things started to go bad. But everything Sally Rand did now was news.

The films of Sally dancing at the World's Fair are grainy and dark, but there is also footage where she is dancing among tables on the Streets of Paris and she is quite obviously nude. This is 1934 and you are having your coffee or your beer and there is a naked woman with feathers dancing around you. Even today this would be news. It would not be as sensational as in 1933, but nudity is still a surefire way to get some press, and the strange sight of a woman switching out ostrich feathers to cover her breasts and her loins would make it even more of a story to break into the national consciousness.

But Sally worked it as well. She never knew how long the feather dancing would last. After all, she had made it once before in Hollywood and watched that dry up and blow away. This had the obvious end date of the fair closing. Who might want to see her then? She was tied to the Chicago World's Fair in a way that would never leave her. It was her well, her springboard, her money machine, her publicity fountain, and she had to make as much money and garner as much publicity as fast as possible before the well ran dry.

Somewhere, Sally Rand began taking amphetamines to keep up her grueling schedule that included up to sixteen performances a day at the fair and a vaudeville show at the Chicago Theatre at night. It was probably around this time she began taking amphetamines to keep her going. Benzedrine had recently debuted and would earn Sally a reputation as a nonstop talker and a whirl of unflagging energy.[1] But all good things must come to an end. Chicago had agreed to keep the fair open after an infusion of two hundred thousand dollars from Congress and a request from the president to keep the fair open for the good of the country. People might just buy their way out of the Great Depression. But even here in the halls of Congress, Sally Rand's name came up. An Ohio congressman brought up the seediness of Sally's performances, to which an Illinois congressman replied, "The fan dance show is one of those places you have to pay to get in and pay to get out. You have a good time while you are there."[2]

An article appeared in a Chicago newspaper during the first year of the World's Fair of 1933. "Sally Rand Tells Troth" is the headline. There is no evidence anywhere else of an engagement. The caption under the photo reads, "Sally Rand, above, whose trick waving of fans and bubbles has won her wide fame, today announced her engagement to Charles Mayon, a radio dealer of Springfield, Mass. She said that after her season ends at the Chicago Fair, she will wed Mayon in Florida and then retire, 'to live a quiet life, raise children and cook dinner,' with fans and bubbles nowhere around."[3]

Already she wants to get away from the fans that have made her world famous. This would be a lifelong ambition even as she did everything to promote her fan dance as a source of income and fame. But would she have walked away from it all to go have a quiet domestic life with a husband and children? The assumption has always been that Sally

Rand chose her life of fan dancing all over the country, but maybe the fan dancing life chose her. This is not what she would portray to the press. She liked to portray a happy starlet, a professional celebrity who was smitten with her life. But the twelve to twenty shows a day at the fair had allowed her to see what a grind fame and fortune could be, and probably how lonely as well.

The fantasy of a quiet life of domesticity surrounded by children and a loving husband would haunt her all her life, and she would attempt several times to parcel one together and escape the fan dancing. But she always returned out of economic necessity. Charles Mayon and Sally Rand will not get married, and Sally Rand does not refer to this engagement again. Obviously, it didn't work out.

A call from Hollywood. This is what Sally Rand had been waiting for. The World's Fair was merely a springboard West to get her Hollywood career back on track. She would never give up the idea that she was first and foremost a Hollywood actress if not a bona fide star. Paramount Studios wanted her for the film *Bolero* with George Raft and Carole Lombard. She had an exit plan. Let's back up though and go over that second year again at the fair. Because Sally Rand had started to remake herself even before the fair ended.

Sally was almost thirty and a now-or-never mentality fueled her on. She now entered the respectable homes of Chicago, the white glove set. Sally Rand's patrician accent was created during these visits, carefully emulating the speech patterns of Chicago's Grand Dames. Sally Rand became an expert with the media, giving out as many interviews as she could. She worked on an Eleanor Roosevelt accent that the Grande Dames would recognize.

Unbeknownst to Sally Rand, there was another rising starlet on the other side of the fair. A fourteen-year-old named Frances Gumm was at the fair with her mother and sister playing at the Old Mexico Cabaret not far from where Sally Rand was playing on The Streets of Paris. Judy Garland would become a star in six years with the *Wizard of Oz*, but now she was part of a terrible dancing and singing act. One night she fought with her mother and left the fair and went to the Biograph Theater. She saw a man in the lobby she thought she recognized as a movie star and asked for his autograph. The man obliged and then was shot dead in an alley three hours later. John Dillinger, a gangster star in his own right, had crossed paths with another nascent star. This story would be told twenty-five years later by Judy Garland, showing how the World's Fair drew people in and changed lives forever.

When Sally Rand left the fair during the summer of 1934, she was a different person. The girl who had ridden a white horse bareback to the opening ceremonies had been left behind for the star who was leaving to go conquer Hollywood and the world. The glitter of the Chicago World's Fair of 1933 would sprinkle the world as Sally Rand charged ahead to cash in on her newfound fame until all the glitter was gone. Sally had pushed the barriers of sexuality, albeit unknowingly, and become a symbol of resolve against the titanic effect of a Depression that had decimated the American populace. People could forget their troubles for a little while when they entered the darkened theater and fell in love with the girl dancing under the blue light. "She was never described as sexy; it was always wholesome, charming, pert . . . she was everyone's sister, neighbor, sweetheart."[4] When the fair would close in September 1934, Chicagoans would riot and steal everything that wasn't nailed down. Even the magic of a World's Fair finally succumbed to the dark night of hard times in the end.

CHAPTER FIFTEEN

The Road Ahead

1935

THE LIFE ON THE ROAD WAS JUST BEGINNING FOR SALLY RAND. THE World's Fair will be the last single venue in a single place for some time. The rest of her life she will mostly be on the road. The sixty-one boxes at the Chicago History Museum tell a distressing tale. The letters and the replies to creditors, divorces, foreclosures, tax liens, government subpoenas, lawyer after lawyer after lawyer then accountant after accountant show a life spinning out of control. The most distressing qualities of the letters is each one is from a different hotel in a different city. Sally Rand would never get off the road.

When I was giving a speech for my book *Al Capone and the 1933 World's Fair*, a woman stood up and said she had seen Sally Rand perform. I was in a suburb of Chicago and the woman went on to explain how she had been in a bar in the town of Oswego in the 1960s and Sally Rand had performed there. Sally was in her sixties by then. A sixty-year-old woman dancing naked behind ostrich feathers. Then I found out she had performed at the Pheasant Run supper club at one time in St. Charles, Illinois, in the 1970s. The truth was Sally Rand in the end would perform at bars, high schools, fairs, rodeos, just about anywhere that paid and a few places that didn't.

But let's go back to the year after the fair. Sally had achieved the dream so wrapped up in the American consciousness; she had become famous. People knew who she was. How that fame would be monetized and used in the arc of her life after the World's Fair would define her. If fame is a pile of money, and many times it is not, the variations on the story of a star or any famous person is how they use that achieved status of permanent notoriety; and what does it produce and how fast does that pile of money slip away. Sally had vaulted herself into the starstruck limelight of America with a movie industry cranking up like a roadster and a media infrastructure that would need constant copy to keep America glued to their radios, in theaters, and finally glued to television. Sally now had to sustain the glow, the effulgence of dancing on the rim of the world in Chicago where a World's Fair and a city used her to promote a fair, a metropolis, and even the government used her to try to jump-start a stalled economy.

Sally was part of this matrix. But her usefulness as a promotion tool had ended, and now she could no longer rely on the publicity department of the World's Fair and Chicago and the reporters looking for daily stories in 1933. Sally Rand had been spawned by the fair in its strange duality of shining a light in the darkest times the country had seen, but now it was up to her to keep it shining. She would have three husbands, one son, three ranches, star in several movies, dance all over the country, dance in the Sam Houston Coliseum for the astronauts who would be heading for the moon, appear on *To Tell the Truth*, take Las Vegas by storm, be sued, file for bankruptcy, get jailed, be chased by her adopted son's mother, not pay her bills habitually, get in fights and bite not a few people, all the time trying to leave her fans behind to become a serious actress. All the time trying to resurrect a moribund Hollywood career. This is her duality. An American sex symbol who would like nothing more than to take the sex out of it. But the feathers paid the bills, and Sally Rand's stardom was dependent on those ostrich plumes.

Sally Rand's career is the arc of a star that shoots across the sky and then finally flames out. After the World's Fair closed in1934, it is amazing how long Sally Rand kept that star burning. But let's now pick up on our story: Sally Rand is heading toward her next engagement, her next dance, her destiny.

CHAPTER SIXTEEN

The Vortex

1935

IF SALLY RAND HAD A MISSION IT WAS TO RETURN TO HOLLYWOOD. That was where she belonged. The great wrong done to her by talkies would be corrected and she would take her rightful place as a Hollywood star and give up the fans forever. The World's Fair of 1933 was nothing more than a mighty springboard to catapult her back to the West Coast into DeMille's or some other director's good graces. She was an actress in her eyes, and a Hollywood star had much more respect than a fan dancer at a Chicago World's Fair.

Before branding became the buzzword it is today, Sally Rand defined it. Sally came off the World's Fair with an amazing new toy, fame. What she had thought of as a stunt to get her a job at the World's Fair had turned into a career. She was now world famous and the question was how to cash in on that fame as quickly as possible. She was essentially going forward to market *Sally Rand.* The feather dancer was the vehicle, but the name had cash value and she didn't know how long that would last, and she still had her family to support.

In the Papers of Sally Rand are lots of letters home to her mother and also to her father, who had crept back into her life after she became famous. Sally apparently bore William Beck no ill will for abandoning her along with her mother and brother and running off with a French woman and starting a new family. Sally's family is complex. She had begged her mother, Nettie, to come to Glendora along with her stepfather, Ernest, and then had to leave. Other relatives made the trek as well. Then Sally bought them the "ranch" that produced oranges, and then she had to provide the capital to make the ranch a functioning enterprise.

Sally Rand for two years had been making incredible money. Thousands of dollars every week at a time when a quarter could buy a dinner. A dollar could buy a very good dinner. During the fair years, she performed twelve to sixteen shows a day. Every time the theater filled up, she went on, and it always filled up. Many times, she then went to the Chicago Theatre on State Street to give the same performance. She had become a cash cow for the fair, and nobody wanted to miss the opportunity to milk her white-hot fame.

So, Sally Rand was now the provider for the Beck family, and this required her to never stop. Why she took on her entire family and supported them is complicated. One reason would be that Sally Rand went from a child to an adult on the road and never left behind the girl trying to please her parents. In a letter written in 1935 from her father to her brother, Harold, he questioned "Helen's" financial situation. "I am afraid that her good luck is rather running out again. I do not know anything about her financial affairs, but I believe she had to borrow money on an insurance policy to finance this show of hers. . . . with all the thousands that she earned the two seasons in Chicago and then have to go and borrow money in that way to finance her show, it sounds funny to me."[1]

The truth was Sally did have to finance her own shows, and cash was immediately such a problem she had to wire her father to go to a safety deposit bank and get her insurance policy. Capital for her shows would be a problem that would not go away as she had to hire dancers, finance sets, and provide transportation. Her father still was not sure where her career was headed and suggested to his son that he and "Helen" pursue a "magic writing business."[2] Obviously, some sort of get-rich-quick scheme. But it shows that all the Becks wondered if Sally Rand's fame and more importantly her fortune would be short lived.

Her mother often chastised Sally in her letters for not writing more. A letter to her mother in 1937 by a girl in the show had to stand in for a letter from Sally. "Sally doesn't get much time to write you, but she thinks of you. I know because she talks of you so often. It was hot, sticky hot in

Sally's dressing room. She has been rushing about all day doing publicity and attending a press party . . ."[3]

Sally was now a career woman monetizing a name or ensuring she got every penny out of her brand. At a time when women had just gotten the vote twelve years earlier and vocations open to women with little education went from a waitress to a maid to a hatcheck girl and men were the entitled breadwinner with women expected to remain at home and raise the children, Sally Rand not only became an independent career woman but she also was selling sex, a commodity that was frowned upon by the public eye.

Her father and his new wife came to see her show. Her grandmother came as well. They still saw her as Helen, but Sally was morphing into the new star who would pay the bills for everyone. "I must come to the rescue,"[4] she wrote in her one of her letters, chafing under the new yoke of breadwinner in chief for her extended family. It is no wonder she lost all her money eventually. She had no real guidance in investing or planning because no one understood the type of fame that had come her way. She wasn't a movie star though she had been in many films. And she had no real product. She wasn't a singer nor was she an extraordinary dancer. She produced no tangible art except for her feather dance. What Sally Rand really had was *Sally Rand*. She had become a name and an act that went with that name. Today she would have had agents and financial planners banging on her door, but in 1934 she had no guidance for how to handle the amazing amount of money that came her way. To make matters worse, she would end up with three husbands with no earning power and who would drain her of money.

But it would seem her dream of a return to Hollywood was coming true. First up was *Bolero*, directed by Wesley Riggins. He was an old friend of Sally's and a part was written in for her. George Raft was playing the lead, and Sally would be one of the many women he conquered in the film. Carole Lombard would eventually get the man in the film after Sally passed on Raft's amore. William Frawley of later *I Love Lucy* fame and Ray Milland would round out the cast. The problems began when Sally realized the part written for her was just a moment where she danced with her fans. This would begin a lifelong schism between the way the world saw her and the way she saw herself. Director Riggles relented and added some other parts for her.

When you watch Sally Rand in *Bolero*, essentially it is the World's Fair of 1933. She is shot rising from a bed and she does her fan dance. A cabaret audience applauds at the end. It is easy to see why Sally was upset. Hollywood had taken her back but simply to cash in on the novelty act she had created in Chicago. There was a no great reckoning of a thespian talent. Naively, Sally thought she could go back with her newfound fame and push her way into the ranks of serious actresses. Hollywood would never see her that way. But she did get top billing after Lombard and Raft, and she was paid twenty thousand dollars for her role. It allowed her to pay off the note for her mother and stepfather on the ranch in Glendora.

This, too, would follow a pattern. Sally would have a big payday, and family and other obligations would move in and suck it up. She was already habitually in debt and would all her life be hounded by debt collectors, lawyers, judges, tax liens, and foreclosure proceedings. She would make great money, but her mother and her stepfather were on her back for life and the ranch would become a money pit.

The movie was a hit though, and George Rand and Carole Lombard would be paired again but not with Sally Rand. In 1937 Sally had a part in *Glorified Scandals*, a stage production at the RKO Boston. A Boston paper described her role: "Sally in a towering feathered headdress and a wisp of chiffon scarf, descends a flight of silvered stairs where she is joined by her maidens attired in glittering robes. At the end of the intricate ballet Sally is whisked in a flash of flame across the stage and up into the wings."[5]

Her second Hollywood film would be the 1939 *Sunset Murder Case*, a film designed for her by National Pictures. In this film she is clearly the lead and is listed as the major star. It is a straight-up noir murder drama with gangsters, and Sally Rand is at center as the girl next door in danger. The film, directed by Louis Gasnier, immediately ran into trouble. The original title *The Sunset Strip Case* was shelved when censors balked, but Sally Rand being hired for her fame as the fan dancer of the Chicago World's Fair would become the film's biggest liability. Lawsuits broke out across the country as censors objected to anything with Sally Rand head-lining. Then Grand National the studio collapsed and essentially left the film without distribution. It fell to indie status and was finally distributed in 1939 and then just disappeared under the concussive effect of a terrible film released the same year *Gone with the Wind* came out.

But before it disappeared, the critics had their say. Movie reviewer Sterling Sorensen pulled no punches. "Miss Rand is perhaps the poorest actress seen in years of movie going and her supporting actors are mere puppets. The inanities and downright 'hamminess' of the characters kept yesterday's audience constantly amused."[6] *Sunset Murder Case* is trite and hackneyed, and Sally Rand is not a good actress. She simply has no delivery. Her voice fades away much as it did twenty years later on *To Tell the Truth*. The other actors are just as bad, but this is Sally Rand's vehicle. This is her film to shine as she is in 80 percent of the scenes. Grand National tried to take a B movie actress and hit a home run on the back of her fame from the World's Fair. It was not enough.

But, saying that, there is something there. Sally Rand, while terrible at playing the character Kathy O'Connor, is very good at playing *Sally Rand*. In the scenes there is a vulnerability, an effervescence that comes through. You can see the Ozark girl with the pluck and verve who ran off with a circus to Hollywood and then crashed a World's Fair. She is that Depression-era figure whom you root for to make it because she does come across as sweet and innocent and yet sexy. It is a strange com-bination, but that is what enticed audiences at the fair. She is a lot like your daughter or who you imagine your daughter to be. Maybe if the film had been good and she had been cast in a different role, she might have shined, but the truth is Sally Rand was best at playing Sally Rand.

The film was shown in New York City initially, then a few theaters nationwide before it ended up on YouTube to be viewed by people curi-ous about Sally Rand and not at all curious about *Sunset Murder Case*. Hollywood had once again given Sally Rand her walking papers. It was as if *The Jazz Singer* had just come out again and her lisp had done her in. The difference now was that Sally Rand was famous. But fame always has a clock and hers was ticking.

Sally then danced at a swanky club in Santa Cruz, California, the Rio Del Mar Club. While she was dancing a squad of police burst into the club and raided it for illegal slot machines. Sally kept right on dancing as people were arrested. Newspaper articles played this up, but Sally Rand knew more than anybody, the show must go on.

As early as 1933 Sally had signed with the William Morris Agency in New York City to handle her bookings. What she had done was inherited an act at exactly the time theaters all over America needed something new. Vaudeville was fading and strippers were still off to the side. There was burlesque but that also had a limited audience. What Sally Rand had inherited was a national name with an act to go along with it. The only comparison today would be a rock band with a number one hit that was going on tour. The venues lined up to get the hottest latest act in America, and in 1935 that was Sally Rand and her feather dance. The money was nothing short of amazing during Depression-era America. Her agent at William Morris was in a frenzy booking the dates.

Received a wire from our Chicago office, saying Butterfield Circuit again showing some interest and doing everything possible to open this territory up immediately following Albany. The two towns I spoke to you about at 3,500 were Troy and Schenectady. I have definitely turned these down, as I feel this offer is very unfair. The people who own these two houses are same management who control Albany, where you are getting pro rata of $5,250.[7]

This is made more incredible by the very fact that Sally Rand had been sleeping in alleys and eating leftovers from restaurants just a few years before. Truly, at this juncture she had fulfilled the "Horatio Alger" motif of a rags-to-riches American success story, and this, too, was part of her draw. The hillbilly from the Ozarks who had failed in Hollywood had carved out an original path not dependent on the whim of an entertainment industry. Sally Rand had become a name and a name was bankable.

Her William Morris agent sent her a new list of booked engagements for 1935.

Duluth, Minnesota; Superior, Wisconsin; Hibbing, Minnesota; Grand Forks, N.D.; Fargo, N.D;. Aberdeen, S.D.; Mitchell, S.D.; Sioux Falls, S.D.; St. Cloud, Minnesota; Rochester, Minnesota; Winona, Minnesota; Eau Clair, Minnesota.[8]

These are rural small towns with theaters where she was usually expected to perform for two days. Many times, it was a fifty-fifty split with the house with seating capacities of usually 1,000 to 1,600. The prices varied but fifty-five cents was an average. Sally's pay many times for several days of back-to-back shows was in the thousands. But her big draws were the cities where she was guaranteed a salary at different venues of two thousand dollars a week. "There are several cafes and restaurants in Philadelphia, Boston, Buffalo, Detroit, Kansas City that could play you from two to four six weeks and pay you $2000."[9]

Essentially, Sally Rand was perfectly positioned with her act to take advantage of a hunger for a tasteful yet sexy and most importantly famous act that could play in large theaters, restaurants, or cafes. But, as early as 1934 she recognized that two things would hurt her: censorship and the time limit of the type of fame bestowed upon her by the Chicago World's Fair. In a letter to her agent, she writes, "I have recognized for some time the fact that this 'legion of decency' business and the picture censorship situation will do a great deal to hurt me this year on the road. It is very unfortunate, particularly at this time, as I know my time of earning is very short."[10] Sally goes on to speculate about new venues, including South America. Censorship by the Hays Office in the motion picture industry was rippling across America and having a chilling effect on burlesque and any dance that could be regarded as lewd or indecent. Under Will H. Hays, a politically active lawyer, the Hays Office initiated a blacklist, inserted morals clauses into actors' contracts, and developed the Production Code, which detailed what was morally acceptable on the screen.

Sally did have a prescient vision; censorship would eventually curtail her income and be a constant thorn against establishing the legitimacy of her act. Her agent responded by saying yes, he recognized censorship as a problem but "this situation is only an obstacle until we succeeded in knocking it down."[11] The truth was Sally Rand was corresponding with the William Morris Agency even while finishing up with the fair in July of 1934 when she was still dancing at the Italian Village. She knew even as she was dancing that she had a marketable act that would have a time limit.

Saying that, Sally let her agent know how successful she had been in Chicago during the World's Fair when she was also performing at the Chicago Theatre.

> *I set the highest box office record ever made in the United States. It was $75,000 during the week of August 18th, 1933 at the Chicago Theatre, Chicago Illinois and played an eleven-week engagement at that theatre . . . during my eleven-week engagement there I never played less than $56,000 per week. The prices in the theatre were 25, 50 and 75 cents. I broke the box office records of every theater in which I played during the season.*[12]

Sally also claims to have broken the box office records at the Oriental Theatre as well. The question here is why these people were flocking to see a "stripper" who hid her nudity with ostrich feathers. The answer is that she had become a phenomenon of sex, grace, art, and hope. She was sheer escapism that would only be supplanted by movies eventually. But movies had not taken hold with the titanic force we have today. Sally Rand's feather dance had become famous for the twisting of sex and the higher art of ballet. Simply, there was nothing like this shining portal in the black well of Depression-era America in the early 1930s. People wanted to escape into another world, and for fifty cents they could.

In 1935 she took her bubble dance to New York City and stayed eighteen weeks at the Paradise Club. She then played Akron, Boston, Chicago, and Los Angeles with girls who roller skated and danced. She promised a new dance the following year to the audience, but even then, she contemplated getting away from fan dancing. In a letter to the people who owned the Taft Theatre in Cincinnati, Ohio, Sally proposed a show with a one-thousand-dollar rental fee for the theater and 10 percent of the gross. "I feel that 10,000 would be the minimum that I would do in Cincinnati . . . I have an excellent show with headline vaudeville acts and a line of twelve girls. We give a sixty-minute performance full of comedy, singing and dancing . . . for my own security I would advertise extensively and if I did not do 10,000 or over I would go very badly in the red."[13] Here we have Sally Rand the businesswoman taking over her bookings very early in her career. She did away with the William Morris Agency probably when she realized she could keep the agent's commission for herself. Throughout most of her career, she would take care of every aspect of her shows from booking, to logistics, to paying the bills. This would eventually overwhelm her, but in 1935 the fruit was ripe for the picking.

She maneuvered herself into speaking gigs and told people she would go to France one day when her popularity faded. She spoke to ladies' groups on beauty and gave cooking classes at universities and even gave a speech to the Illinois legislature on "Art for Art's Sake." Then a speech to the YMCA on the dangers of communism. The feathers and nudity were gone, replaced by a button-down conservative ensemble consisting of a marine suit and a hat, talking on her own rags-to-riches story. In many of her photos in newspapers, she looks more like a businesswoman rather than the fan dancer Sally Rand. She is clearly trying to use her name and bend it in a different direction. If she could export Sally Rand into a serious profession, then she might get off the road and get the respect that being a "stripper" did not engender.

In the meantime, no opportunity was turned down. She joined Jack Dempsey in his restaurant in New York City and judged a cocktail-mixing contest. She tried to keep the bubble dance going, feeling it was higher art and easier than dancing with the seven-pound feathers. But the public wasn't buying, and she even tried attaching wings to herself to emulate the dying swan, but it simply didn't work. Sally Rand the name was Sally Rand the feather dancer who had danced at the Chicago World's Fair. It would be a like a rock band not playing their hits at a concert. People wanted to see what she was known for.

There were incidents on the road as she performed almost seventy-eight days straight. A sailor tried to bite her buttocks, and she got in his face and swore a blue streak that put the sailor to shame. Then she performed with unknown actor Humphrey Bogart in the *Petrified Forest*. The Lakewood Theatre was a respected one that often led to Broadway. Sally Rand desperately wanted to get her acting career going while she was still a hot name. Her belief was that if she didn't transition into something else soon, she would be back on the streets in Chicago.

This was uncharted territory in many ways. She was attempting to run a business on a single act that had no precedent. Mae West was making money in movies using sex as a draw, but she had an entire industry behind her. Mae West wrote plays, screenplays, produced, and starred in her own movies. She was a bona fide movie star. Sally Rand often worked out of a trailer, driving grueling hours to the next gig. Local critics in Skowhegan, Maine, gave her good reviews and the audience applauded with many curtain calls.

Meanwhile, she had an orange grove to manage from afar and money went back to Glendora for maintenance of the ranch. Sally Rand was finding out what every small businessman knows and that is that the margins are close, and one nonpayment could spell bankruptcy. Because she was a one-man band, she had to fund her shows and that meant transportation costs, the dancers, the food, the lodging, and then at the end finding many times she barely broke even. She needed the big paydays to put her into the black. She would write her mother, "I put forth every effort and the result is far from what it ought to be."[14]

The problem was she could not be in two places at once. She sent the money back home and assumed it would be spent in the proper places, but she had no idea. She was running the "Sally Rand Show" 24/7 and it took all her energy. And she had an image to uphold. To the press she was the star Sally Rand. Again, she had no agent, no manager to help her cultivate her image. No one knew how untethered fame worked. We are used to people being famous for being famous, but Sally Rand was a groundbreaker in the mid-1930s.

She often performed with thick white makeup that made her itch, and always she wore a blond wig as she felt her own hair not full enough. Reginald Marsh, a famous painter of his time, did a nude painting, *Fan Dancer*, at Jimmy Kelly's steakhouse in New York City. Marsh probably saw Sally perform. The woman in his painting is holding a large fan above her with her breasts exposed with one knee raised. It was Sally Rand with men leering all around her. She had become part of the cultural reference points, and the restaurant in Greenwich Village hung the painting for all to see.

Sally then played the Biltmore, where in her last week she made over five thousand dollars. She was hit with rocks and cigarettes in some performances, heckled at others. She performed in the rain, snow, sleet. If her balloon popped, she performed. If her feathers wilted, she performed. If her plane was late, her car didn't start, or her music didn't play, she performed. Sometimes she had no feathers and no balloon and still she performed. Photographers took her picture in a race car at Daytona Speedway and then she went for a drive on the track going over a hundred miles an hour. There was nothing Sally Rand was afraid to do.

And still she wanted out. Sally Rand wanted to get back to Hollywood, and to that end she was continually reading scripts, plays, books, anything that might be a vehicle to get her to the next phase of her career. Surely it couldn't just end in the dusty arenas of fairs where her trailer was parked next to cattle trucks. Still, a hundred million people would attend World's Fairs in America from 1933 to 1940. That was a hell of an audience.

At the California Pacific International Exposition, she performed twice a day, alternating between her bubble dance and her feathers. It was 1935 and she managed a trip back to Hollywood, where she ran into Cecil B. DeMille at Paramount.

"Don't you recognize me?" she quipped. "I hear you're looking for a girl to play Calamity Jane in your new Gary Cooper picture." The director admitted he was.

"And that she is supposed to be the toughest, most glamorous most beautiful woman in the West. Have you thought of me C.B. I could play that role."[15]

DeMille said he had thought of her and then cast Jean Arthur. Sally Rand did not realize that her inability to deliver a line without swallowing the words had shredded her as a serious actress in Hollywood. Even though she had a speech coach who had managed to submerge her lisp, she had no projection. DeMille saw Sally Rand as a commodity that had not worked out after silent movies gave way to sound, and while he appreciated her fame as a feather dancer, sagely he knew that was not enough for the silver screen. Lesser producers would make movies banking on the Sally Rand name, but the scripts, the actors, and Sally Rand were all B movie material.

And then there was the morality of her act. Forces in America coalesced at times to block her performances. Ministers in Cheyenne petitioned to keep her out of a local fair. Then there was the weather; wind blew down her tent or freak hailstorms dented her trailer and her Lincoln. Fire up the coffee, smoke another cigarette. She hit the road with her own All Star Revue with fifty other acts that she approved. She had to do everything, auditions, lighting, design, payroll. Logistics. She commented to a reporter at this time she would get married when she was sixty after she made her fortune.

But for now, she was an advertiser's dream. In fact, many of the articles that are in the Papers of Sally Rand are advertisements for other products. If television had been in the public domain then, Sally Rand would have popped up on lots of commercials. She was a name, and a name sells. She was now taking planes to venues and arriving just in time to hit the stage and then back into a cab and heading for the airport. She made a stop in Cleveland and rode in a St. Patrick's Day Parade with a bishop who was none too thrilled to share his car with a fan dancer.

In 1940 she would campaign for John Nance Gardner, a Texas Democrat running for president. It is curious she wasn't an FDR adherent after the president had bailed the country out of the Great Depression and been a huge proponent of the Chicago World's Fair that gave her a career. Sally Rand's anticommunistic stand and her own hard work ethic lead to an assumption that she was more conservative than not. In an interview with journalist Earl Wilson, Sally Rand gives her view on social programs, "Miss. Rand then went back to the subject of retirement. She is violent, almost, when discussing unemployment insurance as it works in California. 'I'm revolted, aren't you?' She demands . . . 'the rest of us work out tails off . . . I'm against security from the cradle to the grave anyway. My ancestors worked like dogs for a piece of land to raise a potato on.'"[16]

One can understand her resentment of those who would retire on Social Security or even unemployment insurance. She had no safety net. It is hard to know if Sally paid into a Social Security fund, but she certainly did not have unemployment insurance. If she stopped dancing, then she stopped eating. Feather dancing was a vocation, and even though it pushed the edge of morality, it was not itself a declaration of a liberal outlook. One could be a feather dancer by day and a conservative by night. Sally Rand was proud of her work ethic, and she yearned for a middle-class lifestyle even while on the road.

In Boston she was brought low by a piano wire that snapped and sent her twenty feet down onto the stage. It was logical that Sally Rand should add flying to her performance with ostrich feathers, but like the ostriches she was not meant to leave the earth. She could barely hobble out for the curtain call. Then a moment of fantasy. She was asked to address the freshman class of Harvard. This more than anything so far showed how far the stardom of Sally Rand had reached. Clearly Harvard did not want a stripper talking to their 1,500 freshmen but a woman who had become a symbol of hope, a woman who had become a cultural fixture, a star that could bring the perspective of a celebrity to the eighteen-year-olds of an Ivy League school.

Her speech was titled "How to Be Intelligent though Educated." Sally Rand wore a gown when she spoke to the freshman. It is amazing that a conservative institution of higher education would deem her worthy of such a speech, but we have little appreciation for the celebrity culture of the time. Sally Rand at this point was everywhere. Other universities would engage her to speak, and one reason was that she drew the crowds. Sally would speak at a luncheon for Sigma Delta Chi, a national professional journalism society. The title of her speech was "Sociological Effects of Advertising upon the American Public." Another speech given to the Atlanta Exchange Club traced her career, and she finished by telling the clubmen her philosophy of life was "Not how much can I get, but how much can I serve." Sally was playing to the crowd and we see how she could morph into whatever people wanted at that moment. Sally Rand was not altruistic, she was a survivor.

Universities do call on unlikely people to speak, but tickets sell, and Harvard was willing to look beyond the feather dancing roots. But the dichotomy of Sally Rand's fame was evident in the fact that John North of the Ringling Brothers felt she was too tawdry to join their circus. A curious schism. The enlightened, educated class of Harvard clashing with middle-class sensibilities. Middle-class morality would always be a problem for Sally. The esoteric realm of celebrity would allow her to hobnob with movie stars and university presidents, but her profession would keep her son from being invited to a kid's birthday party. Middle America was not enlightened and certainly not progressive in the areas of sexuality in early 1940s. Sally Rand would find some doors open and many closed to her.

And the Benzedrine kept her going through all of this. Benzedrine was a new drug, and there was no "war on drugs" campaign to tell people they shouldn't be taking speed. Judy Garland, as others in the entertainment industry, would use uppers and downers to get movies done, with David O. Selznick famously taking B_1 shots to complete his epic *Gone with the Wind* in 1939, and one wonders what else was in those syringes. But Sally Rand was self-medicating while keeping an incredible schedule. During this time of high income, she bought cars and stayed in the most expensive hotels in New York City.

Even though she was riding high, Sally admitted to being lonely on the road. She told a friend in a letter, "Do you know what's been hard. I've never had a girlfriend. A real lasting relationship. All the time when other girls were going to school, forming friendships, learning all the sweet good things about life, I was knocking about, making trains, one-night stands in small towns, seeing a girl I liked for a week, maybe and then never seeing her again. Now I'm little afraid of women. I guess that's the only thing I am afraid of. They seem so secure, so regular in their routines lives, so different."[17]

Sally was a misanthrope. She had a driving force that had her running off with the circus in her teens and crashing in on Cecil B. DeMille when she was in her twenties and then crashing the World's Fair in Chicago. That kind of drive is unique, and she would never shake her desire to also have a "routine life," but it was never to be. She was caught up in the American current of mass culture and for good or bad, Sally Rand was wedded to a life few would see, that of American Fame.

In 1935 she became Sally Rand Enterprises and incorporated and performed at the Golden Gate International Exposition, where she came up with the "Nude Ranch," a bevy of young girls on horses and in chaps and cowboy hats riding around naked. She pitched the idea to the New York World's Fair and got nowhere when they decided nudity was not to be part of the fair. This must have crushed Sally Rand as Chicago would have been a dry run for the New York World's Fair. Then during this time of seeming prosperity, Sally writes a letter on December 7, 1937, to her mother from New York City, lamenting she is broke.

"I hate to write a blue letter, and this is really not a blue letter—it is a statement of the way things are. There is just not a speck of money to be had and no jobs at this moment and I am broke, which of course always makes me feel very badly. I cannot afford to go to a hotel, and so I am living in this awful little place at 152 W. 49th Street which is Ralph's apartment and full of trunks and files and costumes and all the junk which it seems I have to carry around with me."[18]

It is amazing that Sally Rand just four years out of the World's Fair of 1933 is broke and living in a seedy part of New York City. But her existence was dependent on cash flow from her performances, and she had debt and show business had the propensity to dry up quickly. It is a theme that will increase with time's passage. In the dark night of three a.m., Sally Rand must have had moments of horror where she realized that all she had really was a fan dance at the World's Fair in Chicago to pin her fame on and that was capricious at best. Who knew how long she could carry feather dancing as a way to produce income? All Sally Rand could do was to keep on keeping on before the fairy dust of fame and fortune ran out.

CHAPTER SEVENTEEN

Cashing In

1935–1940

SALLY RAND HAD FOUND A NEW AUDIENCE. AS ONE PAPER PUT IT IN describing her show, "As usual, a good percentage of the audience was composed of business executives and prominent men's club officials and politicians who came to applaud their entertainer."[1] Professional men wanted to see Sally Rand, and she was booked into convention shows where lascivious men after a few drinks could watch the most famous sex symbol in America.

People were going to movies and vaudeville was fading into history. But Sally Rand kept cashing in on her newfound fame. She headed for New York City for a booking at the NTG Paradise Café. She used her bubble and danced to "Moonlight Sonata." She would stay eighteen weeks and then organized a bevy of showgirls heading onto the road. Ziegfeld had died the year before, and many of the girls she used were former dancers from the Follies.

In 1936 she entered into a financial contract with the owner of the Music Box Burlesque hall in San Francisco and brought new life to the old hall with her extravagant Star-Studded Review with sixteen performers and herself. She then was booked into the San Diego Exposition in Balboa Park. This was close to Glendora and lasted for a full year. It made sense to replay the success of the Chicago World's Fair with a similar venue. Her bubble dance was enhanced by an outdoor arena in front of a pool that reflected back. She was so close to the audience a little old lady tried to burn her leg with a cigarette. A nudist colony protested her appearance, but it reeked of a publicity setup with the nudists parading around the fair in sandwich boards. But it always added to the box office revenue. Sally Rand knew one thing very well: any publicity was good publicity. She branched out into more speaking engagements, speaking to ladies' groups, colleges, and even the state legislature of Illinois. She hosted a dog show, a baby beauty pageant, and even a cornhusking competition.

Sally talked of being an actress and constantly pushed back on her Ozark roots and the fact she took off her clothes for a living. Being a stripper did not fit the image she wished to project in her conservative dresses, gloves, and hats. The fans had gotten her to where she was, but she wanted to drop the wings like extra ballast.

But the reality was her fame at the World's Fair had launched her in a way that she didn't even understand. She had seeped into the cultural consciousness of America and in that way left behind every stripper in every burlesque show in America. The fan dance was nothing until it was launched on the mega platform of the Chicago World's Fair of 1933 that transformed Sally Rand into something else. This was something the fan dance could not achieve in a strip club.

Still, the public was fickle, and Sally performed seventy one out of seventy-eight days. Hard to know how much Benzedrine Sally Rand actually used. In 1933 it was marketed as a decongestant. People took out the paper strip inside the inhaler and swallowed it for the euphoric effect. Companies caught on and produced Benzedrine sulfate in a tablet form. Benzedrine was marketed to cure narcolepsy, obesity, low blood pressure, or pain. It would later be given to combat troops in World War II and Vietnam and to cure kids of laziness or "neurological disorders." Sally Rand would use it to cure fatigue. She was in her thirties, and it eventually become her drug of choice along with the nicotine from chain-smoking.

And there were hazards. A serviceman tried to lift her dress and bite her. Another audience member shot nails at her. She was banned from one show in Providence by a minister who saw her as a moral degenerate. The money flowed in and flowed out. A lot of it went to the ranch in

Glendora. Her mother and stepfather could not make it without Sally. She had a Filipino servant named Alfredo and two Pekingese dogs, Snoofy and China Boy. Pictures in newspapers during this time show a successful young woman stepping off planes, taking interviews, sitting on a couch. She has a Lincoln Continental, a trailer, a ranch. She is making it outwardly, but she is leaving a landscape of unpaid bills. The lawyers are very polite as this is before the giant bill collection companies. The letters follow her as she makes her way across the country. A dog kennel wants $150, an airline wants to be paid, a florist, a club in St. Louis wants $250. Some of the later letters begin to get nasty. "I suppose you consider that you have shaken me . . . I am convinced that everything you promised me was part of a scheme or plan to avoid paying me. I have never been treated so shabbily by any client."[2]

Another letter from a lawyer states, "Jacks of Hollywood tells us that they got no money from you. It is about time you stopped stalling and paid your bill. $310 is due and it must be at my office by return mail."[3] There are many of these, and as time passes so do the amount of unpaid bills. But Sally Rand is moving fast, and many of the letters miss her as she goes from one venue to another. Sally wanted to stay in the limelight. The road. This was to be her life if she wanted to make money. Her stage was blown down at one event. A man with a slingshot attacked her at another. Hail and a freak wind collapsed a tent at another venue. Bees attacked her. Her venues were carnivals, expositions, and county fairs. She talked of marriage. "I have the primitive urge for children," she admitted to reporters and went on to say a husband would have to get used to her "individualism."[4]

In a sense Sally Rand never understood her own fame. A woman dancing behind ostrich feathers would assume that sexuality was behind the masses of people clamoring to see her. But it was *Sally Rand* they wanted to see, and a stripper would not have done. But she would many times go into ventures thinking more stripping, more nudity, would provide more money. It was not true. In 1936 Sally Rand found herself in Fort Worth, Texas, to perform at the Fort Worth Frontier Celebration. The fair was part of two fairs that had been ongoing in Fort Worth and Dallas for a hundred years.

Texas loved Sally Rand. She threw out the first pitch at ball games. She gave interviews and speeches . . . Texas declared November 6 "Sally Rand Day." Bill Rose was a promoter with the fair who owned an outdoor 4,500-seat amphitheater with a revolving stage surrounded by water that shot forty feet into the air. Portions of the stage were made from steel. Sally Rand and other dancers would have to dance fast or burn their feet.

Rose immediately complained that Sally Rand's feather dance was dated. She switched to her large rubber balloon dance. She then came up with her promotion in tandem with Billy Rose: "Sally Rand's Nude Dude Ranch." As mentioned before, this is when Sally recruited fifteen girls for her show that would consist of cowgirls outfitted in gilded cowboy boots, holsters, guns, and green bandannas around their necks. Ten-gallon hats kept the sun off their faces, and except for G-strings they were nude.

Sally dressed up like a cowboy and received a share of the price of admissions from Billy Rose. The show did not work. It put sex front and center in a ridiculous format. The cowgirls, while titillating, added nothing extra. Sally Rand was essentially a rubber stamp draw for the show, but it was not enough. The magic of Sally Rand's dance to "Clair de Lune" was missing, and the show became a dusty, dirty burlesque in the hot plains of Texas. Sally Rand's connection as a symbol of hope with a Horatio Alger twist was not to be found. This would confound her every time she tried to extract the sexuality of her act for profit.

The problem with being a cultural icon is that it is almost impossible to define and even harder to monetize. The easy conclusion would be that people liked to look at a beautiful young woman dancing behind ostrich feathers, but Sally Rand stood for the intangible elements that people assigned to her. It was the totality of her act that produced the transportation to another world, something people desperately wanted during the Great Depression. It was at its essence a very simple act, but it was the combustion of the various parts that allowed Sally Rand to transcend the appeal of a mere stripper.

The costs of the production far outstripped the receipts at the gate. Sally left the fair with $41,500 in unpaid bills from her Nude Ranch. The fair overall lost $97,000. Since the Century of Progress success, fairs in general during the Great Depression were having trouble remaining solvent. Sally took her 10 percent royalty and hit the road again, leaving behind a failed show and unpaid bills. They would be added to the people who had already been left in the lurch by her. A local church in Fort Worth, the Calvary Baptist Church, had the last word on Sally Rand and the Nude Ranch, calling her an insult to decency.

It didn't matter; Sally Rand was long gone. In 1941, her father would write Sally a long rambling letter. It was full of the woe of his financial situation that punctuates most of his letters. In the middle he gets to the point, "Now I think of something else. About a week ago I asked you for a loan of a small amount of money to pay off an account in which they were crowding me . . . as not having heard from you about it I surmise that perhaps you are having difficulties."[5]

It was twenty dollars her father wanted. She did send her father some cowboy boots that he claimed were "not only too small, but too fancy to wear in and about this muddy crude and backwoods country."[6] Her father will write long letters complaining about his wife, his children, and the price of wood. It is amazing Sally responded at all. But to the world, including her father, Sally Rand had money to burn.

At one show she is peppered with rocks. Another show in Denver and Cheyenne ended when six ministers shut it down. But she put the Fort Worth Frontier Celebration on the map with her publicity. She was pretty and good copy and in 1936 still gliding on the ether of the Chicago World's Fair. Sally had a part in *Little Foxes* in summer stock theater. Karl Malden would later write about performing with the "ex stripper." "Her burlesque days were written all over her, especially in her hygiene habits . . . She just kept dousing herself with perfume and shoveling on the makeup, layer upon layer, until it began to cake and separate so that you could see the dirt buildup in the creases around her neck . . ."[7] Malden noticed her writing her lines on items on the stage. "There's no way she's going to know her lines by opening night."[8] Malden was the one who choked on opening night while Sally performed flawlessly.

Another letter to her mother in 1939 revealed how close to the bone Sally was living. She was still supporting Nettie and Ernest, but she was tight. "You may count on $50 a week and God willing and helping, as much more as I can possibly squeeze out I am having to pay back debts, many of them, and since these people gave me credit I cannot let them down, and must pay back what I honestly owe them . . . something very swell is going to happen to me and I will be out in Hollywood doing a picture and everything will be hotsy totsy."[9]

Sally would increasingly bet on the big paychecks that were fewer and fewer.

The Chicago World's Fair was the Super Bowl compared to the fairs, summer stock, and other venues Sally Rand now played. Many venues lost money on her performances, and when local churches protested it hurt her ticket draw. Unlike the World's Fair in Chicago, where her arrests brought in more people, the moralists in the smaller towns and venues could shut her down and many times they did. This was a disaster as she had the fixed costs of her show and transportation. Life on the road was rough. A husband would be nice. Maybe a big strapping cowboy who could take care of her. That would work just fine.

CHAPTER EIGHTEEN

The War Years and the Cowboy

1941

SALLY WAS IN THE PAPERS CONSTANTLY SELLING PRODUCTS FROM MILK to beauty products. She barely made shows, jumping in taxis at airports, arriving just in time and taking her feathers on the fly. Planes, trains, automobiles. Bills, lawyers, managers, and always another show. But there was that cowboy again. He had shown the nude cowgirls at her Nude Ranch how to lasso with a lariat. Maybe it was time.

Could there be a more perfect match? The hillbilly from the Ozarks who danced her way to fame at a World's Fair and the rodeo star from a Montana ranch family. Sally Rand was ready for something. She was thirty-eight years old in 1942. She always played with her age. Thurkel "Turk" James Greenough would be her first official husband, though there were rumors of an earlier one. The Cheyenne Frontier Days put the two together; she was there to dance, and he was there to ride and win the bronco-busting contest. Sally Rand was all of five feet tall and he was six-foot six. She wanted his autograph after he busted the cows.

Turk did come from old West stock, but from a rodeo family, and he usually went to the rodeo with his sister and brothers. He was one of eight. His father was a roughhewn man who supposedly cut wood for Calamity Jane. Western lore abounded in the Greenough family, and you can see "Turk" spinning lassos and pulling out his six-guns. He was a performer of Western culture the way Sally was a performer in the East, but Sally's fame was worldwide while Turk's was a provincial or at least regional fame.

Still, there was attraction, and Sally and Turk hit the nightclubs and drove around in her Cadillac. He introduced her to his parents and she loved the Red Lodge ranch. It wasn't much of a jump. She was from a rural culture and because of her lack of education was forever covering up her Ozark humble beginnings. Successful women many times will choose a man who works with his hands or one who brings the salt of the earth with him. Undoubtedly, between lust and loneliness Turk offered the kind of manhood Sally always admired. Tough, self-reliant, a showman, someone who didn't rely on anybody. In short, a cowboy.

World War II had broken out. All ambivalence about Japan's intentions vanished when the Japanese bombed Pearl Harbor on December 7, 1941. America First, the most popular isolationist movement at the time and headed by Charles Lindbergh, withered and died and Lindbergh was disgraced. The entire country went to a wartime footing with rubber drives, scrap drives, rationing books, and blackouts, and stars in Hollywood switched to pushing war bonds and making patriotic war films.

The USO flew stars overseas to entertain the troops. Pinup girls such as Rita Hayworth, Marlene Dietrich, Betty Grable, Jane Russell, and Ginger Rogers were adorning GI lockers in barracks all over the country. It is curious that Sally Rand wasn't a pinup girl, but she was close to forty and not exactly Hollywood royalty. Still, she never took her act on the road to the troops. She complained that her act was not an outdoor act and the wind would blow the feathers. One could see women-starved GIs wanting to see a fan dancer who is only five foot tall and still very attractive. Sally did sell war bonds as many stars did. She headlined a rally in San Francisco at the Golden Gate Theatre. One could argue she was as iconic at the time as Rosie the Riveter in terms of recognition. Yet there is a curious gap in her career, and this might be due to her marriage to Thurkel James.

Sally wrote a letter to Turk's parents outlining their life together. "I want a family, as big a one as we can feed, and the means with which to do it for as long as we live and they after us . . ." She then speculates on

After Cecil B. DeMille discovered her, she became a silent movie star. Sally Rand with legendary costume designer Adrian in the silent movie *Red Dice*, 1926.
PHOTOFEST

Cecil B. DeMille called her the most beautiful woman in the world. Sally Rand publicity photo, 1930.
PHOTOFEST

The Fan Dance allowed her to become famous overnight at the 1933 Chicago World's Fair and become a symbol of hope with her rags to riches story. Publicity photo, 1933.
PHOTOFEST

Sally Rand returned to Hollywood in 1934 with the ostrich feathers that made her famous. Publicity photo from the movie *Bolero*, 1934.
PHOTOFEST

She became the #1 financial draw and made the Chicago World's Fair profitable during the worst year of the Great Depression. Publicity photo on top of a building at the Chicago World's Fair 1933.
PHOTOFEST

She always claimed that "Rand was quicker than the eye" but her nudity was often covered by a body suit. She danced up to seventeen times a day at The Chicago World's Fair of 1933. Publicity photo on a rooftop of the Chicago World's Fair.
PHOTOFEST

The 1933–1934 Chicago World's Fair made Sally Rand famous.

The 1933 Chicago World's Fair A Century of Progress was built during the worst year of the Great Depression and promoted the idea that science and consumerism would rescue the American economy.

COURTESY OF THE LIBRARY OF CONGRESS

Sally Rand traveled the country by air extensively at a time when most people had never flown. She even had her own pilot's license.
COURTESY OF THE LIBRARY OF CONGRESS

Sally Rand was a sought after speaker who spoke at Harvard several times and cultivated a conservative business persona.
COURTESY OF THE LIBRARY OF CONGRESS

She broke the boundaries of sexuality for women in movies. Sally Rand in the movie *Sunset Murder Case*, 1938. Her comeback in Hollywood did not last and she had to return to the road.
PHOTOFEST

She never felt nudity was something to be ashamed of and would be arrested her entire life for indecency. Sally Rand publicity photo, 1930s.
PHOTOFEST

Her fame spanned forty years in radio, movies, and television. Sally Rand as a contestant on *The Dating Game* during the 1960s.
PHOTOFEST

the ranch she will buy for Turk and her. "I want it to be permanent and definite and so located that neither flood, nor draught, nor earthquake, nor landslide can affect it and, in a place, where the government can't take it over."[1]

It is the old Sally Rand dream of having a perfect domestic life of home and hearth and children. But Turk carried some baggage beside his lasso and ten-gallon hat. He had a wife, Helen Greenough, along with three children. It seems Turk had married in 1933 and then vanished in 1940. Just like a cowboy. And he claimed to have thought he was divorced as Helen Greenbough had left a few times for Nevada to seek one. Or so he claimed. This should have been the first warning bells to Sally Rand that everything was not OK at the OK Corral. But after attorneys and a strange phone call where Sally got on the phone with Helen, the wandering cowboy filed for a divorce. This little interlude will inform Sally's approach to domesticity. She wanted a family and she wanted it now and she didn't care about convention. This would haunt her later.

A flight to Los Angeles for the happy couple to get married ended in a summons demanding child support. The cowboy was glum. Helen had filed suit and named Sally, and she wanted one hundred dollars a week. She claimed she was flat broke. Again, one would think Sally would hit the brakes, but time was wasting. It was time to get hitched come hell or high water. In a letter to Turk's parents, Sally wants them to be there for the wedding. "Now! If the divorce comes through on the 12th, Turk and I want to drive out with the car and the station wagon on our way to California, pick you up."[2] There were some last-minute jitters on her part and his apparently. Turk claims in a later book (amazing there was one) he wanted out and went through with the marriage only when Sally became hysterical at his reluctance to wed. But they were married in 1942, and the odd couple of show business began their married life apart. The wedding night was less than perfect.

Turk received his draft notice two months after the wedding. Sally wrote his sisters and painted the scene of her husband's departure. "It was quite sad. We stayed in the car and waited until 8:00 o'clock . . . no one could say anything. There wasn't anything to say. One felt sort of dead and bewitched. . . . we all got out of the car and Turk left us very quietly to take his place against the curb."[3] Sally went back on the road while the cowboy who never had any real responsibility beyond what time to show up at the rodeo headed for basic training.

Even before they were married there was trouble.

Sally would go to his rodeos and the audiences would hound her for autographs. Turk was an old-world man who was the king of his castle or at least his ranch. Sally eclipsed him in fame and earning power. He was reduced to living on her income and throwing in his small rodeo winnings. The truth was Turk was at sea. He had been the roustabout cowboy in Montana having kids and leaving families and doggone it, things just happen, but time had marched on and he suddenly realized he had no real way to make a living.

Six weeks after she was married, Sally was back on the road. She then went to Hollywood and headlined at the Orpheum and stayed on and off with Turk's parents on their ranch. Sally bought Turk a ranch called Piney Dell near Turk's family ranch, but it didn't help. She claimed to be pregnant and then mysteriously she wasn't. Some pointed to rumors of abuse for the loss of the baby. Sally even tried to get Turk into the entertainment world with a role in a film, but it didn't work out. Nothing seemed to be working out. Sally was navigating performances and suits and stayed with Turk's family while he was in the army. They clashed. Her father-in-law, Ben Greenough, mistreated his wife and Sally refused to speak to him after she had been at the family ranch a few weeks.

Sally wrote her mother. "Uncle Sam is really giving me the works. Turk and I have been married but three months and along comes the draft to take him away. And now I'm down to my last bubble and that ain't good. But it seems my country needs both my husband and my bubbles more than I need them. So, I'm not crying. We'll all make sacrifices to win this war . . ."[4]

Then Sally wrote her mother a secret letter explaining that Turk had gone AWOL and was in military prison for two months. "What I am about to say is extremely private, a confidence between mother and daughter in which I know that I can trust you. Turk got himself in a jam, was AWOL, was put on trial and has been in the guardhouse for the last two months . . . he is a very willful person completely lacking in self-discipline. I was truly afraid he would do some foolhardy spectacular thing, and either be shot or put away for good . . . his own unfamiliarity with the theatre and his complete disapproval of the kind of work I do in the theatre and his lack of trust in me has made things very difficult."[5]

The cowboy just couldn't get used to conformity and was in shock that he couldn't just wake up from a hangover staring at the pinwheel stars in Montana. Then he showed up one day at the family home and said an officer had tried to show him how to ride a horse. He, a rodeo star! Sally stared at him and demanded to know what his plans were. He shrugged and told her he had quit the army.

Clearly the cowboy and the army were not going to get along. After his stint in the guardhouse, he started to write letters of disapproval. He didn't want his wife dancing nude in front of others. Sally ignored him and stayed on the road. The army had enough and let Turk go because of an injury, but there were reports of psychological problems as well. In World War II the United States needed every solider they could get, so it must have been a severe incident that cemented the break between the armed forces and the cowboy.

Things became worse with Turk out of the army. Sally wrote him a letter from the road. "I was so unhappy and miserable when you left yesterday morning. Why oh why do we have to quarrel? Surely, we can find some way of living together without quarreling. I can't stand it! When you are harsh and cross it simply crushes me and leaves me dead and cold!"[6]

Sally bought another ranch for the wayward cowpoke, Red Rim Ranch, in Wyola, Montana. Turk had no idea how to run a ranch she found out. He was a showman. A rodeo cowboy. After that he wasn't much. He couldn't make money, and he began to drink while Sally tried to find someone to run the ranches. She had hitched her wagon to a fallen rodeo star. It didn't help that her fame was only growing while his feeble light was flaming out. Turk became paranoid and then had a full-scale nervous breakdown. One suspects the army detected his psychological flaw early on and that was the real reason they mustered him out. Sally Rand's friend Holly Knox saw it this way. "The frustration of her frequent absences and the war turned him more and more to the bottle.

On more than one occasion, he hit her in a drunken rage. She was finally pregnant, albeit not happily so, because of the state of her marriage. She miscarried, and this also did nothing to cement the failing relationship."[7]

In a reflective letter later, Sally summed up her marriage and the problems. "My marriage on December 6th, 1943 to this cowboy was not successful. He was a man who had never been regimented. He had lived on a ranch in the open country of Montana all his life, very free and without conventional restraint. The regimentation, and to him, senseless restraint imposed by military discipline were destructive to his personality. His experiences overseas were extremely disillusioning. He was sorely wounded and returned extremely disillusioned and embittered and a very changed person form the simple, honest, kind man I had married. His mind was more wounded than his body and he was not psychopathically [sic] able to take up civilian life nor human relationships. Upon the advice of the psychiatrist who had charge of his rehabilitation, I severed the relationship for my safety and for his better chance at rehabilitation."[8]

This is interesting in that Sally claims Turk was suffering from a paranoid schizophrenia or early PTSD or at least some inability to cope with changed circumstances. Also, Turk never did go overseas. He made it as far as basic training. Leaving him for her "safety" is certainly code for domestic abuse.

Sally stayed on the road for another two years, and in the last year of the war, 1945, she filed for divorce. The two ranches were put up for sale and the divorce was handled quickly. In a show at the Stickney Avenue Fair, Sally told reporters, "I had tried very hard to make a go of the marriage, but my husband would take no responsibility. He humiliated me in my work. He was a changed man after his release from the Army."[9] In a letter to her mother in 1945, Sally reveals her yearning for a quiet domestic life. "I know it is wrong to let any one person simply destroy your life, at the same time it wasn't just Turk. It was what Turk represented . . . all the things I had wanted all my life . . . a home, peace, quiet, things of my own that I could touch and feel and put away and take out and use and say . . . these are mine."[10] Sally then writes her mother a reflective letter and recognizes her own self-destructive tendencies. "I swear I work like a dog . . . I try hard. I do the best I can. I know that there is something wrong with me . . . that I approach things wrong. There is something I do that isn't constructive but what it is . . . I don't know . . . if I could just simplify things a little bit it would be so much easier."[11]

Certainly, the whirl of Sally Rand's life would wear anyone down, but the truth is she is all alone. It is her career. Her business. And no role models to go on. Like any pioneer, Sally Rand was having to test the waters for others to follow by taking modern celebrity to another level. She simply had no choice.

Turk went back to his ex-wife with his tail between his legs. He had been secretly carrying on a correspondence during the war years and sent her money. They tried the rodeo circuit and starved and then finally ended up in Las Vegas. Turk turned forty-five and took a security job. The cowboy hung up his spurs. Turk's imprisonment by the army and then his eventual dishonorable discharge must have left a funny taste in Sally Rand's mouth regarding the war effort.

After the marriage collapse, Sally was in Chicago and announced she would donate a pair of her ostrich fans to the Chicago Historical Society. The society refused with a statement, "The Board of trustees at the Chicago Historical Society feels that the fans used by Miss. Sally Rand at the Century of Progress . . . do not . . . have sufficient historical interest to warrant their acceptance by the museum."[12] Almost thirty years would pass before Sally Rand's fans were accepted by the museum. But at this point, Sally Rand had yet to become a legend. The jury was still out if she would endure as something more than a footnote to the 1933 World's Fair.

Sally stayed on the road. The 1940s were not the 1930s, and while many people enjoyed the boom the war years brought to the economy compared to the Great Depression, Sally Rand's income fell. The costs were high and the bookings not as lucrative, and she had bought the ranches and still had to support her mother and stepfather. During this time her car was repossessed, and she was down to her last hundred dollars many times when she wasn't paid. She was stranded in Miami from nonpayment, and then there were the nonstop debt collections that resulted in judgments, fines, suits, and warrants.

At the Club Savoy in San Francisco, she was arrested again. Her attorney famously stated in the courtroom, "I can show more nudity among the classics."[13] The judge then ordered the entire courtroom to the nightclub for the 9:30 a.m. performance. So, in the year 1944, a judge, lawyers, possibly a jury, all went to the Club Savoy to watch Sally Rand perform her bubble dance. The war intruded here but to Sally's favor. The bubble is usually clear and Sally Rand's naked body is visible through the sphere. But because of the quality of the rubber and the kind of materials being used during the war, the bubble was fuzzy, dense, opaque. Sally Rand was a blurred figurine dancing behind a globe. She also made sure she did not turn her backside to the judge as she usually did in performances, and we can assume she did not toss the bubble up in the air and give her customary full frontal. She was found not guilty of the charges, and the war years drew to a close with her still on the road.

There might be other reasons Sally Rand did not become more of a wartime icon as so many other celebrities did. Even pinup girls went through a wartime board that mirrored the Hays Commission in Hollywood. Hairstyles were altered so that women in wartime factories would emulate practical, safer styles while blasting rivets into the wings of planes or welding tanks. Sally Rand for all her stardom was still an outlier. She represented a breach in morality while the world was confronting evil on a plane no one had ever contemplated. A clear sense of right and wrong rolled through America, and deviation from this code was suspect. A woman dancing naked behind feathers, while on one hand harmless, represented a breakdown or a moral decay. The kind of degeneracy that might lead to a breakdown of other codes of ethics desperately needed to defeat the Germans and the Japanese.

The truth is that Sally Rand would have gladly accompanied Bob Hope or Lucille Ball or Ginger Rogers overseas on USO tours if she was asked. The hard reality was that Mom and Dad didn't want to get a letter from their son describing a naked woman behind some ostrich feathers. We can be sure; Sally Rand was never asked to go with those other stars entertaining the troops. Still, it would have been a welcome relief from dusty fairgrounds, lawsuits, and cowboy husbands.

Chapter Nineteen

Hellcat

1944

HER MAID ALWAYS HAD A CIGARETTE WAITING FOR HER BACKSTAGE, where she took a couple of drags and then went back on stage to perform. Nicotine, caffeine. These were her drugs of choice to keep her moving. Reporters talked about her incessant chatter and the way her voice squealed and how she talked with rapid-fire speed ordering her maid about and talking to her "male dresser." Of course, she was jazzed on speed. The girl from the Ozarks was cashing in, and she could not miss a beat.

Sally fell from a catapult in Boston to the stage and nearly broke her leg. A man fainted in Dubuque while Sally danced, reportedly from the raw sex appeal of her act. She made lots of money and incurred lots of debt. The Papers of Sally Rand are so loaded with debt collection letters from lawyers it is overwhelming even for the historian. From bills for dancers she employed to haberdashers, Sally Rand put her image and herself first and left many people with unpaid bills.

The next engagement. The next article in the press. The next check. This was important. She had the advantage of leaving. Many of the lawyers, small businesses, municipalities, banks, and agents trying to collect money from Sally Rand could not catch up with her. She was always leaving, and she didn't have time to even file her taxes. The government was quickly added to the list of those trying to track down Sally Rand. Western Union telegrams flew back and forth.

"Must know immediately about payroll report due Monday. Also, must have money immediately or impossible to complete income tax, please wire something today sure and call tonight as I must make plans."[1] Frustrated accountants and lawyers working for Sally were also stiffed. She was a cyclone, and the best anyone could do was try to keep up with her. "Please rush money so copy court decision. Also, phone bill past due."[2]

Sally justified the nonpayment surely with the thought that one big smash out of the park with a hit movie would take her off the road. Many times, Sally waited until a court proceeding to settle. And these were not small debts. At a time when the average yearly income was around seventeen hundred dollars, Sally Rand was being sued for debts upwards of ten thousand dollars. One debt amounting to $4334 in a suit that Olive I. Kephart brought against her dragged on until a judgment was rendered and only then did Sally pay up. It is amazing how polite the letters to a woman who would not pay remained. "We were assured by Miss. Robertson that you would mail us a check." "Our clients have instructed us to institute suit against you and we are giving you this final opportunity to communicate with us regarding this matter."[3] Many small businesses could not afford attorneys and tried to cajole a payment with polite entreaties, "Sally, I would certainly appreciate it if you could send us another payment on the bedroom. We are operating on a slim margin."[4] Her accountant was added to the mix many times as she used different ones for different problems. "Sally, Thanks so much for the very clever xmas card . . . now send me a check will ya?"[5] Certified letters, telegrams, and hand-delivered notices were hitting hotels Sally had just left.

But the show must go on. The Paramount Theatre in Los Angeles would let the hellcat out of her cage and become one of the many legal problems she would have to deal with. The incident would become legend and would presage other Sally Rand "catfights." Sally was performing behind a scrim when one Ray Strandford decided to get a picture of the feather dancer holding her seventy-two-inch balloon over her head. Sally lost control and the bubble floated off, and Ray shoved his camera through the curtain. CLICK! The sound was like a rifle shot to Sally, who was paranoid about being caught in a compromising position. She was older, and while in great shape, her act was all about illusion.

Ray and his girlfriend Hazel Drain were already beating it up the aisle when a five-foot tigress in a robe ran after them. Sally demanded the picture, and a struggle ended with Sally biting Hazel, the camera destroyed, and Ray's shirt torn. The press coverage showed a full photo spread of Sally Rand with her father, speaking at Harvard, and behind were her fans under the banner, *Fretful Fan Dancer*. The reporting is light, almost jocular. "Ray Stanford said Miss. Rand tore his clothing and scratched him. Miss. Hazel Drain, his companion, said she was bitten on the arm by the irate fan dancer. Miss. Rand denied biting the woman but admitted a little pinching."[6] But the article also pointed out a prior incident where Sally Rand had bitten someone. "Back in 1933 she walked into a Chicago police station, displayed a bruised eye and demanded the arrest of a night club manager. She said he had 'clouted' her in an argument over salary. He showed tooth marks which he said were Sally's."[7]

Another article had a smiling Sally with a headline, "Sally Wouldn't Bite Anyone."[8] Clearly, she was still a media darling. This would not be the last time Sally Rand would bite a person. Assault charges were initiated, and Sally was given a court date. She missed the date, of course. In the Papers of Sally Rand are many notices of missed court dates. A warrant was issued, and Sally agreed to show up for a new date in October. On the seventeenth of the month, she was held until she could post bond and ended up in a tiff with a policewoman who wanted her picture taken with her. When Sally refused, she ended up in jail, where she burst into tears.

A trial was held for her attack on the couple with the camera. Articles made light of the trial while Sally kept the jury and judge entertained with a re-creation of the event. Sally complained that the lipstick on Hazel's white sweater did not match her own and she had no fingernails to scratch her with. The jury and the judge were not buying, and she was turned down on her offer to perform for the courtroom. She lost and was sentenced to a year in jail and fined two thousand dollars, which was later reduced to a fine of one hundred dollars. The couple then sued her for $150,000, but ultimately the suit was dismissed in 1945.

The question here is why would Sally Rand with her time constraints not have settled with a plea bargain? It is amazing, but she would time and again end up in court wasting time when she could have settled. It was as if one part of her forever remained the naive hillbilly from the Ozarks. She did attack the couple and she did bite the woman. Then, of course, there is no bad publicity, and this had to be her driving force. The trial was covered by the newspapers, which took pictures of her with her fans and balloons. Publicity was the fuel that kept the Sally Rand airplane aloft. So, for a hundred-dollar fine and the cost of her attorneys, she generated probably thousands of dollars in free publicity. Another lesser known incident occurred in Hamilton, Ontario, when her baggage car was left near a tunnel. Sally stormed into the office of Mr. Warnick and told him what she thought of his railway. A struggle ensued over some telegrams, and Sally scratched the railroad man's face with her nails. No charges were filed.

It was during this time Sally filed for bankruptcy protection. She was being sued by Billy Rose for taking the Nude Ranch idea. She had left the Golden Gate Exposition owing sixty thousand dollars. Even though she appeared in *Life Magazine* and had incorporated as Sally Rand Enterprises, things were not going her way. She neglected to list her ownership in the orange ranch she had bought for her mother and stepfather. The trustee of the bankruptcy discovered she held title in joint tenancy with her parents, and Sally had to scramble and get a new lawyer. Her lawyer addressed her ownership in a letter to the trustee. "In the proceeding she omitted to list in her assets the joint tenancy which she held with her mother and father in the orange ranch."[9] The lawyer then claimed Sally didn't know she had been listed as a "joint tenant by her parents until she was cited for a supplemental examination last spring."[10]

The truth is Sally had a history of playing fast and loose with the truth. She didn't want the orange ranch in the bankruptcy as there was a chance the trustee could take the ranch and force a sale to satisfy debts and turn out her mother and stepfather. The lawyer then compounded the oversight by claiming Sally never invested any money in the ranch, which was not true. Sally regularly sent home money to fund the ranch and helped with expenses. She is scrambling to keep what she can, and it will not be her first bankruptcy. The proceedings were amended as the mortgage and taxes were in arrears, and a payment schedule was set up for the orange ranch as well by the trustee.

Sally gave a speech to some businessmen in Seattle, explaining, "one of the reasons why I went bankrupt was that I was credited with too much business acumen. As I got deeper and deeper into business and my reputation was built up, businessmen began to fear I would outwit them."[11] This seems to be code for saying she got no business advice at all. Later she would tell columnist Lloyd Shearer, "I thought I was going to mint a small fortune form the Fair at San Francisco. Instead I was taken to the cleaners like Grant took Richmond."[12]

In 1939 Sally would go further and spell out the details of her financial situation in a column under her own byline. "No stocks, no automobiles, no annuities, not even a Rolls Royce. Just $8,067 worth of clothes and jewels, for even a fan dancer must have clothes for leisure moments. My creditors are trying to squeeze $64,638.00 out of that . . . going broke on $174,830 a year? It's easier than getting the $174,830 in the first place."[13]

Sally Rand was not a good businesswoman. She knew how to make money, but she could not control her debts. Many times, her shows would not break even after she paid her dancers and transportation costs and shared her profits with the hosting venue. In the end she pawned her watch and diamond ring for cash. It was all becoming a grind. Where was the family life she now craved? A husband. A baby. Cigarettes, nicotine, and an empty hotel room were awful in the dead silence at the end of the day. She was in her forties and the math of diminishing opportunities was playing out, even for Sally Rand.

CHAPTER TWENTY

The Instant Family

1948

SALLY WAS INVITED TO SPEAK AT THE SOUTHEASTERN COMMUNITY Theatre Conference in 1948. A letter lauded her "ability as a speaker and your ability as a producer and manager as well."[1] She also wrote an article for *Billboard* magazine about life in the carnival business, "I'm with It and for It!"[2] The next year Sally passed on performing at the Illinois State Fair because of the polio epidemic and she did not want to "be charged with attracting the public to a crowded area and thereby be guilty of contributing to the risk of spreading this tragic and fearful disease."[3] This disease that attacked mostly children would have new meaning for her.

Sally now performed with a baby lying in a fan box backstage. The scent of pancake makeup, smoke, hot lights. Girls changing all around the baby. The music. Sally gave a fistful of money to Sunny Nivens, another dancer, and told her to take the baby and go to New York City and get a hotel room and not to open the door for anyone, even the police. Sunny took the baby and disappeared out the backstage exit while Sally peeked through the curtain. The mother was out there somewhere. She had been asking around, and she wanted her baby back. But Sally could not give up her son. Not now. He was really all she had.

In an article in the *Daily Mail*, Sally is shown writing a letter to her son. It is an interview she gave at the Anderson Fair. "'Give a child enough food, enough rest, and enough love and he'll be happy and contented,'[4] is Sally Rand's advice to parents . . . She speaks with authority as she talks about her own son, a five-year-old Irish lad with big blue eyes, long curly lashes, and dark curly hair, whom Sally adopted when he was eight days old."[5] The article then veers and gives an idyllic picture of an idyllic life. "'He's a happy well integrated child,' Miss Rand says with motherly pride . . . whether traveling with his mother and enjoying the merry go round, the clowns, and theatrical life or staying with his grandmother and grandfather on their ranch in California, where he can ride his own little sorrel pony and attend his advanced nursery school."[6]

The whitewash that is the Sally Rand publicity machine is in full swing. The article finishes up with a Hollywood rendition of her life. "Ambition and hard work carried her through her years as a vaudeville trouper and motion picture actress and stage star to the top in the theatrical world and to international acclaim. Study and work with ballet and dancing masters of the United States and Europe prepared her for the development of her original and famed solo dancing with the ostrich fan and the bubbles."[7]

Another article covering Sally when she held up her baby at the Cushman Club in Boston said, "the baby was a great surprise as well as a delight to everyone as Sally's motherhood was not generally known . . . so it turned out she had adopted the little boy even before, as she said it, it was born, sight unseen. 'So of course, I didn't know what it was going to be.'"[8] But there is another article dated 1948 in the *Fresno Bee*. It is a picture of Sally giving her adopted son, Sean, a bottle. The caption reads, "Fan Dancer Sally Rand feeds her adopted son Sean between acts of the Royal American Shows in Jackson Miss. Sally said she adopted the boy in Birmingham Ala, but adoption agencies there deny the fact."[9] So, the first lie is out there. She did not adopt a baby.

In a letter in 1953 to lawyer Al Caleare in Key West Florida, she complains about having trouble getting a proper birth certificate. "Remember, I took care of all this adoption deal before Sean was born. [She also has changed the spelling of his name from Shawn to Sean.] Remember the day in your office when the father and mother both signed—I was there remember I paid all the hospital and Doctors, etc., and left it to you to obtain his proper birth certificate. There was no doubt of my adoption of him even though I did not get to Key West to pick him up till September—I paid his mother's doctor and hospital bills. His doctor bill for circumcision; his hospital bill for every day he was in the hospital—till I picked him up."[10]

There are problems here. Holly Knox's rendition of events has Sally Rand dealing with the young mother with the father nonexistent. Now a house she bought in Key West starts to make sense as it is rarely mentioned in her letters. Did the mother stay there while pregnant or did Sally have plans to settle in Florida with Sean at one time? But things get even more strange. In her letter, Sally states, "This birth certificate is for a child named 'Robert Hepler.' I know no such child. The school authorities would know no such child."[11]

The lawyer responds, "in reference to the birth certificate I forwarded you, it is the only record that is on file with the Bureau of Vital Statistics in Jacksonville Florida and the original certificate of birth cannot be altered."[12] What this seems to imply is that when the baby was born the name of the father was given to him, Robert Hepler. Sally said she could not get to the hospital until later. The lawyer further tells Sally, "I cannot file adoption proceedings in the State of Florida for you to adopt Sean Orion Rand as neither he nor you are a bona fide resident of the State of Florida."[13] The lawyer then continues and says, "It is true that I have in my possession two signed Affidavits by the parents of Sean Orion Rand giving their consent to the adoption of him by you."[14]

The lawyer's offers to turn it all over is also telling. He writes Sally Rand in a different letter that "your North Beach house had been condemned as a fire menace and will be torn down by city authorities. In the past six or seven months there have been at least three small fires on your premises . . . also the city and county tax certificates have been sold to individual buyers . . ."[15] So, what is going on? A young dancer told Sally she would give her baby to her. Sally bought property in Key West, probably knowing she would need residency to adopt in Florida and giving the young mother somewhere to live. She doesn't get down there until after the baby is born who now has the last name of either the father or the mother, Hepler. Sally has two affidavits that are functionally worthless. Sean Rand will later tell author Leslie Zemeckis that his father had died on a ship when a gun exploded. The house falls behind in taxes and goes into disrepair because its function was never to be a place for Sally Rand to live. It appears that Sally Rand raised the baby as Mark Hepler until he turned eighteen and then adopted him as Sean Orion Rand.

Of course, this is only revealed seventy years after the fact by the letters in the Papers of Sally Rand. Sally wants a son and like the rest of her life she will have to make it up as she goes. This would account for the little mention of her property in Key West. She knows that she has not a chance of adoption because of her profession, age, and marital status. So, she takes a dancer's baby and raises it under the guise of legal adoption. The North Beach property slips into foreclosure several times before the government eventually takes it for back taxes.

Apparently, Sally had tried to adopt a baby once before. A dancer had a baby she brought with her on tour, and Sally became attached to Baby Paul. She began to pester the young mother to let her adopt her son. The dancer, Lorie, and Sally got into a physical altercation. "She was the only one I ever hit but she called me terrible names, really a gutter mouth. She called me a whore. I slapped her. She tore into me. I don't know what happened. I think I just took off. I kneed her. Next thing I knew I just ran."[16]

The cover story is the perfect life the article portrayed. This is all betrayed again by the Papers of Sally Rand. There is a letter she wrote to a friend admitting to loneliness on the road. "I'm not married. In many ways I would like to be, for all of us who are unmarried life can be very lonely, especially as one grows older one seems to need the companionship and very closeness of another human being...it is difficult sometimes not to have a strong masculine chest to lean on."[17] Also tucked away in the papers is a prescription. It is among all the newspapers articles and suits and letters from lawyers requesting money. It is a strange prescription, given by one George L. Cook, MD. The ingredients are:

15 drops of whiskey

1/4 aspirin

1 white tablet

Pinch of sugar

One or two teaspoons water

The instructions are: "Mix and give for restlessness."[18] That's it. It is obviously for a baby or a toddler. An early psychoactive drug. The Ritalin of its time. The child would certainly be knocked out with the whiskey. It was probably for a crying baby. And then there is another strange item mixed in with some letters. "General Instructions for Infant Care. The following information is intended to serve as a guide in the care of the young infant. Obviously, only general rules can be given, for the details of the care of the infant depend upon individual circumstances and individual attention."[19] Then there is a letter from Babyville, a New York City babysitting service. "Babyville is comprised of individuals who associate themselves for the purpose of serving parenthood."[20] And then a picture of Sally Rand holding a baby. Where did all this come from? This instant baby and instant motherhood.

No one was going to give a baby to a forty-three-year-old woman who made her living dancing naked behind ostrich feathers. Family life could not be solved between court appearances, arrests, dusty state fairs in the middle of nowhere, and the incessant money problems. The best she could hope for was providence to provide her with a family. The traditional route of a baby of her own was increasingly remote with her age now a factor, a rumored abortion, and a stable man nonexistent. The road was hell. She was stranded in Miami when a show didn't pay. Her car was repossessed and then wrecked. She had been arrested at the Club Savoy. The Iowa State Fair said they didn't need a stripper. Sally Rand's career was a grind because the minute she stepped away from her fan dance, the money and the fame vanished over the next hill. She writes a poem in a hotel room, titled "Defiance":

> Oh Gods! Take back your stinking gift of life
> I fling it in your face
> For me there is no light, no love,
> For my head no resting place
> Why are we created

With such capacity for pain
Are you blind or just indifferent?
Are we expected to be sane?[21]

Where was the love missing in her life? Between the hotels and the fairs and the endless driving in her Lincoln with a trailer in tow behind or catching a plane to another booking. The bleak existential state of her soul is laid bare in her poem. It would be a knock on her dressing room door in Tallahassee, Florida, that changed her life. Holly Knox has the scene this way and we can only assume this is how Sally told her it went.

Sally did not like to be disturbed before a show. The knock persisted.

"Ok come in and make it snappy."

The door opened to a young girl with beautiful eyes asking for a job.

"I need a job, mam. I've had training and I really need a job."

Sally was short a dancer and she was hired. It was several months later she noticed the girl putting on weight. In a scene in her dressing room straight out a B movie, Sally confronted the young girl.

"Are you pregnant dear?"

The girl broke down and told her the father was a married man and her own family refused to help her. Sally was angry.

"But what in the hell am I supposed to do with you?"

The girl cried and shook her head. Sally leaned forward.

"Do you really want this baby? It's rough out there going it alone."

The girl looked up.

"This baby needs to be born and I will have it. But I do plan to adopt it out. The father wants me to and so does my family. I've decided to do it."[22]

Who knows where this really happened? Maybe some fair or the backstage of a theater in a small town. But Sally Rand lived an improvised life and took shortcuts when nothing else presented itself. She saw the writing on the wall. This was it. She leaned forward.

"Would you let me adopt your baby? I have been trying to adopt for a couple of years. I would be an excellent mother. I'll keep you working till you show too much and then support you till the baby is born."[23]

The girl was happy to let Sally Rand have her baby. Her name was Imogene Younger Hepler. She was set up in an apartment or maybe the house in Key West until she was ready to deliver. This was the one-in-a-million break Sally needed. "Getting little Sean had been a dream come true for her. Numerous doctors had assured her that she would never bear a child. She was determined, however, and when she reached a large city, she would make it a habit to check with adoption agencies . . . and the answers were always the same. She was not employed in a stable profession. And most important in the years of the 40s; she was not married." When people questioned her profession, she responded, "so what . . . some people are plumbers and taxi drivers, and everybody has a right to make an honest livelihood."[24]

Sally Rand would solve the first objection with a new husband, Harry Finkelstein. He was a dark-haired, green-eyed smooth talker who had been her manager for years, and Sally's version told years later to Holly Knox painted the marriage as one of convenience. It is over lunch at Sardi's in New York City that Sally broached the subject of adopting a child with Harry.

"In this business . . . you. Sally Rand?"

"Of course, me. I'd make a hell of a mother. I have a house on the coast. My mother lives with me. It would be perfect and look at all I could teach him about life."[25]

Harry was skeptical. At this time, he is married to stripper Georgia Sothern. Sally and Harry had been having an affair for years, and it came to a head when Georgia caught the two in a room and there was a scene. The police were called, and Sally was charged with disorderly conduct. According to an affidavit filed by Sally's lawyer, a bribe was attempted to influence a judge against Sally, who had been lying down in her room with the door open when Georgia entered. There was a "morality clause" in Sally's contract that Georgia wanted to be invoked so she would be fired. The truth is she was livid with the woman stealing her husband. The case was dismissed but the disorderly conduct would stick with her after some newspapers picked up on it, and it would keep her out of the Illinois State Fair.

Sally went to the US Attorney and friends of the governor to change agriculture director Roy Yung's mind, who had made the decision not to let Sally Rand perform. A newspaper article laid out the controversy with the headline "Sally Rand With or Without Fans Banned as Fan Dancer." The article went on, "The curvaceous fan dancer has been refused permission to appear at the big exposition . . . her nemesis is Roy Yung . . . who got his dander up and put his foot down when the dancer attempted to book an appearance at the fairgrounds."[26] Sally told the press, "It will be a big disappointment to me if I am not allowed to appear at the fair."[27] But Yung would not budge, citing the disorderly conduct incident two years before and the attendant bad publicity. Georgia had her revenge against the woman who stole her husband.

The divorce from Georgia came through in 1949, and Harry and Sally were married the following year. Sally had her baby and was living in a large trailer on the road with a secretary and a nurse. And she had a husband; the instant family was complete. As long as she could stay ahead of the birth mother who decided she wanted her baby back. The problem was Harry never stopped having affairs. Sally was an affair and every other stripper her manager could bed would become affairs as well. Sally writes to Harry and throws down the gauntlet.

> It is normal for a man to want sex and for a man to get it, but it only takes a minute and doesn't leave a scar. And it's more fun if the broad thinks you're wonderful and terrific. But by God you don't have to make a career out of every whore you lay nor bring her flowers and jewels . . . why don't you be smart? Dames to lay are a dime a dozen. Finish your court at night. Call your wife, let the dame wait. Feed her, fuck her, send her home. Or get up and go home and forget about it. You got laid. What else do you want? Love? That you got from me.[28]

This is an amazing letter in that Sally gives Harry permission to have extramarital sex as long as he doesn't tell her about it. "You're a damn fool. But I'm a bigger one to write like this, to plead, to care. But the day will come when I don't."[29]

In the Papers of Sally Rand is a letter from Harry begging Sally to give him one more chance. There is a groveling letter written from a hotel in New York City to Sally in another hotel. Harry pleads with her to take him back, professing his love. "Please Sally give me a reprieve. Give me the opportunity to prove my love to you. . . . I promise before God you will never know an unhappy moment. Inherently I am a good boy. I never wanted to be bad . . . let us not destroy our lives."[30]

Sally's return sixteen-page letter shines light on her religious beliefs and the sordid details of her marriage. "According to you you have no place to go, there is nothing else you can do. You must depend on your divorced wife for food, shelter, spending money and laundry . . . your letter pleads with me to believe you, that you are all though with lies, your very life day by day and minute by minute is a lie . . . you feel that you can accomplish the fulfillment of our physical and material needs and desires by cunning, craft, deceitfulness, shrewdness, instead of by work, industry or thrift."[31] Sally then tells him to go to a psychiatrist, get a job, live simply, and no more women and he must find religion the way she had with Christian Science. She lists the requirements for her wayward husband.

"Reading the daily lesson. Help and instruction at least once a week form a Christian Science practitioner—both of these things for one year. You change your name. You have plastic surgery on your nose. That you are sexually capable and potent with me."[32]

The last two requirements are strange, but Sally believes deeply in Christian Science and lets Harry know that she "wants to achieve and obtain membership in the Mother Church and in a branch church and I desire to have class instruction with a teacher. I would like to become a lecturer . . . I want to raise Sean and my other children in the Christian Sciences Church and I need their early father's help."[33] Further on she lets Harry know she wants "to get out of show business"[34] and live a quiet life in Glendora. "I expect go get out of show business this year. I must be with Sean . . . mother cannot handle him alone and he needs his mother—also his father when he has one." Sally then explains she is not prejudiced but wants Harry to get a nose job to lose the burden of being a Jew. "You have carried the burden for so long—if you are to make a new life, if we are to make a new life together this is one burden I insist that you be rid of. Let it also be a symbol of the new man."[35]

This could be anti-Semitism even though Sally cloaks this "one burden" as a psychological fix for Harry. America in the 1940s was very anti-Semitic, and Harry doesn't fit her ideal Christian Scientist husband. But this also fits with Sally's idea of remaking yourself. A person can become someone else through sheer will. She had gone from Helen Beck the hillbilly from the Ozarks to Billie Beck to Sally Rand, a world-famous celebrity. Others could do the same.

Then there is the sex. "I don't want any remembrance of our former humiliation because of this lack in our marriage. In other words, I don't want any hangovers of yesterday's failures."[36] Harry obviously had a hard time performing sexually, and Sally puts this next to a new religion, a nose job, and fidelity. "And you will have to stick this out for a year, at school, at a job, supporting yourself and studying Christian Science."[37] Sally also requires him to change his name to get rid of his "Jewish burden."[38]

Harry promises to do anything to win her back, but it is the prisoner facing the gallows who will do anything to avoid his punishment. Even seventy years later Harry's letters reek of disingenuousness. "Darling I want to be with you always. I now feel I am a different person, the kind of person you would want me to be."[39]

In Milwaukee, Sally was arrested along with Harry for indecency when some police came to the show. Sally revealed she was forty-six and had to call her brother, Harold, for bail. To get her and Harry out would require fifteen hundred dollars. It is interesting to note that neither Sally nor her husband/manager had enough money to get themselves out of jail. The truth was her cash flow was terrible. Many times, she didn't get paid, and the cost of her shows with dancers and transportation costs and lodging left her continually in the red.

Another suit came her way from the owner of Cavalcade of Amusements for slandering him on a radio interview in Chicago. It is during this time in 1951 that Sally posts a five-hundred-dollar bond for Charles

Cecil Pearson, whom she met in 1948 during the Royal American Show. She writes an affidavit attesting to his character and in this affidavit, she lists the properties she owns. There is the ranch where her mother lives at 325 North Michigan Avenue, Glendora, California, and 1434 East Sierra Madre Avenue in Glendora, and a residence in Key West, Florida, at 918 North Beach Key West. Nowhere else has the property in Key West been listed, and this points to the possible scheme to establish residency in Florida. In a letter dated July 24, 1949, a friend tells Sally, "your old house is boarded up and looks very dreary as we pass it. . . . you will see for yourself once you get back to Key West."[40]

Posting bail for Charles Pearson throws up more questions. There seems to be a question of loyalty to the United States with Charles Cecil Pearson. A follow-up letter from a lawyer in the Papers of Sally Rand furthers the mystery: "I am afraid I have some bad news to convey to you at the present time. Last night at 6:00 I was called by the immigration Bureau and informed that the examiners down here have decided to refer the Pearson case back to Detroit for further questioning of Pearson and allow him to obtain additional information as to his moral character."[41]

Another letter from the government informs Sally that Pearson, "apparently neglected to keep the appointment." It becomes clear now that Sally wants Pearson of Canada to become a citizen so that, as the government put it, "he may assist you in your traveling show."[42]

What is the truth? Sally met Pearson while performing in Canada and was married to Harry at the time. Her motivation in trying to get his citizenship could well have been so her boyfriend could travel with her. After he didn't show for his immigration hearing, there is no more correspondence.

Sally returns to Harvard in 1951 to give a speech to the freshman class. This time it did not go well at the annual Smoker. Sally read a poem and spoke on the evils of communism. The restless freshmen stared at the older woman, waiting for a joke that never came. She was suddenly the older woman, slightly strange, and then the crowd turned surly. A freshman pelted Sally with a penny. Then another flew out. Sally tried to continue with her speech. The pennies rained down with other objects with the laughter of the freshman echoing in the hall. Sally Rand retreated off the stage with tears streaming down her cheeks. The cute blond who had wowed the freshman of Harvard almost twenty years before was gone and had become the middle-aged woman pelted with pennies from freshman who had little idea who she was.

Sally Rand has now been on the road over twenty years since the Chicago World's Fair closed. She has a cheating husband and a child whom her mother looks after in California unless he can join her at a show. She is three years from fifty and living out of hotels and trailers and is constantly in debt and constantly in legal trouble. Then Harry went back with his ex-wife, Georgia, and they had the dueling letters that are amazing in length. Sally's sixteen-page epistle laid out the road to salvation again for Harry, again, quit screwing Georgia, become a Christian Scientist.

Sally writes a will and gives Harry one dollar and bequeaths the rest of her estate to Sean O. Rand and appoints her brother as executor. The marriage between Harry and Sally is annulled in 1953 by Sally on very interesting grounds. The decree sites, "That the defendant perpetrated a fraud on the Plaintiff in inducing her to enter into the marriage ceremony. 2 That these fraudulent representations of the Defendant pertain to the essentials of the marriage relation. That the defendant was totally impotent, lacking in physical capacity to have physical intercourse."[43]

The annulment is based on the fact her husband could not have sex. This is suspect as Harry had multiple affairs while married and then went back to his former wife. Of course, there might have been a problem just with Sally. One must wonder if the annulment was necessary to make sure he had no rights to the child Sally Rand had not even formally adopted. The decree went on to state that Harry would renounce all marital rights with the annulment to property and assets. Basically, he got nothing for his time with Sally Rand and, of course, no rights to her son. Sally would later write of the marriage in a letter to a childhood friend, "This marriage was never consummated for reasons that do not bear discussion at this time. Suffice to say I find being single is better for me in this pleasant maturity that I am enjoying."[44] She then goes on to explain her adoption of Shawn on August 1, 1948, "when he was eight days old."[45] As there was no birth certificate, this is the closest we have to an actual date when Sally took the baby.

In an illuminating letter written to herself at the time, Sally takes stock of Harry and her general situation with men.

If a guy his age isn't successful, he's not going to be. And every guy that's married has syphilis, shankers and leprosy as far as you're concerned . . . Just face it—who the hell is going to want to marry you, a widow, without money with a young problem son, too witty, too bright, and too adult to dominate—men in your age bracket don't want problems, young children . . . they want to get laid? For a dinner and a couple of drinks they can get a 20-year-old, beautiful . . . so what is left for the fortyish widow—frankly nothing . . . so stop it, stop beating your head against the wall. You're not in love you're lonely, you want a strong shoulder to cry against, a little fun, you don't like to sleep alone, you want to get laid while you can still enjoy it . . . answer, keep busy, it's not going to happen . . . it's a problem, you just go out with the married couples, you have to get used to it, get more physical exercise, when you have to go out of town . . . get it . . . watch your accountant, he or she . . . now tear this letter up. I told you it wasn't going to be a pretty letter and it isn't . . . and you're the only person I could ever write it to because I love you deeply and I don't want to see you destroy yourself. . . . Sally.[46]

It is a letter of recognition. Maybe something darker. A possible contemplation of suicide with the "destroy yourself" reference. Sally knows her own demons. She knows she has a destructive side, and it also shows how lonely she is in the life she has chosen. The life on the road is lonely. There is no blaring television to take the edge off. Maybe a radio. Mostly silence. She calls Sean a "problem son," which explains the whiskey and aspirin concoction. But she must keep her own counsel. We can see the little girl who ran away with the circus here. It is the young girl who at an early age chose the road less traveled and has a destructive side that manifests itself in broken marriages, debt, bankruptcy, assaults, arrests, and a life so uncertain she must dance to eat. Sally Rand to the public is successful and famous, but, like many celebrities, the facade hides a dark lonely place.

Sally noted in a letter written October 23, 1953, her father, Colonel William Beck, had died "three springs ago." Sally had been unusually close to her father even though he had left her as a child. In a letter soon after her earlier movies in Hollywood, he had written her and urged her to "just keep going girl-of-mine and we will see your name in electric lights on Broadway before very long. You will be the greatest Beck of the whole crowd yet."[47] He goes on to say that the Beck line had not done very much. "With a poor environment, no high education and small initiative, they were inclined to meander in a small circle and never get very far."[48] The elder Beck then pointed to his own circumstances and maybe some perspective on why he abandoned his family for a French woman. "I grew up handicapped with that same environment and have had to struggle against it all my life . . . if I could have had an illustrious family behind me . . . I would be something worthwhile today."[49] He also comments on her changing her name from Billie Bick to Sally Rand. In another letter eight years later to his son Harold in 1933, he chides him bitterly for not standing up to his mother and complains about the way the "Groves" were taking advantage of Sally's new wealth.

"When I think of the way that her house has been overrun by the Grove clan and other grafters and of the terrible expense accounts that she alone has to pay for their support, food, clothing, cocktail parties, and wasteful vanities, all imposed upon a little girl who in order to succeed must work nearly every minute of every twenty four hours, facing jail and other court sentences, and her unnatural mother who with a complacency and indifference and sangfroid that smacks of some form of dementia was and is willing and ready to bleed her girl of every farthing it makes me mad enough to commit murder."[50]

It is one of the few times the issue of Sally's support of her mother and her family is brought up. Sally was a celebrity and she did make very good money, and to her rural family from the Ozarks there had to be a feeling that Sally was fabulously wealthy. They didn't understand that Sally had to keep performing constantly to keep this illusion alive as they took advantage of being related to a famous person. They certainly took her money. In this, William Beck probably was sniffing something that was real. Her mother would write her in 1953, "I have been in bed the past three days . . . too much pressure from creditors! I have been holding the bag too many years! We must find a way to get out of debt!" Sally responded with a list of questions for her mother regarding Sean and finances. Her mother wrote again listing debts she had to pay and telling her daughter, "I am so distracted with this financial pressure that life is not worth living."[51] In another letter her father in 1947 asks Sally to write a letter to Senator Truman to help him get a new appointment to get him away from the farm he has been working. William Beck's letters are usually lists of woes besetting him that angle around usually to a request for some favor.

In 1949 in a letter he complained to her about the hospital. "For God's Sake come and take me out of this brutalized dump before I die of neglect and abuse. The ward doctor, Bremen and I got on fairly well today when an incident happened that set him against me and he said things to me he would not dare say to me on the street with a gun in my hand."[52] Shades of when William Beck murdered another man when he was sixteen. Her father to the end was the supplicant asking his daughter for a favor, saying that a nurse, "sure wanted one of your autographed pictures with my autograph below. . . . I must stop. I am too sick."[53] The man who had left his daughter so easily once before was making sure he kept in contact with her at the end. A final letter told her he was eighty-seven pounds and that his wife "Maria does not want me here . . . she much rather I stayed at whipple or in the hospital or in the Soldiers Home . . . while in the meantime . . . my pension and retirement checks could come through to her . . . I have become the object of the most violent attacks of abuse and vituperation."[54] Her father in the end would turn against the French woman whom he had left his family for. In the end it is the daughter he abandoned that he leaves with his final instructions, telling her he wants to be cremated with his ashes scattered in the old family graveyard.

There is a schedule in the Papers of Sally Rand for the baby for meals, naps, toilet, and bed. Sally will be dependent on others, mostly her mother, to care for the new baby. She is contracted by *Liberty Magazine* to write an article titled "Sally Rand Has a Baby." The article was to cover how she got the baby and life on the road with her son. Sally would cover her tracks with a standard adoption story even though the editor asked if she had any problems as "a show person."

But the gigs kept coming. A man wrote to Sally and pitched a song, "Lonely to You," to use in her act or just to promote it. "To suit the taste of the artist who considers promoting the song, he or she has my authority to rearrange the song if they so desire for an opportunity of becoming a successful number."[55] Sally is still enough of a star where people believe she can change their lives. She went to the Dallas World's Fair and performed and entered into talks for a television show and bought interest in a nightclub.

The reality is though that Sally rarely saw her son when she was on the road. There are many letters to "Sean," who is in the care of her mother. "Your mommy loves you very much and is very lonely without you. I am working very hard to make enough money so that I will never have to go away from you again. We are going to build a new house with a room just for Sean, where we will all live together always and love each other and be very happy. I think a good name for our new house would be 'Casa Coneta.' This means happy house."[56]

Here we see the dream that will not die of a perfect domesticity that really belongs to a nine-to-five world with a house in the suburbs with a mother at home and a father who is stable and a good wage earner. Sally Rand will never give up this dream that existed side by side with the reality of dusty fairgrounds and seedy theaters and nightclubs frequented by gangsters and lecherous businessmen. Sally is haunted by this "American Dream" that will prove elusive for the fan dancer who will never make enough money to get off the road.

To anyone on the outside, Sally Rand was fabulously successful, rich, and famous. Few knew the woman sleeping in lonely hotel rooms or a in a trailer pulled behind a Lincoln in danger of repossession, fielding letters from lawyers regarding suits, debt, tax liens, an alcoholic accountant who cleaned her out, foreclosure notices, subpoenas, judgments, writing snippets of nihilistic poetry and relying on the axioms of Christian Science while her husband slept with his ex-wife, her son was hidden away with her mother, because out there in the unkind darkness was a young mother looking for the child she had given to a fan dancer.

Sally would purchase a series of volumes on child rearing called CHILDCRAFT. A letter details what she can expect from the series. "As you use your CHILDCRAFT you will be even more convinced that this business of being a parent [can] and will be fun . . . CHILDCRAFT will help you to know and understand these things you cannot actually see in your child—his social, mental and emotional growth."[57]

Sally will need all the help she can get between crushing financial obligations, bad husbands, and a constant life on the road. In August of 1954 the government took possession of her Florida property in Key West and sold it to satisfy her debt. Sally was notified of the auction and the application of $7105.20 to her IRS tax bill. She still owed the government, but it gave her some breathing room.

The baby went on the road with her some of the time. A Chicago newspaper makes note that Sally is staying at the Lotte Cushman Club. "With Sally at the club are her mother, Mrs. Annette Kissling, her baby son, Sean Orion, the baby's governess and Bing, a boxer . . . Baby Sean is 10 months old and lively as a kitten. Sally adopted him before he was born."[58] Obviously, Bing was her current boyfriend. Sally Rand is traveling with her mother and a governess on the road with the baby. The instant family needed all the help it could get.

CHAPTER TWENTY-ONE

Changing Times

1949–1952

SALLY RAND WAS BARRED FROM THE OKLAHOMA FAIR IN 1949. REVER-end James R. Greer had deemed her show a "combination of scandal and sordid sex stimulation calculated to attract all the vultures from one [side] of the state to another."[1] Sally shot back and responded, "the statements of Mr. Greer do not originate from sincere and good intentions . . . those ministers hurt her and her three-year-old son who I don't want to grow up to think his mother was called evil by the ministers of Hutchinson."[2]

Sally pointed out none of the complaining ministers had seen the show, and thirty thousand people had paid admission to see the show the year before. She then presented the newspaper with letters attesting to the decency of her show. An Oklahoma newspaper explained, "Sally Rand won't be allowed to wave her fans at the Oklahoma State Fair here next year . . . The Rev Max Stanfield pastor of the First Baptist church of Putnam City who opposed her appearance said today he had been assured . . . that Miss. Rand would not appear in the 1949 fair."[3] This type of censorship or blocking her from performing hit Sally Rand where it hurt most, her pocketbook. But more than that, it reminded Sally she was one step away from being a burlesque dancer or worse a stripper. She liked to view her show as an expression of art, but parts of middle America still viewed her show as obscene.

Sally hit the papers again with more unfavorable coverage. A portrait photographer was trying to collect a judgment. The photo is flattering but the paper revealed this was not the first time Sally had been sued. "More financial woes are besetting Sally Rand fan and bubble dancer—this time all the way from St. Louis Missouri. Suit was filed against her in Superior Court here for the collection of $9924.13 said to be due on principal and interest on a judgement originally for $8795.38 won in St. Louis in 1950 by H. I. Harmon a portrait photographer."[4] The press was not good. Not only had she not won the original suit, but she had been dodging paying the judgment.

In Missouri she danced at the Missouri State Fair and received a letter from the governor's office congratulating her for "building up the attendance and gross receipts for the 1951 Missouri State Fair."[5] The letter went on to say that, "through your personal appearances, radio talks and work on the midway you have been the most influential factor in increasing our gate attendance thirty two percent this year."[6] The Missourians were very happy to have Sally Rand, and it showed the power of her name to still draw people. Governor Smith himself had gone to see the show and told a reporter that "the show that I saw was neither immoral, lewd or obscene. I thought the production well presented."[7]

In 1950 in Texas she was stiffed by a promoter and left stranded. Writing to a friend and explaining why she couldn't pay a debt, she explained her real situation. "I played a week under the auspices of the Junior Chamber of Commerce here. Because the promoter didn't keep his word with them, they said that my contract was no good, so I didn't get paid . . . then I had drawn so much money from the man for whom I was working that here I sit in Miami with 78.00 in my pocket. The finance company repossessed my car. I had to get it out to travel . . ."[8]

The state of Kansas attached Sally Rand's "lands, tenements, chattels, stocks, rights, credits, moneys and effects"[9] for $2548 for a judgment. It is also at this time in 1951 Sally was arrested at the Casablanca Club for a "lewd performance." The Liquor Control Board cited the club on Saturday, December 1, and sent two investigators to the club. Sally wrote her account later in an affidavit of that night. "Now that I know who you are, tell me what you wish."[10] The two investigators demanded she wear more "costuming." Sally then brought out what she wore during the performance. "I showed them a G string, two pairs of panties, and a brassier.

I described to them that these garments were held to my body by liquid adhesive."[11] The two men left but Sally realized she had been named in the citation, and here is where the times had changed.

In the 1930s and 1940s, her arrests were regarded as titillating, good for business, bringing in even more people. But in the suspicious and conformist 1950s, Sally Rand now had to be worried she would be designated "a lewd act." She wrote later, "I then realized that even though I had not been given a citation myself, my name, performance and reputation were involved, that my career and livelihood was in jeopardy and most important of all that custody of my adopted son was in jeopardy."[12] Since her son was not adopted, this is Sally Rand hyperbole. She then agreed to go with one of the agents to the Liquor Control Board in Canton, Ohio, but the damage was done. "Mr. Oneich had notified the newspapers and kept them appraised of exactly what was happening. . . . the result that every wire service in America has a story saying that 'Sally Rand has given a lewd performance.' This means that my living is jeopardized."[13]

A Canton paper immediately put her on the front page with the headline "Sally Sizzles as Agents Here Frown on her Art."[14] The mood of America had changed. Communism was a threat. The McCarthy hearings were unfolding, and the bawdy laugh of early century America had been replaced with morality codes and suspicion. The citation was given because it violated a regulation stating, "entertainment consisting of dancing either solo or otherwise, which may or may not, either directly or by implication, suggest an immoral act is prohibited . . ."[15]

Sally also again cited the real fear it would affect the adoption of her son, essentially admitting for the first time publicly she had never legally adopted the baby she had been raising. Sally again collected letters from theaters, churches, and fairs stating her act was essentially clean. Another article headline blared that the "Liquor Board May View Sally Rand in Fan Dance."[16] The article explained that Sally Rand "may do her act for the Ohio Board of Liquor Control after all."[17] The fact is this was Sally's idea and would not come to pass. But this sold papers, and the story stayed alive. It culminated in a story claiming, "Sally Rand offers Dancing Secret."[18]

Essentially, Sally revealed what she really wore during performances, a closely guarded secret kept from the public that assumed she was nude.

Sally appeared dressed in "a Navy-blue dress with blue and white striped collar and cuffs and her blond hair cut poodle style."[19] She was appearing as a suburban mom of the 1950s vintage. The board demanded to know what she really wore after objecting to a secret statement. Sally then let the world know "she always wore a covering of mousseline de soie—a sheer and filmy fabric over her body, pasted on with a liquid adhesive used in plastic surgery. It is of two thicknesses in some places . . . she also said her fans weighed seven pounds each and have 23 stems."[20] Sally protested, saying, "you wouldn't ask a magician to tell you how he pulls a rabbit out of a hat would you . . . I might as well retire from fan dancing now that my secret is out."[21] But she had defused the idea she was a "lewd act," something she could no longer afford.

It was a year later that the author Holly Knox ran into Sally Rand in 1951. Her book *Sally Rand: From Film to Fans* was probably inspired by this meeting on the road when she hooked up with Sally in Wichita Falls, Kansas. She had been touring with *Guys and Gals* when the show ended, and she heard Sally Rand needed six chorus girls when after a dispute her fan ballet had left her. "Sally was touring the same territory that *Guys and Gals* was with her own vaudeville package. A clever mutual agent must have looked at the map and discovered the proximity of the shows . . . the more girls they could keep working the less trouble there would be for the agent and union . . . Harry Finkelstein drove from Dallas to pick us up."[22]

There were only three girls, but Sally made do. Holly Knox would now be in her fan chorus. It turned out it was a union dispute that had enraged Sally to the point of firing the other six fan dancers. In the Papers of Sally Rand are several suits waged by unions for wages on behalf of dancers. "The six previous members of the fan ballet claimed she hadn't given them a promised raise . . . the Union sent out a representative from LA to check up on her and make sure she paid their salaries. In fact, they were so rigid, they insisted Sally post a bond each week before the girls worked."[23] Sally didn't have the money for the bonds and she found fault with each of the dancers and "made life so miserable for the six girls they were glad to accompany the Union Man back to Hollywood."[24]

The reality is Sally Rand had a reputation for not paying her dancers. "I was aware however, that our paychecks could be in jeopardy, because of her track record,"[25] Knox wrote later. But they were hired, and Holly Knox was introduced to the fan dance. "I couldn't believe how heavy they were, especially in my road weary weakened state. I didn't think I could ever do it correctly. The fans were forty-one inches long, of ostrich feathers with a potential wingspan of 82 inches, six or seven plumes wide. They weighed seven pounds each and were all male feathers. Sally would specify. The weight was awkwardly distributed, but she deftly handled them as if they were little more than cotton candy."[26]

The other dancers protested the wages and the work and asked Knox to go talk to Sally in her dressing room. "It was a gutsy thing to do because after all we were in the middle of nowhere, or so it seemed . . . I blurted out something about slave labor and that I couldn't sing if I was in a state of fatigue."[27] Sally relented and increased the wages of the dancers. She had a profit margin, and here we see the stress of those numbers. Many times, Sally would go into the red for a show where the receipt didn't cover her costs.

The balm of religion was applied before every show when Sally Rand practiced her Christian Science. She was looking for a rock to adhere to in her transient lifestyle. She was now forty-seven and while she had a son cared for her by her mother back in Glendora, the life on the road drove her into the arms of the Christian Scientists. Christian Science was developed in the nineteenth century by Mary Baker Eddy, who argued in a book published in 1875 titled *Science and Health* that sickness was not real and could be banished by prayer. *Science and Health* became the bible of Christian Science. The church didn't require adherents not to go to a doctor, but the emphasis was on prayer rather than medical science. This would result in several prosecutions for manslaughter when parents didn't take their children to doctors and they died.

A pamphlet in the Papers of Sally Rand had a *Relaxation Exercise* from the church with a mantra of thoughts to go over. "I am whole. I am perfect. I am powerful. I am loving. I am harmonious. I am rich. I am happy. Now giving thanks, feeling happy. I take a little breath and a long deep sweeping sigh . . . now I take another breath and a quick sigh."[28]

Undoubtedly, Sally practiced these techniques. Sally Rand, like many self-taught people, was susceptible to the gurus, get-rich-quick schemes, conspiracy theories, and religious zealots. According to Holly Knox, Sally, "had a rule, however, that was not to be violated. She was not to be disturbed a good half hour before she went on. . . . she would use this time for prayer and her dressing room was her temple. She had embraced the Christian Science religion and the *Monitor* was a permanent fixture on her dressing room table among the false eyelashes and the pan-cake."[29] Knox reflected later that," she seemed to derive fresh strength from every session and if there was a predominant reason for her longevity in such an ever youth seeking profession, her meditative prayers might have been that force."[30]

Money became an issue again when Sally passed a bad check for $366 to the Hotel Pittsburgher. She was arrested in Youngstown, Ohio, by two plainclothes policeman who took her to the station as she "ducked reporters and a photographer at police headquarters."[31] Always mindful of bad publicity, she refused "to budge out of an elevator on the second floor of the police station when a photographer attempted to take her picture. She stated, 'I'm not coming out. I don't want my picture taken so where do we go from here.'"[32] Sally hid behind two plainclothesmen and rushed into the chief's office, where the hotel agreed to drop the charges if she made good on the check. The paper put the article on the front page of the *Youngstown Vindicator*.

The plain truth was Sally Rand was broke. A man named Marsh was owed money for a show where he moved equipment and lent Sally money. After many letters demanding payment, Sally finally responded, imploring him to destroy the letter after he read it. "I assure you that my inability to do anything about it now is due to causes beyond my control and over which I have no control—taxes, etc. If I ever get my money . . . You may be sure you are first on my list."[33] The letter was never destroyed.

Sally was invited to speak at another university. Holly Knox was there when Sally was invited to speak at a luncheon with the dean of the University of Oklahoma and the Oklahoma Sooners. Knox was afraid that Sally's profanity would undo her. "I guess I was really afraid that Sally would let a backstage four-letter word slip out. Considering a certain taboo on nudity, I was in a mild state of shock that we had been invited."[34] Sally was living out of a large trailer, and Knox and the other dancers were staying in nearby hotels. The schedule was grueling. "We gave so many performances, sleep was still a precious commodity. Sally's energy was indomitable, and she probably slept about five hours a night. On long hard tours such as this, she used Benzedrine Sulphate to get through the rough spots."[35]

On the day of the luncheon, Sally called Knox to help her zip up her dress. "Will one of you silly broads come in here and zip me up?"[36] When Knox went to Sally's dressing room, she was shocked at the conservatively dressed Sally Rand. "I could hardly believe my eyes. She was almost into a little chic navy-blue street-length dress. The neckline was high with a small white collar caught up with a cameo brooch. After zipping her up, she asked me which hat would look best. She told me that making hats was her hobby. They were both fluffy, little flowered jobs and very pretty."[37]

Once at the university luncheon, Rand shocked Holly Knox again with her deportment. "Not only did she not utter the infamous four-letter word once, but she actually made erudite conversation with the dean. Her knowledge of history and a little French seemed to amaze them all, including three dazed chorus girls."[38] Sally Rand proved once again that she was something beyond a burlesque star. The dean of the university held a question-and-answer session, and again Knox couldn't believe the woman who chain-smoked, danced up to twenty-six shows in one day, and lived out of a trailer could transform herself into the role of cultural star. "She introduced us individually with a sweet compliment for each of us and then smiled at all of them and answered their questions about her profession with a studious solemnity. It was obvious she had been in more than one situation such as this."[39]

But business was business, and Holly Knox found herself on the short end of the receiving line once again with Sally Rand. In 1953, Sally called her again to join the fan ballet. "Sally was exuberant and happier than I had ever seen her. She and Harry Finkelstein had parted ways. Her face was tight which looked like a recent lift had been done. But Sally was positively joyous."[40] Knox had married and had a baby. She and Lucia

Rand (no relation) joined Sally's show and trouble began immediately. "Lucia and my contract called for lodging. But it seemed that Sally had other ideas about the extra rooms that went with the show. She installed Sean and her secretary in them."[41]

This called for another dressing room meeting. Knox went to her room. "When I was finally able to see her and confront her, she was flanked by her secretary and a tall man in a dark suit who was standing over a huge Bible in her dressing room."[42]

Knox pled her case and describes what happened next:

> She took my hand and put it on the bible.
>
> "My dear," she said. "God gave you a beautiful singing voice and meant it to be used. Here you have the opportunity to do so. Go out and sing and forget about small mundane matters." She batted her eyes at the tall man and asked, "Isn't that correct Bishop?"[43]

Knox took a small room with her fellow dancer and let it pass. But the use of the bishop and the bible and religion as a cudgel in her business relations show that Sally Rand viewed religion as not only a balm but a tool. Undoubtedly, she used Christian Science to find some inner peace, but the hackneyed invocation of a religious tenet to keep a woman from getting a room of her own shows the promoter and conniver at Sally's core. She had to survive and if a bible and a passing bishop allowed her to do so then all the better. Sally's relationship with the church and religion would veer all her life from contention to promotion to commendation. For the hustling girl from the Ozarks, she probably saw religion much the same as show business. You had to get the people to the show.

Sally Rand would have loved to have spent her time entertaining university deans and spewing religious dogma, but the ostrich feathers paid the bills and Sally Rand had to do everything. Lighting, design, costumes, choreography. Because Sally Rand was a concept, a cultural icon, she was selling not only the fan dance but *the concept of Sally Rand*. Here is the famous Sally Rand, and the sleight of hand required perfect lighting, makeup, costume, music, and then a bit of magic that had to be generated to the strains of "Clair de Lune." *The Dying Swan* had to take flight every time, and like good fiction it is as important what Sally Rand left out of her routine as it is what she put in.

And then there were the police. Sally was sitting one night in a theater in Okmulgee, Oklahoma, smoking a cigarette. The lights had been a mess on the opening night. She disappeared every time she moved off center stage. She snapped at a stagehand. "Damn it. Will the you tell the GD Lightman to get his ass down here? Those lights would light up the milky way. Doesn't he understand English? When I say soft and blue, I'm not talking about the music. I'm talking about the lights!"[44]

Lighting could not be dim enough now. It was bad enough that the musty theater was only a quarter full. She still had beauty and her body was in good shape, but she no longer had the careless beauty of a twenty-something that would allow for a gaffe in the lighting. Now, the illusion had to conjured, and that meant no mistakes. Timing was everything right down to her costume changes and a waiting cigarette in the wings. "The last strains of 'Clair de Lune' faded, and the audience was applauding with enthusiasm. She rushed to the wings. One of the dancers had a beaded evening dress ready and quickly zipped her up. She took a fast glance in the mirror, fluffed her hair, and glided back to the proscenium arch through the first curtain . . . Joe the manger brought her roses. . . . it had been Sally's idea . . . now and then an admiring fan would send her roses."[45]

Then Sally Rand faced the audience.

"I want to thank you for coming to see me today. I performed for many of your fathers. They were a wonderful audience, just as you have been. God bless you."[46]

She then would head to her dressing room. Every performance generates adrenaline and exhaustion in equal measure. Sally stood in her dressing room and faced the mirror. She was in shape, but the road had steadily worn her down. She had to support the ranch and her home in Glendora. "The more money that came in, the more people she hired, or she would buy a larger trailer or a new Cadillac . . . the really big money slowed down considerably after the Chicago Century of Progress."[47]

SALLY RAND

Sally Rand often had to deal with the fact she was making a living by skirting the obscenity laws of her time. It had been going on for a long time and when the knock at the door came in her dressing room in Oklahoma, she wasn't surprised when the manager of the club told her the sheriff wanted to see her.

"The Chief of Police is in my office Miss. Rand, and he wants to close down the act. He wants to close down the whole theatre."[48]

This story was told to Holly Knox by Sally Rand. It has the feel of some revisionism, but we must assume this played out many times.

"Tell the gentleman I'll see him in your office in ten minutes."

After closing the door, she quickly put on a dressing gown that covered her up to her neck but was well-fitting. She put a ribbon around her hair, took off a little lipstick and left her dressing room. Sally went to the manager's office to find the perfect stereotype of a western lawman "in a brown hat, smoking a cigar."

"Mam . . . my name is Chief Roberts of the Okmulgee Police Department—"

Sally offered her hand, cutting him off.

"Ah yes, Chief Roberts. I believe I've heard about you in Oklahoma City. You have a fine reputation."

"Well mam, that's really nice of you to say that . . . we have to close your show right now . . . mam."

"What's wrong with my show sir?"

"It's your . . . mam. You don't wear any clothes."

"How do you know I don't wear any clothes sir."

"In this state, mam . . . you have to have certain—parts— covered."

Sally felt the anger rising as she pled her case with the Okie lawman.

"Chief Roberts, the whole object of my act is to create the illusion of nudity behind my fans. In states such as yours, I always comply with my bra and panties, to wit . . ."

Sally Rand then unzipped her dressing gown for the Podunk Chief and showed him her bra and panties.

"Are you satisfied sir?"

The chief then apparently backed into an ashtray and knocked it over.

"I see what you mean mam, but we have reports that you were naked as a blue jay up there."

Sally responded. "It's an illusion. The lights are low so that no one can really tell. I'm not a burlesque queen who has to show as much as the law allows to be a success."

The chief had regained himself as Sally zipped back up.

"I appreciate that and if you wear . . . ah . . . what you are wearing now. I'll give you the ok for the rest of the show."

Sally held out her hand.

"Thank you, sir."[49]

It does have the feel of a movie scene. Maybe a bad one. But the truth is Sally Rand used her body to make money and get out of tight spots with the law. She had changed the minds of judges, juries, and policemen with her looks, her charm, and the ineffable quality of innocence that existed next to her sexuality. Sally was right, she was not a burlesque dancer and she wasn't a stripper. She had become a cultural reference point, a star in name who glided from a symbol of hope at the Chicago World's Fair. She was hard to define. Even Sally Rand didn't understand who she was.

Chapter Twenty-Two

Debt and Carnivals

1951–1955

SALLY HAD HER OWN SHOW UNDER A TENT WITH A SEVENTEEN-MEMBER troupe. It was as close to having her own circus as she would come. The tour reached across Oklahoma and Texas, heading farther west to Washington before heading back east. Many reporters asked about her age now, and Sally, who in 1951 was nearing fifty, never gave a straight answer. She had fifty people on her payroll, and twelve showgirls joined her every night in a glorious fan ballet that brought people in by the thousands. The dusty world of small-town fairs was her world. She had come into her fame at the 1933 World's Fair in Chicago, and the fair was always a more democratic crowd. She was truly the star and essentially among her people. Nightclubs often had a more urban crowd that could be difficult, or a more lecherous crowd depending on the caliber of the club.

The Royal American shows were among the most lucrative "railroad carnivals" of their time. Sally joined with a troupe of sixty and hit the road, driving along with the carnival in her mobile trailer home. A boy who cleaned her dressing room, Leroy Neiman, described Sally as a clean freak. Sally was in her element as the fair made its way through the Midwest. She had struck a deal of five thousand dollars a week with a percentage of merchandising, programs, and 50 percent of the gross. Royal American struck this deal because Sally Rand the name was a draw for the entire fair. In shades of the World's Fair of 1933, Sally Rand became responsible for the profitability of the Royal American Fairs. There were setbacks with the high costs and a freak fire that consumed her set.

She then joined Al Wagner's Cavalcade of Amusements, which would bring a protracted lawsuit. The Cavalcade of Amusements would not be a good time for Sally Rand. The money was not there, and they parted ways with Sally claiming she was owed back wages. The suit came to trial in Dallas, and Sally won a $10,517.74 judgment against Al Wagner and his company. A Dallas paper covering the suit showed the fluid nature of Sally's business. "Complaining of Miss. Rand's show in a letter introduced as evidence, Mr. Wagner said he was losing 2000 each week."[1] Sally, on the other hand, claimed, "her contract guaranteed her 3000 a week and that on several occasions she did not get her just due."[2]

Wagner would then turn around and sue her in 1951 for libel from a broadcast from WGN in Chicago where she claimed he owed her twenty-three thousand dollars. The suit was for two million dollars and named NBC as a co-defendant because the station WMAQ made no effort to cut the program. The suit would drag on for years.

The fact was the further Sally got from 1933 the less earning power she had. In 1949 her tax returns show she made $105,252.25 gross income with $55,651 in expenses. She netted $50,000, which was very good money, but it just seemed to slip through her hands. In 1950 she made $90,657 with expenses of $44,183. The public perception of Sally Rand was that she was wealthy, but her pot of gold was getting smaller each year. She could not even pay her accountant in 1950, who wrote her a long letter saying he could not even pay his rent. "Sally I really think that you should send me at least enough to satisfy the landlord and so that I can pay a few debts and get a suit of clothes. It is most discouraging to note that in the last year when you were in difficulties, and were figuring out the payroll, everyone was listed, but I never appeared on the list."[3] Her accountant in desperation told her, "the only thing I can do is pawn the adding machine."[4]

Sally was running a business from afar, and her accountant, who wrote her voluminous letters saying he was existing on "oatmeal and spaghetti,"[5] was tasked with untangling her finances. "Have been working all the time, spent 10 days on the payroll recapitulation. Had to set up three books for this one, a Time Book showing every day who and where employees were engaged in order to show that you did not have 8 or more employees for 20 weeks in order to avoid the Excise Tax of 3 percent."[6]

Sally just didn't have the money anymore. Usually time is the arbiter. It is very difficult to remain in the public's eye over decades and now the World's Fair was in the rearview mirror of Sally Rand's life. Her problems were compounded when several of her showgirls were involved in a serious accident with a train in Indianapolis at 4:00 a.m. on December 18, 1951. A deposition by Frank Lagett, who was driving, showed they were lucky no one was killed.

"There was a very bad snowstorm and visibility was very poor and the road was very slick. I was driving about ten miles an hour and I couldn't see much over 10 feet in front of me. I saw the red flashers of the track just as I was at the track. I started to stop but saw that I couldn't, so I tried to cross the tracks. The Cadillac went across the tracks but due to the slippery road I couldn't pull the trailer over the single track. So, I got out to try and flag the train down."[7]

The train was unable to stop and hit the trailer with the dancers still in the car. Sally would describe the damage to the car in a letter to the insurance company. "When the cowcatcher hit the right rear corner, because of the icy conditions of the road it spun both the car and the trailer around and when the trailer snapped off of the hitch it hit the right side of the car which spun the car around and when the trailer snapped off of the hitch it hit the right side of the car ... the car folded up the trunk as if it were tissue paper, knocked both fenders off and spread the whole body of the car."[8]

Fortunately, the women were not injured, but Sally did not carry public liability insurance or property damage insurance. It led to another court case. The fact she was continually on the road increased her chances of accidents at a time when seat belts were nonexistent. A second accident in 1952 with her Cadillac was far more serious. Three dancers in her show were driving her car to Cleveland when they were involved in a head-on collision. The three dancers were hospitalized with head injuries and internal organ damage. The man in the other car, Harry T. Snell, immediately sued for $30,000. Sally's insurance covered $26,500 and she had to make up the difference of $3,500. Another debt she could not pay.

What's worse, dancers left her show for nonpayment. Sally was still hustling, still having to make her show relevant to a culture now consumed with television and movies and a newly released magazine called *Playboy*. The naughty factor of her act had been all but decimated by sirens like Marilyn Monroe. But the truth was people now had more options. What they used to go to a fair to see they could now see at home on their television. Sally Rand, while still youthful in appearance, clearly was no longer the young girl behind the fans, and her family was still a drag on her, financially and spiritually.

Her brother Harold's career in Hollywood had never taken off. Her mother still needed money for the ranch house and for groceries. The family that had followed her from Missouri had never really gotten to the point where they could make it on their own. *Sally will provide* was their mantra and she did, but it was getting harder and harder. In 1952 a rogue accountant took her money and there were tax liens from the IRS. An International News Service story listed "two tax liens filed with the San Francisco County Recorder today."[9] The liens were in relation to the El Cerrito Night Club. Sally had gone into business with John J. Carey and Sam Neider, who were also named in the liens totaling twenty-three thousand dollars. At this point Sally didn't have the money for a lawyer and wrote the IRS a long, rambling five-page letter. Her claim was that she was not an actual partner in the club. "Mr. Neider, a sharp fellow in San Francisco . . . contacted me about using my name on a night club. I permitted him the use of my name for 1000 a month (which I never received) I was to give my services as a single performer for a percentage of the 'net' and I was to advise them on the booking of various acts."[10] She then explained she was to become a partner using the funds from her percentage of the net. Sally then found out there was gambling going on in the club. "Imagine my alarm to arrive at work and find four '26' and 'boat the dealer' going full blast . . . I lived in a small unfurnished house located in the rear of the nightclub on the parking lot of the club . . . I had my meals at the club and signed checks for them . . ." When the gambling was discovered by authorities, "I knew there would only be one outcome ... I simply took a walk."[11]

The club soon went into bankruptcy, leaving a trail of debts and unpaid taxes. Sally revealed in a letter her mother had just had a heart attack during this time. Her alcoholic accountant, "I am not drinking and have not been for several weeks,"[12] after pleading that he was hungry and needed money to eat and settle debts, pointed out that "the government could step in any minute and attach all sums of money due you, or put out a statement in California as they did so that you could not work in the state of California until you have satisfied the government claims."[13] The government would eventually settle with her by taking possession of her property for the back taxes.

Sally was performing now in venues like Calumet City outside of Chicago. She was missing her son. Things went from bad to worse when musicians at a performance in Philadelphia were not paid a debt of eight hundred dollars and Sally Rand the fan dancer had to perform for the first time in total silence. One can imagine the sound of her heels on the wood floor, the swish of the feathers, the labored breathing of a fifty-year-old woman going through her routine while a crowd stared at her like an exotic animal. Her act depended on the music to transport the audience to a different place, the *Dying Swan* could not die in silence. But there she was, huffing and puffing through her routine while the audience looked stonily on.

The photos of Sally Rand in the newspapers are that of an attractive woman showing off her deluxe trailer or standing in a house under construction with an architect. The photo spreads show Sally Rand working out, extending her legs to the ceiling and proving to the world she was still that girl that caught everyone's eye in 1933. One article showed her supervising the building of a house in Glendora, but the carnival days had ended for her in 1958. The profitability of fairs had slipped, and her act had subtlely become a nostalgia show. Sally Rand had been on the road for twenty-five years and the press still gave her attention, but she had become a cultural totem pole rather than the sexy feather dancer.

An article in a New York paper announced a film, *The Sally Rand Story*, summing up her own film career: "Sally Rand, who never got anywhere in movies, despite her fame at one time, is going to have her life story filmed under the title of 'The Sally Rand Story.'" The rights were acquired by Michael Rose in New York and Sally "had not agreed to play herself on the film but has said she would coach an unknown for the role."[14] No film on Sally Rand would ever be produced, and there is no evidence she was paid for the rights to her story.

The letters to her mother are now concerned with the mortgage on the ranch and expenses. Sally Rand's earning capability had been greatly diminished and from now on she would play in second-tier clubs. Sally had to pay for her own fame now. In Minneapolis, after heading a show called *Gay Nineties*, she drove out to see a billboard. In the night was a picture of herself as she had looked twenty years earlier. Sally must have had a moment where she realized she was now twenty-eight years beyond the World's Fair, and that girl, shimmering on the billboard in the night, had become a phantom of her past. It was no longer the 1930s where she and Jean Harlow would meet with millionaire producers to discuss deals with promised fur coats thrown into movie deals that also had sex as a price. It was back rooms at fairs and clubs and the smell of stale cigarettes in lonely hotel rooms or moldy trailers. The marriages had drained her as well. The cowboy Turk had nothing, and his constant drinking and legal bills left Sally with debt. Harry Finkelstein left her with what she came in with and at the end of the marriage there was only debt.

Sally Rand had to support her home with her mother and other relatives. Even as far back as 1940, the assumptions about Sally Rand's wealth were proved false. A famous journalist at the time, Quentin Reynolds, testified in court about a bogus article written about Sally Rand by *Colliers* magazine. The war correspondent had interviewed Sally Rand and "the article credited Sally with a wealth that didn't exist and even implied that she was on her way to becoming a millionaire. Two months later she admitted she had nothing and was grossly insolvent."[15]

Sally Rand had no fortune. The Papers of Sally Rand bear this out over and over, loaded with debt collection notices from lawyers, banks, stores, friends, haberdashers, the IRS, foreclosure notices. Many times, Sally didn't pay even when she had the money, and she continued to purchase Lincoln Continentals and Cadillacs. The car debt tells a story she liked to keep from the public.

The Harris Bank of Tampa wanted their money for the car. "Up to this time four payments have been paid on your note, amounting to 438, leaving eight payments in the amount of 873."[16] Sally would own several cars, with each finance company left holding the note. The Bar Ken Dog Kennels wanted their money for boarding "Gretchen" in Las Vegas, a large PAST DUE plastered across a bill for $112.50. A private detective she hired for legal proceedings involving an accident wanted his $565. Lawyers who represented her in the Al Wagner suit wanted to be paid. The Memory Chapel wanted to be paid for funeral services for her father, William Beck, in 1949. A doctor's bill for $200 for her second husband, Harry Finkelstein. A nightclub in St. Louis wanted their $307. Her storage locker in Las Vegas was auctioned off but the buyer, "will withhold disposing of your goods for ten days."[17] The American Guild of Variety Artists wanted their $1125.

And there are personal letters where Sally didn't pay friends for services rendered. "I suppose you consider that you have shaken me. The idea of telling Mr. Berman that you had sent me a check was quite a low blow, considering in your heart you knew that it was not so."[18] Sally Rand had bought two lots in Glendora, California, with an eye to building. "Your city taxes on both of your lots will be delinquent February 1st, 1953 and additional interest and penalties incurred if they are not paid."[19] The lawyers were her main nemesis as they acted as collection agencies in most cases. "Jacks of Hollywood tell us they have got no money from you. It is about time you stopped stalling and paid your bill."[20]

An IRS lien was filed against her for back taxes from 1948, and she owed $21,000. Sally rented an adding machine in Las Vegas and did not pay the rental fee of $250. Young Bundy Motors wanted their payment of $250. She is named in two tax liens in San Francisco. Then Sally bounced a check to United Airlines for $37 and they wanted to be paid. A furniture store pleads with her to be paid on a bedroom set. "Sally, I would certainly appreciate it if you could send another payment on the bedroom. We are operating on a close margin now and it would mean a great deal."[21] Lasalle Press Printers want something on her bill. She had her show trailer modified and Vagabond Coach wants their $403. "We were assured by Miss. Robertson that you would mail us a check to cover the repairs."[22] National Theatre Supply wants their money. "You promised to send this, it's over one year old. I am getting hell from my New York office."[23] The American Federation of Labor hits her with a claim for $1,375. "Trust that we can bring this claim to a conclusion."[24] Olive Kephart hits Sally with a judgment for $4,334. The Music Hall hits with another judgment for $617.50. H. I. Harmon wins a judgment of $8,795.

This is but a taste. The letters are voluminous, the dunning notices become more aggressive, the lawsuits more dire. And among all this debt are the newspaper articles showing Sally Rand building a new home, in her luxury trailer, showing off her new son, posing in photo spreads to show how fit she is. In all the photos she is beautiful, smiling, happy. The image of Sally Rand to the public is that of a star, not someone who has to file bankruptcy and negotiate with the IRS on back taxes and who welches on debts large and small. Sally Rand simply did not pay her bills. Yet she made very good money and owned multiple properties, a ranch, a home, multiple cars. She had a secretary and a maid and at times flew around the country in a style befitting royalty. To the public she was of that other world. She was one with the starlets of Hollywood that she had always seen herself as.

The life on the road of dismal hotel rooms and letters on hotel stationery written after days of chain-smoking, coffee, driving thousands of miles and then finding herself alone again was kept from the public. The poetry, the desperate letters to three different husbands, the Christian Science pamphlets, the nihilistic poetry written in the dead of night, betrayed a lost soul behind the facade of the gay Sally Rand. The sheer energy kept her going as her forties passed into her fifties and then her sixties. The awful truth was the only way Sally Rand had to make money was to get up on stage and take off all her clothes and dance behind two seven-pound ostrich-feather fans. They must have felt heavier and heavier as time and circumstance wore her down. The dance routine had become a ritual of necessity as her heels scuffed the groaning, tired, and worn-down floors of theaters in the process of being converted to movie houses. Sally Rand had no vocation beyond being Sally Rand. She had desperately tried to get beyond the fan dancing with her movies in Hollywood, but the truth was she had little dramatic talent.

Even watching the old cinemascope of her *To Tell the Truth* episode she looks shy and awkward, and her speech is barely decipherable. It is as if she reverted to that shy hillbilly from Missouri. But the debt, the suits, the divorces, the deadbeat husbands, the family problems, the lonely hotel rooms, the musty trailer, all vanished when the first strands of "Clair de Lune" played and she hid herself behind the ostrich feathers and became that swan in Anna Pavlova's famous dance that had inspired her back when she was a young girl . . . dreaming of escape.

CHAPTER TWENTY-THREE

The Boy Toy

1955

IN A LETTER TO AN OLD CHILDHOOD FRIEND IN 1953, SALLY DESCRIBED her working life. "During the summer I always play some type of outdoor show business, especially at the large state, regional and country fairs which are a very important part of our American life."[1] Sally likes these agricultural events usually occurring in small towns. "These fairs usually take place after Harvest time . . . Playing for this type of audience is very stimulating. . . . their taste in things theatrical is not to be underestimated and they are very frank in their disapproval."[2] She then returns to nightclubs and theaters for the fall and winter. "Altogether I keep happy, busy and apparently from what I am told there is no outward change in my appearance since 1933 at the World's Fair."[3]

This gives us a snapshot of her life right before she met Fred Lalla. The article in the Las Vegas paper was short. "Fan dancer Sally Rand changed into a simple frock between performances early today for a surprise marriage to a former Los Angeles contractor Fred Lalla. Afterward she slipped back behind her fans for the next show. The dancer, believed to be 52 and twice married previously listed her age over 21 on the marriage license as did Lalla, who said earlier he was 35."[4] Sally Rand had found her boy toy.

A flight provided the meeting ground. Fred Lalla was a former boxer with dark brown eyes and slicked-back hair. He had a wife who was twenty-five and three children. When the five-foot-tall blond started talking to him in the airliner, he had no plans to leave his wife and children. By the end of the flight, he was already thinking about it. As a former boxer the drug of low-level fame surely added to the mix as he and Sally went for drinks. Sally Rand was still famous and a woman of the world, and he was a handsome contractor on his way to Las Vegas.

They had both flown from Chicago, and Lalla had two residences in California so he could be close to his job. This allowed Sally and Fred immediately to begin living together in Eagle Rock, which was about three hundred miles from Lalla's wife and kids. Perfect. Sally writes to him from the road, promising to be a good wife.

"Dearest Love don't worry about the drinking business. I never drank as much in my whole life as I did the days you were here, just because I was excited and happy. But you and I both know that Lalla's girl and Lalla's future wife could never be one to drink too much or get tight . . . So put your mind at ease and your heart at rest, it will never happen. Also, as to language and four-letter words, I know how totally unbecoming the bad language is and I apologize for acquiring such an ugly habit, there's no excuse for it and I'm very wrong."[5]

Desperate is a word that comes to mind as Sally is already changing herself for the younger man. Promising to drop the hard edge of the road she has been on for twenty-five years. Apparently Sally drinks and swears too much for her boy toy. Sally has spent her whole life in theaters and clubs and her salty language was legendary. Drinking has not surfaced but with the chain-smoking, the stress, it would fit that she would drink heavily. She was an earthy woman who had lived a pedal-to-the-metal life, and one can see how different Lalla's experiences had been from hers already.

And Sally was a lustful woman who demanded sex when she wanted it. The young brown-haired stud is a sexual conquest for the older woman. Lalla's divorce took ten months, and there are the pictures of him putting wedding cake in his new bride's mouth. Fred wears a loud tie and still looks pugnacious with challenging eyes and a smirk that broadcast to the world: look what I just caught! Sally Rand looks like a fifty-year-old woman who couldn't be happier.

In a letter to Fred's parents, Sally encourages them to come join them in Nevada. "Las Vegas is fabulous, because the town is expanding so rapidly—the business opportunities are wonderful. There are really four lots available, so we could build a house for you and a house for us and an income building on the center lots."[6] It was the celebrity talking flush with cash and a new man and now a new life. The unvarnished truth was Sally had monstrous debt, tax liens, and a cash flow problem. But part of Sally's allure to Fred and his family was undoubtedly that fame equaled fortune. In Sally's case the opposite was true.

Lalla's wife went to the press and demanded alimony. "If he'd rather have her than his own family then it's alright by me, but he better send me my 50.00 a week."[7] Mae Lalla was pretty with auburn hair and made good press. Sally was the older famous woman who had stolen her husband. Mae had to go to work in a box-cutting factory while Fred and Sally whooped it up between her shows at the Hotel Last Frontier. Sally called Fred "Pops" and he called her "Mother." Freud would have a field day with these appellations.

At the divorce trial, Sally Rand did not come off well. Mae said Sally called her and asked to pick up the kids, so they could see her father. "I thought she had a lot of nerve and wouldn't allow it."[8] Sally Rand did have a lot of nerve. In a letter to his parents, Fred paints his marriage to Sally in a religious context. "Sure, mom and dad I miss my children, sometimes I believe I can't stand it, but when I look to God for help and understanding, he's always there. I only ask him to show me his ways, the good and the right way. I am so grateful for giving me my wife, Sally."[9] Then Sally wrote his parents in a sort of tandem *breaking-the-news letter* where Lalla wrote on the back of her letter. "I am so grateful to having Fred for a husband and father for Sean. I could not have dreamed that I could be so blessed . . . I didn't know exactly how God would work it out for me. I didn't question . . . I had wanted a family all my life and when I had the opportunity for adopting Sean . . . it was like a miracle."[10]

Sally then trashes Fred's marriage to Mae, saying, "it was destined for tragedy," pointing out Mae's "sad and sordid premarital experiences."[11] Sally was destroying the other woman who might compete for Fred's parent's affections and painting herself as saving their son. All this of course was to battle the image of the older woman, the famous older Sally Rand using Fred as a boy toy and destroying his family in the process; the term homewrecker was certain to be getting a lot of use among Mae and her supporters.

It is during this time Sally performs at the Last Frontier Hotel in Las Vegas for a record-breaking thirty-two weeks from 1954 to 1955. One cannot help but feel a little sorry for Fred Lalla. He probably thought of Sally as a fling; an interesting affair with an older woman. Then the promises of fame and fortune were out there for the Las Vegas contractor saddled with a wife and children. Like many he thought he could walk into Eden where responsibilities vanish and drink the pap of the American Dream of the rich and famous.

There is a picture in the Papers of Sally Rand of Fred with his three children. They are all less than age ten and he looks like a happy man who probably should have stayed married. Sally Rand was a worldly, famous, beautiful woman in her fifties who overwhelmed the less-than-successful contractor. The letters he wrote while Sally was on the road of tending their garden and mooning over her absence are part love letters and part pathetic. He was spying on his ex-wife to see if he could catch her with a man to get custody of his kids. "No dice as yet, just mugging, I guess they do their screwing in the car . . . you know how badly I want the children."[12] Fred was living in the desert of Las Vegas with Sally's son, a man who had given up an independent life for the life of a concubine. Sally made the money and the decisions and, more than that, Sally was gone. Lalla wrote her many love letters that showed he would not last long with his wife on the road.

"Baby, if you were here now, I'd say some real juicy things to you like kissing your neck and around your nipples and such wonderful nipples . . . ooohhh . . . I'd squeeze you so very tight . . . I'd take your beautiful face into my hands and kiss you so tenderly, so juicy, and I might even stroke your bottom so gently, by that time my Love, we'd be out of this world."[13] Obviously sex for Sally and Fred is the glue of their relationship, a welcome change from the philandering, impotent Harry Finkelstein.

Sally and Lalla set up their home in Las Vegas. The pool in the backyard was perfect. She could watch her long, slim, tan boy toy swim laps while she sat under an umbrella with a Manhattan and a cigarette. Sean was six and lived with them, and if there was a moment of domestic tranquility for Sally Rand it was here. Living in the desert was a long way from the road, and she had a steady gig at The Last Frontier and the Silver Slipper. But as with all things that are not quite balanced, this brief interlude of tranquility spun out of control. The luster of being married to Sally Rand eventually wore off, and what Fred was left with was an older woman who could have been his mother and who had to return to the road. Even as Lalla wrote love letters, he addressed their age difference. "Believe me darling you held your age so wonderful, hell baby I'll probably catch up to you a lot sooner than you expect . . . a young gal just doesn't understand, you baby I know you do, our age difference! Best thing in the world for us. . . . the difference in our ages like you said is all on our side."[14]

The affairs began quickly and spiraled into a confrontation at the Silver Slipper between shows. It is during this confrontation according to Sally Knox that the Chicago gangster Vito, who had threatened Sally Rand back in 1933, surfaced. He had been responsible for the death of Ed Callahan, her old boss at the Paramount. That Sally Rand had interactions with gangsters is entirely plausible. She was operating in an underworld of sorts, and while her claims that Al Capone offered her a job don't ring true, the interaction with Vito in Chicago could well have happened. Sally claims there had been a contract put out on her when she didn't work for Vito in 1933. It is hard to know how much of this is true, but Holly Knox, who interviewed Sally Rand, claimed the conversation ran like this:

> She faced a short stocky and dark looking man. He was the prototype of a hood, but a well-dressed one who might have had his position elevated.
>
> "Still chewing somebody out, huh, Sal?"
>
> "It's just a loving discussion, Vito. What brings you to Las Vegas?"
>
> "I came to see your show Sal. You have always been one of my favorites."[15]

Vito then mentioned he heard that Sally had a child. The ominous tones of the conversation are there with the implied threat of bodily harm to her or her child. Fred Lalla was never introduced to Vito and for Lalla maybe that was a good thing. He had enough troubles of his own. Mae had remarried, and Fred was not comfortable with his kids having another father. Sally had to hit the road again, leaving her wayward husband on his own. Then there were the domestic logistics of any divorced family involving kids. Sally was not around a lot of the time to do her part of the shuttling and it fell to Fred. Life with Sally Rand was not all that it was cracked up to be.

It is during this time Sally gave an interview to a Denver paper and proclaimed she was writing her life story. "The little blond from the Ozarks revealed Tuesday that she is writing the story of her life . . . the story of Sally Rand's life will span a period of over 30 years as a night club entertainer, movie actress, and more recently a television performer."[16] The year is 1955 and Sally Rand must have seen another revenue stream in publishing for an account of her life. She gives another rendition of the night at the fair that began her career. "She will tell how on a chilly May night in 1933 when the fair was just getting underway she accepted a dare that led her to getting a chance to perform her fan dance on the 'Streets of Paris.'"[17] With all the animals barred from entering the grounds, Sally hired a boat to bring her to the fairgrounds astride a big horse. With only her long blond tresses hiding her nude charms, Sally came riding down the 'Streets of Paris' portraying Lady Godiva, winding in and out and around a group of Chicago's leading socialites who were seated at a milk fund dinner."[18]

This memoir was to also tell the story of her years in Hollywood with Cecil B. DeMille and "her leading role in one of the all-time great movies *King of Kings*."[19] This of course is not true as she had a bit part in the movie. But we see Sally beginning to repackage her past and elevate it. She is always selling *Sally Rand*, and the article winds up noting her thirty-two-week engagement at the Tropics Nightclub in Las Vegas and noting her adoption of her "baby boy, now six years old, with the adoption coming at a time when she was not married."[20] The paper put "when she was not married" in bold type. This is curious, but the paper wanted to stress the oddity if not unique situation of a woman adopting a child without a father. "Proclaiming her current marriage to a Las Vegas contractor 'a very happy one,' she said that her biggest role of her life now is that of a mother and housewife."[21]

This book will never see the light of day. In the Papers of Sally Rand there are fragments of a manuscript, essays, diaries, but no full manuscript. She never mentions it again. Writing a full book might have been too daunting, or a contract might have never materialized with a publisher. Sally Rand was still performing many shows, and she would go back on the road and her life with Fred was anything but happy. He was out screwing around and for her to sit down and write a book at this point does not really go with the reality of her life, which is one of debt, travel, and child rearing from afar.

It's during this time that Sally managed a quick visit to Chicago for the twenty-second anniversary of the 1933 World's Fair. "Sally Rand blond and breezy, bounced into the Loop Thursday night to relive the Century of Progress exposition. She and some old friends experienced that wonderous world's fair again by pooling their memories."[22] In the Chicago paper Sally is shown with E. M. Lee, a former guard at the fair, greeting her at the airport. The Century of Progress Association threw a party at Toffenetti's restaurant in Chicago. "I'm still doing the fan dance with the same equipment,"[23] Sally told them after flying in from Las Vegas.

It had to be bittersweet. The girl who had crashed the World's Fair in 1933 and rode the whirlwind was far different from the woman just barely hanging on with impossible debt, lawsuits, and a philandering husband half her age. Seeing those people from 1933, she must have wanted to click her heels and go back to that simpler time where survival and fame operated hand in hand and she had emerged victorious. Had twenty-two years really passed? Chicago must have seemed like a refuge against the grind of her life on the road. Then, of course, the question that had begun to nag her with increasing frequency: what did she have to show for the years but debt and dissolution.

But she flew back to Las Vegas and tried to salvage her marriage. In a letter to Fred, she implores him to get moving again and make some money. Apparently, Fred Lalla did not like to work. Her advice has a Christian Science ring to it. "Achieve a premise. Analyze the contributing factors. Arrive at a conclusion. Then damn it, get off your lazy ass and ACT . . . I'm not saying you are lazy, to the contrary I think you keep busy as hell and try hard and are sincere, but just being physically busy isn't enough."[24]

The truth was Sally's career dwarfed Fred, and he found solace elsewhere.

Phone calls and letters sounded a familiar pattern while Sally ran a household from the road. Sally and Fred stumbled through eight years of marriage as the desert interlude ended. Sally had a half-hour television show during this time on KLAS TV. At the time it was the only television station in Las Vegas. It was a show where Sally interviewed celebrities and discussed books, music, and the home. The pay wasn't great, and the show was short lived, and Sally still had to support her family through all of this.

In a letter she detailed her mother's situation and her stepfather's. They were doing no better with the orange ranch. "She and Ernest have worked 26 years like dogs and have never been out of debt the present income from the fruit isn't enough to take care of them. . . the yield has gone down and down, they owe taxes for 2 years on the ranch over 800." Sally then totals up their debts, including the mortgage on the ranch. "Can you imagine what you would do if you owed fifty thousand dollars, couldn't get a job, and didn't know where your next dollar was coming from. . . she's seventy-one and earned some peace and serenity."[25]

The truth was her mother's situation was not so different from her own. As long as she danced, she could make money, but she simply couldn't pay her mounting debt. But nothing could stop the disintegration of her marriage. Sally wrote a letter to herself. "My husband has shown an increasing and groundless jealousy. He has indulged in almost daily temper tantrums, uncontrolled, unbridled, and of an intensiveness . . . I have never witnessed. These temper tantrums increase daily. I have been accused of everything . . . he knows the name of."[26]

It is likely he was abusing her. Sally left Lalla in 1955 for almost two weeks, and Fred kept a diary of days, cataloging his lovesick moments.

"Long night as every night without my beloved, can't sleep, walk the floor, read and read, wake up at 4 AM . . . I love her, dear dear, beloved wife Helen, my love. I miss you . . . called my beloved wife, talked to her, so wonderful to hear her voice, much call back, if 2 find out what she wants. . . . darling love you, gone 3 days . . . lit our candle prayed."[27]

Fred is guilt sick as well as lovesick. His diary has the remorse of the serial abuser. Sally's dream of a domestic life of stability is betrayed by her son's recollection of his grade school years. "In the 2nd grade, I went to school in Vegas, Glendora, Chicago, and Tampa Florida . . . I did all that in the second grade and then in the third and fourth grade I was back in Glendora with my grandmother, they had a battle. She'd say that's no place for a kid out on the road. So, they brought me back out here and I went to a local military school in Glendora."[28]

The marriage will struggle on, but by 1960 it was all over. In an affidavit Sally wrote in a custody hearing for Fred's children, it paints the losses Fred suffered not from Mae, his ex-wife, as was intended, but really from his marriage to Sally Rand. "He had lost his wife, his children, his home and his business. His once flourishing contracting business came to an end . . ."[29] Fred was a victim of sorts. Sally Rand moved in a bigger world that had seduced the younger man into destroying his life by promising a glamorous life with a glamorous woman. His kids suffered most being shuffled between homes and not having their father.

In a rare assessment of her own mother, Sally pointed the finger finally at Annette for being a financial drag her whole life. "Fred's condition was further aggravated by my aged senile mother whose greed for my economic support and whose vanity and vicarious status depended upon being 'Sally Rand's mother.' She hated him passionately and senselessly. She never missed an opportunity to downgrade him."[30]

Several things are interesting here. Sally finally calls out her mother for not supporting herself, but also, we can see Annette looking down her nose at the young Italian stud who had hooked up with Sally, probably seeing him as a gold digger. The truth was Sally was in bankruptcy and there was no gold to dig, but her mother was certainly fearful there would not be enough Sally Rand pie to go around. Also, there could be the old prejudice of early twentieth-century America against Italians.

Sally at a point had to admit her mother might be onto something. Later she would admit, "He wouldn't go to work at all. I guess he thought it was beneath the husband of Sally Rand. No amount of ranting and raving would help. I guess he thought his best work was done in the bed."[31]

Sean Rand's take on Fred was nicer than his mother's. "He was nice to me. He actually saved my life one time when the car door flew open and he reached out and grabbed my leg while I was flying out the door . . ."[32] It was during these turbulent years Sally Rand was held up in Baltimore in 1957 in her dressing room for $524. The "barefoot negro" struck her in the nose and fled.

In 1964 Sally wrote to Fred and blamed him for the way her life had ended up. "I earned the right to not be alone. You and you alone took it from me, stole it, exactly as if you had taken money from my purse. You stole my time, the only time I had left. You stole my love, that I can give to no one else, my money, that I can never earn again, and the pleasure of my child, who needed me and whom I needed. . . . I could never stay home and be with him because of you."[33]

The boxer would go on to marry three more times. It would be the last for Sally Rand. Lalla was her last stab at the domesticity she had fantasized about all her life. She had talked about hanging up the fans and settling down into the tranquility of hearth and home many times. If there was a midlife crisis for Sally Rand, it was probably here. The young man whom she could still snare even though she was now nearing her mid-fifties. Later she would sum up her longest marriage, to Fred Lalla. "He was wonderful in bed, but I couldn't get him to do anything else. Like work."[34] Sally Rand had leveraged her name for money and for sex. It just didn't have enough equity for family.

CHAPTER TWENTY-FOUR

Cultural Icon

1957–1965

JOHN KENNEDY HAD COMMITTED THE UNITED STATES TO GOING TO the moon before the Russians. The race was on, and this led to the sleepy town of Houston becoming ground zero for the space race, or Space City. The new astronauts had been lauded and trained and taken all over the country. They were America's new Knights in Shining Armor, and in the year 1962 the space race had taken on dire consequences. *Sputnik* had been launched the year before by the Russians, essentially opening another frontier in the nuclear cold war. America had yet to catch up to the Russians in satellite technology, and so the gauntlet had been thrown down to put a man on the moon by the end of the decade.

Tom Wolfe would capture this race in his book *The Right Stuff*, which would be made into a movie. The fact Sally Rand would be asked to dance at this kickoff of America's new Mission Control in Houston and inaugurate the space pioneers is amazing and speaks to the longevity of Sally Rand's cultural appeal. This is up there with speaking to Harvard and shows the neat designations of a fan dancer who happened to stumble into being famous simply do not fit.

Sally Rand in her sixties still embodied hope. Hope that something better lay in the future. Why else would the powers that be ask Sally Rand to dance on the world stage for astronauts, government officials, the vice president, the cultural elite of the country? There is a flight component that goes back to Sally Rand's original concept of her dance. The

Dying Swan. Flight. It is about fighting against the darkness and taking flight. But the planners must have seen a component of hope for the future that the people related to in the Great Depression.

Sally Rand would confound the designation of just another stripper time and time again by a culture that recognized her as something much more. The advent of television would also deem her a cultural icon with the most popular game shows on television, *To Tell the Truth* and *The Dating Game.*

In 1957, she would appear on *To Tell the Truth*, which is based on four celebrities guessing which of three contestants is telling the truth about his or her identity. The celebrities ask the contestants various questions about their past with the moderator keeping track of the questions. In Sally Rand's show they all claimed to be Helen Beck. The fact Sally Rand was requested to be on this show speaks volumes on her longevity and her place as an enduring part of American culture. The show only works if the audience knows and *recognizes the celebrity* in question. In 1957 the producers of *To Tell the Truth* deemed Sally Rand as still culturally significant to be on a show that was broadcast to millions of people. When this show is watched we see a woman who speaks in quiet voice, so quiet we can barely hear her. It is amazing that quiet voice was behind the long reign of Sally Rand.

The show is grainy. One camera swings from the emcee to the panel that includes Carl Reiner and Kitty Carlisle. Television is still just getting rolling. Geritol is more prominent than the emcee or the panel. The three women who claim to be Helen Beck are all in their late fifties. They all have blond hair and are in dark blue dresses. The questions from the panelist are about Sally's days working for Cecil B. DeMille. No one can really answer the question about what movies were made with DeMille. Number 2 says *Bolero*. Number 3 is asked where the movies were made. She replies, unsteadily, DeMille Studios. She really doesn't have much of a clue.

Number 3 is interesting. She can barely speak. She is almost afraid to speak. Her voice is thin, weak, delicate. The other women have much more confidence. But the panelists all guess correctly that number 3 is Sally Rand. She stands up and everyone applauds and then she smiles, and we see a glimmer of something else. It is amazing this demure woman has been making a living dancing nude behind fan dances for twenty-four years. But she has. Was it from trying to conceal her lisp behind a put-on patrician accent? There is fear in her voice when she speaks. This is what destroyed her movie career. She fades in front of the camera. She falls away. The silent movies were her medium. She does have an expressive face. But the voice is that of a child.

The panel is impressed, at least they seem to be. Carl Reiner claims to have seen her perform. Kitty Carlisle applauds her effort to return to college after fan dancing. This is a fiction but good copy for television. *To Tell the Truth* specializes in taking American icons, legends, and pawning them off as somebody else. The panelists stare at Sally Rand with the respect of a younger generation for an older, yet some of the panelists are in their fifties as well. She has become part of lore, of legend, a nostalgia trip into the wild world of the Chicago World's Fair in 1933. She is not someone who is a stripper, rather she is a cultural totem pole. One of the other panelists identifies herself as an old burlesque dancer. *To Tell the Truth* contestants must reach the television audience as recognizable icons, stars, leaders. The television executives who make these choices cannot have someone the audience does not know. This is the wow factor. The moment when Sally Rand stands up, Mom and Dad must have that moment, *so that's Sally Rand, the famous feather dancer.* In short, to be on *To Tell the Truth* in 1957, you still must be recognizable, you still must be a star. No small feat for a five-foot woman who danced in a World's Fair twenty-four years before.

The show is tight, and Sally Rand is not allowed to say anything about her life. You can almost hear the panelists and the audience yearning to ask her questions. What had she done since the World's Fair? What was it like to dance nude behind ostrich feathers for all those years? What was America like during the Great Depression when you performed? Did you really act in silent movies with Cecil B. DeMille? A star. A star. The life of a star. Helen Beck smiles, holding her hands together. She could tell them about the life of a star.

But now America was going to the moon, and Houston had been chosen as the Command Center for the new Apollo program. Houston was just an oil town in Texas until the government dropped sixty million

dollars and proclaimed Houston would be Space City for the new program President Kennedy had created by throwing down the gauntlet to
reach the moon before the end of the decade. And now Houston Control
was throwing the biggest Texas-size party it could manage with four tons
of barbecue and gallons of whiskey to welcome the seven new astronauts
to their new home. There was an even a Mercury Six capsule behind all
those convertibles with waving astronauts.

Houston was putting on the dog, America was heading for the moon.
Houston would never be the same. To welcome the seven astronauts and
hundreds of NASA employees, there was a morning parade through
downtown, with the fresh-off-the-plane astronauts and their families
waving to the sweaty thousands on the sidewalks. The parade wound its
way to the Sam Houston Coliseum for the main event. A nineteen-year-
old Elsie Wilmouth, just named Miss Houston, welcomed the astronauts
after they each received a hundred-dollar LBJ Texas hat. Then Gene
Barry of the television show *Bat Masterson* spoke and did a short performance, and then, around two in the afternoon as the lights dropped,
a band picked up, and a spotlight centered on two giant ostrich feathers,
and a sixty-year-old Sally Rand began to dance.

Tom Wolfe in the book *The Right Stuff* would describe the dance this
way: Rand, he wrote, "winked and minced about and took off a little here
and covered a little there and shook her ancient haunches at the seven
single combat warriors. It was quite electrifying. It was quite beyond sex,
show business . . . the Venus de Houston shook her fanny in an utterly
baffling blessing over it all."[1]

So, the astronauts watched the woman from the Ozarks perform to
"Clair de Lune." They were to take America to the moon. This was the
center of the world. America had to beat the Russians to the moon and
man had to extend his footprint to the cosmos. And to welcome the
astronauts to the world of space travel was a hillbilly from the Ozarks
who thirty-one years before had crashed a World's Fair party. Or to put
it another way, a fan dancer from the 1933 Chicago World's Fair had
been called to usher in the future for the entire country in 1964 and
had landed one more time in the center of the national spotlight. Sally
Rand held the stadium of astronauts, dignitaries, and citizens of Houston

transfixed the same way she had thirty years before in the worst year of the Great Depression.

In 1983 the movie *The Right Stuff* would immortalize this scene with a twenty-something actress playing Sally Rand. It would be the emotional payoff where the astronauts watched the beautiful young woman floating though the darkness like a young swan. In this moment, the astronauts were connected to something bigger, something beyond space travel. This was no stripper. This was even beyond sex. Sally Rand embodied an eye to the future. She embodied leaving the earth. She had embedded herself in American culture and now Americans were going to another planet. She had shown Depression-era people thirty years before what a poor girl from Missouri could do and pointed the way to the future. And now, dancing in the silence of the Sam Houston Coliseum for the world, she was doing it again.

In both cases, it was nothing short of amazing. The reality was the sixty-year-old Sally Rand had been living out of hotels and trailers for thirty years and was chronically broke, in debt, chain-smoking, and getting over the rough patches any way she could. It was a strange intersection of sex, technology, dreams, legend, hubris, and human frailty. Only Sally Rand could pull that off.

Chapter Twenty-Five

Jail

1964

SALLY RAND USED THE LAW FOR HER BENEFIT. HER ARRESTS AT THE World's Fair only increased her notoriety. It was part of her publicity machine. The arrests were not dramatic. In a *Chicago Tribune* photo, Sally is being walked to court by a detective in a straw hat. Sally looks beautiful and unconcerned, but the photo would do its job and that night more people would come to see her fan dance at the World's Fair. This became standard in the Chicago years. An arrest would put her in the hands of a matron who would get her before a judge. The judge saw a beautiful young woman who described her dance as art and said no one could see anything because it was all behind her feathers. A light fine was sometimes issued, and she would return that night to the fair and give the exact same performance.

It was all in good fun, and the judges and the police did not mind the publicity of arresting a star like Sally Rand. Sometimes the arrests would veer into comedy. In 1946 while performing at the Savoy Club in in San Francisco, she was arrested by six police officers who took her down to a judge who gave her immunity if she was arrested for the same offense during the trial period. She was arrested again wearing long underwear and a sign, CENSORED S.F.P.D. The judge had enough and went to view the show himself and emerged, saying that "anyone who could find something lewd about the dance as she puts it on has to have a perverted idea of morals."[1] He cleared Sally Rand of all charges.

But things did not always turn out this way. Sometimes the law turned against Sally Rand, who played a cat-and-mouse game with the lawyers, judges, and small businesses pursuing her for money. Her best defense was to leave for another venue. This was at a time when mail moved slowly and catching up to a fan dancer on the move across the country was tricky. But on two occasions Sally Rand's luck ran out and she ended up in jail. In Milwaukee in July of 1949, Sally was arrested with her husband/manager Harry Finkelstein after performing at a local fair. This arrest followed a pattern of all her arrests for fan dancing. The difference here was there was no friendly judge and she was jailed briefly.

The second arrest that put her in jail didn't follow any script at all and was more sad than comical. She was now sixty years old and it was 1964. She was scheduled to dance at the Colony Club in Gardena, California. It was Christmas Day and it was Sally Rand's opening night. It is depressing enough that she had to dance on Christmas Day in a strip club at age sixty. Even though the club was "a showcase for Burlesque Greats" it was still a watered-down strip club featuring a woman dancing behind ostrich feathers. Two officers approached the owner with a warrant for Sally Rand's arrest. She was no longer the young woman being arrested for showing off her beautiful body. She was the older woman being arrested for failing to appear in court over a debt proceeding. Sally had shrugged off court appearances for years and rarely did they ever result in a warrant. Many warrants were threatened but few ever came to see the light of day.

But now on Christmas in a smoke-filled club there were two policemen waiting to arrest a sixty-year-old woman who was still taking off her clothes in nightclubs. It did have a pathetic tang. Gone was the payoff of publicity, the push that allowed Sally Rand to make even more money as newspapers showed the young beauty escorted by smirking detectives. The club's owner begged to allow her to perform before they arrested her. The two cops waited until after the midnight show and then arrested Sally Rand for failure to appear.

Photographers had a field day as they snapped pictures of an older woman, drawn and downcast. "Oh Feathers"[2] was one of the captions. Sally Rand was booked and then she was sent to jail. So now she is behind bars. The woman who had danced for astronauts and become a star in 1933 and remained in the cultural stream for three decades was now in a jail cell for nonpayment of debt and a failure to appear in court for that debt. The truth was people didn't really care that Sally Rand had gone to jail in 1964. It is amazing the local papers covered her; she was no longer big news.

If there was a failure for Sally Rand, she must have confronted it now. She had become a star in the United States and had a healthy run of thirty years. But she had never risen financially above being a hustling fan dancer who could never afford not to dance. The grind of her existence was that she never could get to the next phase, and sitting in a jail cell in Gardena, California, on Christmas night at age sixty was the hard proof that for all her success she was broke, and worse, she was alone. Sally Rand had paid a high price for fame and she was still paying it. The one thing doing Sally Rand in at the end was simply age. No amount of illusion could bring her away from the fact she was incarcerated with no one to lean on but herself. Jail, was finally, jail.

Sally would later say she only spent twenty-three minutes in jail after paying a bondsman fifty-five dollars to get out. Twenty-three minutes or an hour, the result was the same. Sally Rand liked to bend facts, and the truth is she had to get the money and probably had to borrow it for the bondsman. In 1965 Sally was arrested one final time for dancing in the nude in Omaha, Nebraska. She and the nightclub owner, George Earl, were taken to the police by patrolman Vern Presher, who "testified that he saw Mrs. Rand withdraw the feather fans that shielded her unclad figure. He timed the nude for six minutes. 'She went beyond the bounds of propriety.'"[3]

Sally and the nightclub owner posted a three-hundred-dollar bond, and she could finish her run at the club. A month later she had to return to Omaha to defend herself on the charge, which was "removal of clothing on the property of another person."[4] The judge ordered the law rewritten when he realized anyone taking a shower would be liable. Sally had brought a yellowed wrinkled clipping with her from the 1946 trial in San Francisco with the judge's comment, "anyone seeing anything lewd or base in her act, had a perverted mind."[5] Sally Rand opened up at least one judge's mind on sexuality in Omaha, Nebraska. Really, she had been doing that for thirty years.

CHAPTER TWENTY-SIX

This Was Burlesque

1965

STARS BECOME TRAPPED. GEORGE REEVES COULD NEVER BREAK FREE OF his role as Superman, and some blamed his suicide on his inability to ever get free of his television persona. The public makes an association with a person and it never goes away. Many television actors have this problem where a series permanently types them into a single role. Sally Rand had a similar problem. The public saw her as Sally Rand the fan dancer, and over the years she continually tried to shed the ostrich feathers and become an actress in Hollywood or even a public speaker. But nothing paid the bills except for fan dancing, and she always had to return. She had one more chance in the 1960s to become someone other than Sally Rand the feather dancer.

Show business eventually becomes a caricature of itself. The times move on. In 1965 the Beatle invasion was at its peak, Americans were dying in Vietnam, and television dominated the landscape with situation comedies like *Batman, Gilligan's Island,* and *Green Acres.* College students were protesting America's involvement in Vietnam while growing their hair, burning their draft cards, and getting stoned. Sally Rand belonged to an era that had simply disappeared. Burlesque was dead and strip clubs had given way largely to adult films. But there was a niche in the new culture, and burlesque star Ann Corio had found it. She came up with a retro show called *This Was Burlesque.*

Sally could have taken a few cues from Ann Corio. Her story, while different, had similar veins. Born in 1909 in Hartford, Connecticut, she snuck away at age fifteen and began performing as a chorus girl in burlesque shows. She had managed to carve a career out from the burlesque days that went all the way into the 1980s. It didn't hurt that she was gorgeous and had a figure that put her in *Yank Magazine* during World War II as one of the pinup girls. While Sally was still in Hollywood, Corio was playing at Minsky's Burlesque in Manhattan and stayed on the burlesque circuit until it was closed by the mayor of New York City in 1939. During this time, she played with up-and-coming comics Abbott and Costello and Burt Lahr.

She then went to Hollywood, where she was recognized for her body and cast in *Swamp Woman, Jungle Siren, Call of the Jungle*, and *Sarong Girl*. Always in a scanty costume, Corio put forth her biggest asset, her body. The low budget films were poorly reviewed. Always a dancer, she went back to New York City and performed consistently on the stage as an actress all through the 1950s, doing summer stock theaters. Then with a young producer, she put together a self-produced off-Broadway show, *This Was Burlesque*. It became a sexy cult hit in New York City's East Village in 1962 and would run on and off Broadway for thirty years. It was a nostalgia show with sex packaged in that television would pick up on and a small startup Home Box Office would record several times to broadcast. It was loaded with lots of women dancing in practically nothing with Corio directing and performing. She then wrote a book, *This Was Burlesque*, in 1968 and released two albums, *How to Strip for Your Husband*. In a way she was out Sally Randing Sally Rand with her savvy business instinct. But Ann Corio had something Sally lacked, and that was real talent as an actress who could pull off serious roles and understood timing, comedy, and the importance of the dramatic moment.

Corio was covering all the bases in a way that would have made Sally Rand envious. She had made the leap away from just a burlesque performer years ago and morphed into a Broadway dancer, performer, director, producer, and then finally an author. Sally Rand could never clear her fan dances, try as she might. Every time she tried something else, she had to return to the circuit for money. Corio would go on Johnny

Carson several times in the 1970s and kept *This Was Burlesque* alive in summer stock productions.

But there was a moment when Sally Rand saw an opportunity to leave her fans behind permanently. In 1965 *This Was Burlesque* was still running in New York City. It was a successful show that Corio was headlining along with directing and producing. Then she was hospitalized and required surgery. Someone had to step in and replace the Burlesque Queen. Sally heard about her predicament and called her home and offered to step in. Corio accepted her offer, and Sally stood in for the Queen of Burlesque in the show. The problem was really the same one Sally had with the movies and even her small part on *To Tell the Truth*. She really wasn't a burlesque dancer. She had never really done the circuit. Since *This Was Burlesque* actually is *This Is Burlesque* and all that the name implies, it was a genre in which Sally was not experienced. She did not have the time to learn the "talking woman" parts of the many sketches of the show.

Sally Rand did not have verbal acuity. She simply could not project, and this is largely what kept her from becoming a successful actress or for that matter a performer much beyond doing her feather dance. Sally stayed with the show for four weeks, but then Corio returned. By now Sally Rand liked it. She was performing on Broadway in a successful show. She had elevated herself beyond the fairgrounds, gymnasiums, bowling alleys that had become her bread and butter. The sweaty grind of the road, the hotel rooms, the stress of putting on her own show was gone. She was in a production and she hoped to remain, proposing to Ann Corio she become a permanent part of the show.

Hard to know what Ann Corio thought of Sally Rand. In a way Sally Rand was her own show. She was *Sally Rand*. But Corio was the star of her world. She had written, directed, and produced a successful Broadway show and in this way, she was a step up from Sally Rand. Corio wore the laurels of a real hit apart from herself that was not dependent on her getting onto the stage. Sally still had to stoke up some cigarettes, drink some coffee, and pick up her feathers that each year became heavier and heavier. Of course, Sally Rand wanted to stay with her show. Sally was already in her sixties and Corio was in her mid-fifties but had not suffered the grueling life on the road.

Ann Corio declined Sally's offer and continued on with *This Was Burlesque*, which would run longer than *Chorus Line*. Sally Rand picked up her feathers and returned to the road that was her real home. Ann Corio would outlive Sally Rand by almost a quarter of a century and die one year short of the millennium.

CHAPTER TWENTY-SEVEN

Frozen Feathers

1965–1970

TEX AVERY LIKED TO MAKE IN-YOUR-FACE CARTOONS FOR ADULTS. WE know them as Looney Tunes. In the Warner Brothers cartoon *Hollywood Steps Out*, Sally Rand is a bubble dancer. She would not allow her name to be used, so she became Sally Strand. In the cartoon produced in 1941 is James Cagney, Humphrey Bogart, Clark Gable, Bing Crosby, Jimmy Stewart, Bette Davis, Paulette Goddard, Edward G. Robinson, Kate Smith, and Greta Garbo to name a few. Hollywood royalty. And one *Sally Strand*, though a hatcheck girl says *Sally Rand*. Avery's cartoon is straight Looney Tunes, which is an over-the-top short film in a Hollywood night-club where Sally Strand is the star attraction with her bubble until Harpo Marx pops it with a slingshot and she is revealed wearing a barrel.

The cultural markers of the 1940s were in Tex Avery cartoons. These shorts were played before movies and audiences needed instant recognition for the sight gags to work and for people to understand Tex Avery's spoofs that abounded in his work. The fact that Sally Rand is included in this cartoon that has Hollywood royalty speaks volumes as to where she fell in the cultural history of the United States in the middle years of the twentieth century. She is introduced by Bing Crosby while everyone sits around and watches her do her bubble dance. She has star billing in a cartoon of stars.

This was not some throwaway cartoon. Tex Avery was at the peak of his career when he made *Hollywood Steps Out*, and he was taking on just about every movie star of his time. Yet Sally Rand is in the center, and the American audience who watched it in the 1940s, 1950s, 1960s, and beyond recognized the stars, and they recognized Sally Rand. It is dead center in the golden age of animation and stands as a testament to a time when cartoons spoke to adults and made cultural statements and often lampooned politicians, movie stars, and public figures of the time.

By the time Sally Rand was in her sixties, the cartoon had been out for twenty years and was still being played on television. The world of burlesque had vanished long ago, television was dominating the culture, and Sally Rand had become historical in her own time. She would tour in the 1972 nostalgia revue *Big Show of 1928*. The cultural revolution of the 1960s put her in the same category as silent movies, the Three Stooges, and nostalgia revues. Essentially her act became a look back to a different time. It was during this time she gave a pair of her fans to the Chicago History Museum. The museum had turned down her feathers four decades before, but now they saw the historical value of Sally Rand and, by proxy, her fans. She had endured and the fans would be of value. They were put into a deep storage faculty underground and frozen. Those frozen feathers were supposedly from the Chicago World's Fair of 1933, but there is some doubt as she told her son later the fans were not the originals.

Sally's act was one of illusion, but age would have its due. When a reporter knocked on her dressing room door in the 1970s, "a little old lady in a neglected robe answered the door."[1] Something about sixty. A line was crossed for Sally Rand though she kept performing, driving herself, chain-smoking, never stopping. At sixty-two she was still a draw and wore miniskirts and Go-Go boots. She embraced the counterculture with its opening up of sex and drugs, and she might have seen it as a confirmation she had been on the right course with her arrests for indecency all those years. She had been at the vanguard of a more open approach to sexuality. While never overtly positioning herself as a women's rights advocate, Sally Rand by her actions had pried open the lid on women's sexuality.

In the 1960s, women burning their bras and embracing a more free and open approach to premarital sex was all territory Sally Rand had mined starting with her appearance at the 1933 World's Fair. She saw her arrests as good for publicity, but the truth is every time she was arrested for indecency with the attendant publicity it brought into the light the double standard America had for women regarding sex and broke down the wall just a little more.

Sally Rand wore white Go-Go boots and a miniskirt but probably did not smoke pot. At least there is no evidence. Her drugs of choice were designed to keep her performing. Coffee, cigarettes, maybe a few drinks to take off the edge. Besides, she was still working forty weeks a year and didn't have time for getting high. She was still able to bring them in. Her venues had changed though, as she played state fairs and bowling alleys.

The youth culture was something new. Sally Rand did embrace the loosening up of the straitjacket society had placed on sexuality, but the new party was exclusive. She overheard two women discussing her age at a performance. One woman guessed forty and the other guessed sixty. She was realistic enough to know that popular culture had left her and that she would take the work where she could get it. But her act depended more than ever on illusion.

Art is a sleight of hand ultimately, and Sally Rand's swishing fans now had more to hide despite body paint and body suit. The truth is there was still a sixty-two-year-old naked body behind the ostrich feathers, and the light had to be just right and her movements had to be dead on. The illusion was now walking a thin line between the chronology of age and the magic of suggestion. There was a certain reverence for Sally that kept her packing customers in. Her figure was praised for retaining its youthful measurement.

Most of the time it worked, but sometimes things just didn't go right. Sally was asked to dance at the Fan Ball in New York City at the Plaza Hotel. She spent five hundred dollars on some new fans, but things went badly from the start. The lighting, which was so important to the illusion of her performance, was bad. She was not wearing her body suit, and she had slowed down. The young girl of 1933 had a nubile body, but also the fans did move faster than the eye. Now the fans have slowed, and even though she had cut six minutes out of her routine, she was tired and the people sitting close to the stage were flashed with images of the real Sally Rand.

And there were paparazzi now.

The photographers assaulted her as she went through her routine. The press was always on her side before. Sally Rand enjoyed the deference given to stars by the media all through the 1930s, 1940s, and 1950s. But the 1960s were different. The market for the inside scoop or a salacious photograph had arrived, and at a moment when the youth culture was approaching its zenith with "don't trust anyone over thirty," Sally Rand had no protection against a sneering press who wanted to reveal the woman behind the fans.

The midnight ball had Mrs. Dwight D. Eisenhower among its luminaries. Sally Rand was performing in the center of the world when a photographer broke the illusion she had been perpetuating for thirty-five years. The resulting photograph taken from behind showed a naked sixty-two-year-old woman holding ostrich feathers in front of her. It was the antithesis of a generation that was coming of age shouting, "hope I die before I get old."

The photograph was sold off and reprinted in magazines and newspapers that would take the risk of showing nudity. The wrinkled buttocks and her sagging haunches spoke of time and circumstance. The enemy for Sally Rand had always been reality. The naked truth had been avoided when she left Hollywood and ended up in a strip club on State Street in Chicago. The truth was left further behind when she remade herself and became the Dying Swan for the masses struggling though the Great Depression. The truth was locked out as she ran through three husbands and adopted another stripper's illegitimate child. She frequently changed her age, had face-lifts, used tape, body leotards, makeup, wigs, lighting, fans, corsets, dance, anything to stay one step ahead of reality. Then she married a man twenty years younger to prove she still had it. If the fans moved fast enough, then even age could be outwitted and left behind as she moved on to another show.

But this time she could not get to the next show fast enough. The lights did not dim, and she could not vanish into a darkened stage. She should have worn the body paint, the leotard, the tape, the muslin, the adhesive. It is curious why she did not. Maybe she wanted to see if she could pull it off without resorting to covering up. Sally Rand always preferred to be nude. But this was a different age. Reality was hard to avoid. Television caught everything. People wanted to see how things really were. Trust was out the window. President Kennedy had been assassinated and no one took anything on face value. The photograph broke every illusion in the world and showed a woman dancing as fast as she could, hanging on as she had always done by her fingertips, while the world swirled away from her. A woman who was clearly now sixty-two years old, working the fans but, inevitably, slowing down.

CHAPTER TWENTY-EIGHT

The Seventies

THIRTY MILES WEST OF CHICAGO IS THE PHEASANT RUN PLAYHOUSE. It is a dinner theater where people eat and watch a performance. Sally Rand scored a play there called *Night Watch* with Jack Kelly in 1967. What is interesting is her teaming with child star Margaret O'Brien. Sally was sixty-three and O'Brien was thirty years old. Holly Knox in her book has an interview that is illuminating in its historical context.

> *Sally made her entrance at the restaurant.*
>   *"I remember you at the World's Fair," said one of the photographers.*
>   *Sally beamed and then cooed, patting her costar's knee.*
>   *"Baby here wasn't born yet."*
>   *Margaret smiled her tremulous smile.*
>   *Sally went on, "I'm 63 and proud of it."*
>   *She went on to reminisce about her career from the carnival and Cecil B. DeMille to gardening, bookkeeping, stage lighting and "famous people we met."*
>   *"I was once asked to read the Gettysburg Address before General Marshall, General Eisenhower and Admiral Nimitz," said Margaret.*
>   *"I knew General Pershing," said Sally.*
>   *"I met President Truman and I once got spanked for sliding down the bannisters at the White House when Franklin Roosevelt was there," said Margaret.*
>   *"I once fell asleep on Theodore Roosevelt's lap," said Sally.*[1]

We never think we are going to get old. Especially those who are gifted with health and stamina who make their very living with a body that seems to be ageless. Sally Rand floating around in Lake Michigan in the night in 1933, staring at the glittering skyline of the city she had conquered, never could conceive of a day when she would have to be careful with lighting just to make sure she was not revealed.

She is living alone in Glendora. This is the seventies and she is in her seventies. She can still wow her son by taking him to a ball game and introducing him to Casey Stengel . . . one legend introducing another legend. She becomes a grandmother and continues dancing, anywhere. Gymnasiums, senior citizen homes, bars. She takes classes at a local college, gardens. She continues dancing, quipping, "what in heaven's name is strange about a grandmother dancing nude?"[2]

Sally Rand does not know this in 1933. She cannot imagine it and it is not part of who she is. She is an illusion. She lives in the memories of people who have lived in the American Century and she is part of that history. The girl in the darkness of Lake Michigan, waiting to be rescued, is us. People in 1933 were waiting to be rescued from the darkness of a Great Depression and there was this girl, this creature dancing in the darkness with ostrich feathers. This poor girl from the Ozarks who had the guts to ride into a World's Fair and become famous. She was of her time, but what is amazing is that she became part of American culture and stayed there through half of a century.

No one knows what makes anyone relevant. It is almost undefinable. But Sally Rand should have vanished after the fair in Chicago closed. She should have been an interesting footnote to The Century of Progress, but that did not happen. She remained relevant, and what's more she became a star in her own right. A cultural meteor that appeared in twenty movies, cartoons, television, danced for astronauts and then became a legend that to this day is hard for people to put their finger on as to why they even know her name.

Toward the end of her life, Sally Rand gave an interview. "I wish I'd lived a profound life, been able to produce great and wonderful things to advance the state of man. But I haven't. Not many people's lives are very profound. And perhaps those whose lives we look upon as profound don't realize it themselves."[3]

Sally Rand has faded from modern memory. She is historical. But the girl from the Ozarks who ran away with the circus and then starred in silent movies and then lost it all and remade herself in the worst times in history and emerged world famous is very much in the Horatio Alger pantheon promised by America. Rags to riches. Rags to riches. It is the central tenet of America. It is the amazing zircon of American life that people can remake themselves and climb out of obscurity and become rich, become famous. The early twentieth century provided something new. A bright light that young people could run to. "The transformation of popular culture cleared the path for Rand's journey from rags to riches. Juxtaposing precision with grace, concealing with revealing, sexual allure with controlled distance, her disguised nudity and mastery of illusion made Rand's performances the top attraction of the Midway and one of the major revenue draws . . . Rand felt herself transformed into 'a femme fatale, a coquette, a Cleopatra, as soon as she picked up the ostrich fans.'"[4]

It is the light of something more. Something beyond a middle-class existence. This modern beacon has produced stars from Judy Garland to Sally Rand. The girl next door transformed into America's girl. That was the component that took Sally Rand out of the pantheon of just another burlesque star, just another stripper. She was not a Faith Bacon. She had stumbled into something much larger, and she became that alter ego that allows people to reflect themselves onto.

Sally Rand said once that Isadora Duncan was one of her inspirations. It is an interesting thought. "Both women choreographed their own routines to classical music, both introduced unique dance forms, and both inspired imitators." But where one appealed to an intelligentsia in Europe the other was of the common people in America. "Time, popular culture, and the nation's economic circumstances carried the two into different social circles . . . Duncan had performed in revealing tunics that exposed her limbs, a provocative style that pioneered dance as a modern art form. Her socialite audiences defined Duncan's style as art."[5]

Sally Rand came out of the hardscrabble backwoods of the Ozarks and came into the light during the worst economic times in the history of the United States.

"She drew her following from working-class and middle-class pleasure seekers . . . Rand symbolized American consumption-based sex and spectacle as well as a nation stripped of its protective garments."[6]

What is lost on most people is that Sally Rand was a modern businesswoman and self-promoter and while constantly in debt she made amazing money at a time when there was very little money to go around. "An astute businesswoman, workaholic, and perfectionist, Rand performed up to sixteen shows a day. She did her own bookkeeping, and though represented by the William Morris Agency, she negotiated many of her own contracts."[7] She worked long hours and sent money to her mother and other relatives for her entire life. Much of her life was lived out of trailers and hotel rooms where she made her own clothes and cooked her own meals. In this way she mirrors the American resourcefulness of the farmer American, the rural individual who ultimately knows they only have themselves to depend on. Sally Rand, even after three husbands and many relationships, never once depended on anyone but herself for income.

For the man out of the work in 1933 who took his last nickel and went into the darkness and "Clair de Lune" starts to play, Sally Rand was a goddess. Out of the darkness comes this beautiful creature and she dances with wings. She dances like a beautiful swan and something about it brings tears to his eyes. This hillbilly from the Ozarks has taken a moment and transformed it into something ethereal. And for those ten minutes the man has forgotten all his troubles. The Great Depression suddenly has disappeared. And he is no longer hungry. He is no longer of this earth. And when it ends, he is a little sad, but the world is not quite as dark. He hunches up his coat against the cold and heads out into the night. He will remember her name . . . Sally Rand.

Sally Rand's last performance was in her hometown of Glendora. It was on a Saturday, March 17, 1977, that she was to dance at a pageant with her feathers. At age seventy-three, she had been gardening more, and the event at the Glendora Women's Club was unique in that Sally Rand was not having to travel anywhere to make a buck. By all accounts she was just barely hanging on financially. She had been dancing for forty-four years, using the same dance she had come up with as a twenty-nine-year-old. It was amazing, but people were still paying to see Sally Rand dance. She was in debt and had no retirement of course, but she kept dancing. She took courses at community colleges and could still cuss a blue streak. Her mother, Annette, had died in 1970, and she was now for all practical purposes alone except for her son and her grandchild.

Sally kept a heart attack in 1977 to herself and kept going. The truth was that for Sally Rand when she danced, it was 1933 again and no time had passed. But the years, and the cigarettes, took their toll, and the Dying Swan was finally dying. Asthma and acute congestive heart failure would keep her from dying at home.

On August 31, 1979, the girl from the Ozarks who ran way with the circus to Hollywood and then became an unlikely symbol of hope during the Great Depression from a fan dance at the 1933 Chicago World's Fair, and who would remain a culture icon up to her death, died. Her name was Sally Rand.

An unpaid medical bill from the hospital was paid by a mysterious source. It was later revealed Sammy David Jr. paid the ten-thousand-dollar debt, remembering a star who had given him a hand up when he was a young performer trying to make it. This time, Sally Rand left no bill behind.

CHAPTER TWENTY-NINE

The Legacy of Sally Rand

SALLY RAND SHOT ACROSS THE BOW OF THE AMERICAN CENTURY, heaving from the roaring Prohibition-era 1920s into the Depression-yoked 1930s and beyond like a comet proclaiming that times will get better and that grit, determination, and unbridled optimism will see us through. She is a Horatio Alger story of rags to riches. It is simply confounding that a woman who was not great in any known field of the arts should grab the culture and be propelled along with movie stars, sports figures, and politicians and have the same name recognition of her time.

I have given speeches on the World's Fair of 1933, and when I flash a picture of a naked young girl kicking a rubberized ball up, I ask one question: Who is this? And in that darkened room someone in the audience will inevitably cry out, Sally Rand! Eighty-seven years after she danced at the World's Fair of 1933, people still know her name.

It was a really a matter of luck and the perfect act for the perfect time. As Cheryl Ganz points out in *Chicago and the 1933 World's Fair*, "By the 1930s young women experienced new levels of freedom, including sexual expression. Commercialized sex had become part of the public urban culture during the century's early decades."[1] But to say Sally Rand was a stripper who became famous for dancing behind ostrich feathers at the Chicago World's Fair would be to ignore the arc of her life that belongs to that phenomenon of the early twentieth century whereby anyone had the chance to become a star if only they could dream hard enough, work hard enough, and catch a break.

Sally Rand became that American girl of pluck and audacity we associate with a certain type of flapper F. Scott Fitzgerald embodied in his fiction but drained of its urban shimmer for a more working-class version of that female Horatio Alger. She did come from nothing. She was uneducated. She was fundamentally working class. And that is more American than Gatsby's Manhattan-based dream girl. For the American Century was one of building up the country, and this was done with brute strength and with a thriving working class that shined with the qualities of the farm girl gone to the city to find her dream.

She was a hillbilly from the Ozarks born in the echo of the nineteenth century in 1904. She would sit in Teddy Roosevelt's lap and run away with the circus. Sally Rand did dream of becoming famous in her hardscrabble existence in the early years of the century. She belongs to that American arc of history that produced the Bogarts, the Judy Garlands, the Cecil B. DeMilles. She is the slag left over from the forging of Hollywood and star creators such as DeMille, and then she was pushed out to become something apart from the B actresses whom we do not know now. She became the name on her tombstone. There is "Helen Beck" across the top. And then in quotes, "SALLY RAND." The name shouts out a brighter day even in death. The truth is she did become a symbol of hope. "Sally Rand's outrageous behavior made a statement about Depression-era Chicago and A Century of Progress. In fact, Rand became the fair's enduring icon for optimism and hope, a true Horatio Alger, rags to riches figure."[2]

DeMille's moniker, given to Helen Beck on a whim when he sees an atlas in his office, stuck, and more than that it created a persona bigger than life and one that could ride along the American wave from optimism to the Great Depression to War to the changing times that would engulf the country in the later part of the century. The contradictions are there. Rich. Poor. Hillbilly. Speaker at Harvard. Actress. Stripper. Feather dancer. Pilot. Stuntwoman. Trapeze artist. Businesswoman. Debt. Bankruptcy. Foreclosure. Jail. Divorce. A child not hers. Suits upon suits. Beauty, yet covered in body paint, corseted, blond yet stubby dark hair. A ranch but she lived out of hotels her whole life. Chain-smoker. Dancing until she is in her seventies.

A Warner Brothers cartoon immortalizes her as she enters the cultural zeitgeist only to be found years later dancing in unknown bars in Illinois. Appearing on *To Tell the Truth* and then dancing for the Apollo astronauts in Houston. Arrested for biting her manager. Arrested for obscenity four times in one day. Arrested so many times the judge comes to see her show. Living out of a trailer, working the carney circuit. Starring in Hollywood movies. Sleeping in alleys, cars, fields. Known to millions of her time and beyond . . . obscure to the current generation.

But Sally Rand changed America's attitude about sex. She did not start out to do this. Sally Rand wanted to be a movie star, and when that didn't happen, she simply wanted to be famous. But from that drive for American fame she stumbled into the Great Depression and a moment in time and inadvertently changed our ideas on sexuality. Her legacy is with us every time we go to a movie.

"The debate over Sally Rand, the fair's risqué Midway shows, and public nudity influenced later Hollywood production codes. In December 1933, the winter after Rand made the fan dance a sensation, Will H. Hays issued a set of twelve bans for film publicity. Number four illustrated the power of Rand's influence. 'Thou shalt not photograph the so-called fan dance type of photograph in which delicate parts of the anatomy are covered by fans, feathers, lace or other types of scanty or peek-a-boo material.' The next year when Rand danced her fan dance in the film *Bolero*, the Production Code Administration informed Paramount that they needed to eliminate views of dancers wiggling their posteriors at the audience."[3]

The Hays office would have great sway for years to come, and Sally Rand had pushed sex into the open to the point where she was singled out by the very office that would be the final arbiter of morality movies in America. Sally Rand was fundamentally an uneducated working-class woman, and it is amazing she pushed along the concept of an independent sexually liberated woman thirty years before the women's liberation movement would assert itself in the 1960s.

The enlightenment that had produced the flapper was a middle-class bourgeois phenomenon, but working-class women did not enjoy the spoils of that opening up around sex. The media singled Sally Rand out as a symbol of hope during the Great Depression and as the first modern sex symbol of the twentieth century. She had an artist's temperament that with "her experience in circus performance, Hollywood film acting, stage theatre work, and burlesque theatrics culminated in her ability to produce a dance that created a fantasy, both sexual and artistic. She brought credibility to burlesque dancing by taking it into the public arena and presenting it with pride and a level of perfection that made it into an art."[4]

Yet Sally Rand at her peak would make up to four thousand dollars a week in Depression-era dollars. She got fan letters by the thousands. Men proposed to her, propositioned her. Gangsters threatened her. She had seen it all, and yet this girl from the Ozarks must have realized, too, it could all vanish tomorrow. She had seen it before. She was on her way in Hollywood and then it had blown away like the dry sand on the backlots where she did stunts for unknown directors.

The Great Depression had dragged on for four years. In 1933 the world was six years away from a Second World War. The Wright Brothers had flown thirty years before, and Lindbergh had crossed the Atlantic in 1925. In 1932 Adolf Hitler had become the chancellor of Germany, and eight years after the 1933 World's Fair the Japanese would bomb Pearl Harbor and plunge the United States into the biggest conflagration the world had ever seen. Movies now had sound and radio was still king. Only 10 percent of the population in Chicago owned a car. Against this backdrop Sally Rand had broken through the noise of popular culture and come to stand for something more than she was, and this would only happen to a few through the luck of timing, opportunity, pluck, grit, tenacity, and then something peculiarly American that is almost indefinable, perhaps as F. Scott Fitzgerald so eloquently summed up this quality . . . it was simply a willingness of the heart.

This is why to define Sally Rand as a burlesque dancer or a stripper is wrong. Sally Rand, by treating her dance as art, and by pushing her way into the biggest event of her time, produced a flickering dance of hope in very dark times. She became a major media star who became a cultural icon of the twentieth century in America. Dancing for the astronauts, appearing on *To Tell the Truth*, having a Warner's Brothers cartoon and twenty movies along with nonstop media coverage in newspapers and radio clearly established Sally Rand as an agent of social change.

In other words, Sally Rand, while being a symbol of hope and held up as an American sex symbol, also pushed the independent notion that a woman's body was her own to use as she wanted to make a living. "By publicly displaying her body she demonstrated a sense of privileged mobility with a sense of danger but in a safe and self-controlled environment."[5] People could enter another world in the darkness of a theater, men and women, and be transported to something higher by a woman using her body as a tool of art. In this way, Sally Rand was a cultural phenomenon and a pioneer.

So now it is 1933 again. A young scantily clad woman from the Ozarks is riding through the night on a white horse on the opening night of the Chicago World's Fair. It is the worst year of the Great Depression, and she is riding toward the bright lights in the darkest of times with nothing but a cape, a wig, a wing, and a prayer. She is riding toward her destiny, looking for salvation. Just like us.

CHAPTER THIRTY

American Sex Symbol

WE CAN'T CONSIDER SALLY RAND AS AN AMERICAN SEX SYMBOL without considering Mae West. She was older than Sally Rand by twenty
years, born in 1883. She never used feathers or crashed a World's Fair.
Mae West began her career at age seven by winning talent shows and
then entering vaudeville at age fourteen. She debuted on Broadway at
age fourteen and was immediately noticed by a reviewer for the *New
York Times*. She wrote sexually provocative plays under the pen name Jane
Mast and acted with Al Jolson in *A Winsome Widow*. She directed and
produced a play called *Sex* and went to jail for violating moral laws and
served eight days though she could have paid a fine. Like Sally Rand, she
was no fool on what publicity could bring her.

While Sally Rand hacked it out in silent movies, Mae West stayed
in New York City, producing homosexual comedies like *The Drag*,
which ultimately would be suppressed. West then wrote and produced
The Wicked Age, *Pleasure Man*, and *The Constant Sinner*. They were sexy,
provocative, and kept her in the news. Packed houses were not uncom-
mon. *The Jazz Singer* came out, and Sally Rand got her walking papers
and ended up in Chicago at the Paramount Club in a desperate fan dance
to get a job. Mae West was over fifty and headed for Hollywood in 1932.
She made *Night After Night* and took a small role, rewrote her scenes,
and became Mae West, specializing in the double entendre that would
make her famous.

In the year 1933, Sally Rand crashed the World's Fair and became
famous overnight for riding a white horse into the opening ceremonies

with very little on. Mae West starred in *She Done Him Wrong* using her by now trademark shimmy and boosting the unknown actor Cary Grant to stardom. The film was a smash and, like Sally Rand, made Mae West a star and in the process saved Paramount films from bankruptcy. The studio would repay West with plum roles. She and Grant did it again in *I'm No Angel*, which was another smash. F. Scott Fitzgerald, who would later come to Hollywood to assist in rewriting the script of *Gone with the Wind*, would say of West, she had both an ironic edge and comedic timing.

She and Sally Rand were now both in the headlines. The World's Fair would run for two years and keep cranking out copy, keeping the feather dancer top of mind and associating her forever with Chicago's biggest fair since 1893. Mae West would star in *Goin' to Town* and *Klondike Annie*, offending William Randolph Hearst with a flippant comment about his mistress Marion Davies. The newspaper baron tried to suppress the movie and Mae West. Sally Rand returned to Hollywood and flamed out quickly, heading for the road then.

Mae West stayed in Hollywood, teaming up with W. C. Fields after *Go West Young Man* and *Every Day's a Holiday* in 1939. She and Fields would do three films, *My Little Chickadee, You Can't Cheat an Honest Man*, and *The Bank Dick*. Her reign in Hollywood ended when censors finally caught up with her and she wasn't allowed to rewrite her lines, finishing out with *The Heat's On* and *All About Eve*.

In 1943 West played swank clubs, theaters, and radio. An offer to play Norma Desmond in *Sunset Boulevard* came her way and she turned it down. Sally Rand was on the carnival circuit, giving speeches where she could, gathering publicity for just about anything she did. Getting arrested for not paying her debts and getting in censorship battles with churches. Both women would test the boundaries of sexual mores of their time, and both women would suffer from the clamping down on perceived indecency in the 1940s and 1950s. NBC would eventually ban Mae West from their studios for turning a line on its head in a skit, "Adam and Eve in the Garden of Eden." Her radio career ended.

In 1958 West would appear on the Academy Awards on television while Sally Rand appeared on *To Tell the Truth*. Sally Rand talked about writing a memoir; Mae West published her biography, *Goodness Had Nothing to Do with It*, in 1959. She would guest star on *The Dean Martin Show* and *Red Skelton* and make a guest appearance on *Mister Ed* in 1964. Sally Rand would dance for the Apollo astronauts in 1964 at the Sam Houston Coliseum.

Through the 1970s Mae West appeared in films with Tom Selleck, was interviewed by Dick Cavett, and released a book, *Sex, Health and ESP*. She was wealthy after investing for years in real estate. Sally Rand was still doing her fan dance in bars, senior citizen homes, and shopping malls. Sally Rand died in 1979 from congestive heart failure. Mae West got out of her bed in 1980 and fell. She had a stroke, and three months later she died on November 22.

These two women both grew up with the twentieth-century entertainment industry and both pushed the boundaries of sex as far as they could. We cannot consider Sally Rand as a modern American sex symbol without Mae West. But the road diverges early on. Mae West had real talent that allowed her to become a Hollywood star. Her stature soared with her over-the-top sexpot character of a late 1890s madam complete with the swaying hips and bawdy wordplay. Mae West exported that character as a symbol of American sex, and her clever lines, her ability to rewrite dialogue on the fly, her strong literary talent that allowed her to write and produce plays about sex at a very early age put her squarely in the realm of the professional in the entertainment business. She was a heavyweight in this arena, and it made her wealthy and created an enduring fame that gave her work up to the end. Sally Rand could not claim any of this.

Sally Rand did not have an overwhelming talent. She did not have the ability to deliver in lightning speed a line that would upend a whole movie. She did not have the kind of dramatic talent that Mae West instinctively used since she was a little girl. Sally Rand was created by forces beyond her control. Sally Rand was created by the Great Depression. She was thrown up to the world as the girl next door who had nothing really and had made something out of nothing. She was an American sex symbol because America identified with her even when others disapproved. Her career was one of a singular phenomenon pushed on by a little girl's ambition to be a ballerina, to fly like a swan, to be a star.

Mae West was a sex symbol but the fork in the road swerves away at that point. She was anointed by an industry that churned out sex symbols like cereal boxes. Sally Rand was anointed by a country of blue-collar workers, of common people who could identify with her struggles and see something beyond the feather dance, an aspiration for something better when there was nothing better. The hillbilly from the Ozarks becoming a star against all odds is simply more of an American story than the hip-swinging, wisecracking madam with W. C. Fields tapping his cigar in the background.

One is a manufactured sex symbol and the other, the other is the struggle under a carnival tent in sawdust and heat. It is fitting that Sally Rand finished out in gymnasiums and senior citizens homes while Mae West finished out on Dick Cavett. A proletarian American sex symbol is one with the twentieth century where the working class built the country up and had its greatest glory and went through the hardest of times. Out of those very hard times, there emerged a few stars, a few pins of light that shone brightly during the 1930s and then receded as our memory of those hard times faded. Sally Rand is of that America. She will forever be that young girl from the Ozarks riding a white horse into the opening night of the Chicago World's Fair and crashing the party of the upper crust. The more fortunate. That distrust of the rich is very American. We immediately side with the five-foot blond thumbing her nose against all the forces against her. And we revel in her triumph.

The image of Sally Rand on YouTube or in the grainy movies of Hollywood does not do her justice. We are not sitting in the darkness, transported from our Depression-era troubles while a young girl dances her concept of *The Dying Swan*, lifting off from the earth and then slowly dying.

Epilogue

SALLY RAND STILL INFORMS CULTURE TODAY. IN THE YEAR 2020, I WAS asked to give a speech on my book *Al Capone and the 1933 World's Fair*. It was at a church filled with senior citizens. When I arrived, the woman who hired me asked if I would do her a favor and, in my PowerPoint slide show, skip over the pictures of Sally Rand and her fan dance. She smiled tightly. "We don't want to shock anyone." I assured her the pictures were of Sally with her large rubberized ball and there was no real nudity. But yes, I would skip over the pictures.

In fact, there was nudity, Sally was kicking her ball up with one foot, her body a white nude perfectly formed. So, during the presentation, I flashed up the slide of Sally Rand and was about to click my pointer, when I paused. And instead of going on, I stayed on that sepia slide and there was Sally Rand, all of twenty-nine, kicking up her giant rubberized sphere at the Chicago World's Fair, looking as naked as the day she was born.

I lingered for a few seconds in the darkness while she kicked her giant ball up one more time in 1933. I knew then I wouldn't be coming back, so I shouted out into the darkness.

"Who's this?"

And sure enough, like a thousand times before, a voice came out of the darkness.

"Sally Rand!"

Acknowledgments

Many thanks to the Chicago History Museum for tolerating the man who rooted through sixty-one boxes of the Sally Rand Papers for days on end. And more thanks to John Russick, the curator of the museum, for taking me down into the walk-in freezer in the basement of the museum to see Sally Rand's fans from 1933. One is afforded so few glimpses of those who lived before, and for that, I am grateful. Thanks to the good folks at Lyons Press and Rowman and Littlefield and my agent Leticia Gomez for finding another home for one of my books. And of course to my family for enduring.

Notes

PROLOGUE
1. Hazelgrove, William. *Al Capone and the 1933 World's Fair* (Lanham, MD: Rowman and Littlefield, 2017), ix.
2. Papers of Sally Rand. Chicago History Museum, *Chicago Daily News*, August 16, 1933.
3. Ganz, Cheryl. *The 1933 World's Fair: A Century of Progress* (Champaign: University of Illinois Press, 2012), 13.
4. Ibid.
5. Ibid.
6. Ibid.
7. Ibid., 1
8. Hazelgrove, *Al Capone and the 1933 World's Fair*, ix.

CHAPTER 1
1. Hazelgrove, William. *Al Capone and the 1933 World's Fair* (Lanham, MD: Rowman and Littlefield, 2017), 135.
2. Terkel, Studs. *Hard Times: An Oral History of the Great Depression* (New York: Pantheon Books, 1970), 437.
3. Ganz, Cheryl. *The 1933 World's Fair: A Century of Progress* (Champaign: University of Illinois Press, 2012), 9.
4. Ibid., 11.
5. Hazelgrove, *Al Capone and the 1933 World's Fair*, 205.

CHAPTER 2
1. Terkel, Studs. *Hard Times: An Oral History of the Great Depression* (New York: Pantheon Books, 1970), 437.
2. *Frontiers, A Journal of Women Studies* (Pullman: Washington State University Press, 1978), 35.

3. Haskell, Arnold Lionel. *Balletomania: An Updated Version of the Ballet Classic* (New York: New York Performing Arts, 1979), 112.

4. Balanchine, George, and Francis Mason. *Balanchine's Festival of Ballet* (London: W. H. Allen, 1978), 194.

5. Terkel, *Hard Times*, 437.

6. Papers of Sally Rand. Chicago History Museum, Box 25, Letter from William Beck to Mrs. Rosa Steward.

7. Ibid., Box 19, As told to Lloyd Shearer.

8. Ibid., Box 8, William Beck letter to his daughter.

9. Ibid., Box 8, William Beck letter to his daughter.

10. Ibid.

11. Ibid.

12. Ibid., Box 25, Partial of a book.

13. Ibid., Box 51, Partial of a book.

14. Ibid., Box 39, Newspaper article unspecified.

15. Knox, Holly. *Sally Rand: From Film to Fans* (Bend, OR: Maverick Publications, 1988), 4.

16. Ibid.

17. Ibid.

18. Zemeckis, Leslie. *Feuding Fan Dancers* (Berkley, CA: Counterpoint Press, 2018), 24.

19. Ibid.

CHAPTER 3

1. Papers of Sally Rand. Chicago History Museum, Box 10, Newspaper article, undated.

2. Zemeckis, Leslie. *Behind the Burly Q* (New York: Skyhorse Publishing, 2013), 32.

3. Ibid.

4. Zemeckis, Leslie. *Feuding Fan Dancers* (Berkley, CA: Counterpoint Press, 2018), 33.

5. Ibid., 36.

6. Ibid., 37.

7. Ibid., 36.

CHAPTER 4

1. Albritton, Laura. *Hidden History of the Florida Keys* (Charleston, SC: History Press, 2018), 105.

2. Papers of Sally Rand. Chicago History Museum, Box 30, *Los Angeles Times* article.

3. Papers of Sally Rand. Chicago History Museum, Box 15, Letter to a friend.

4. Knox, Holly. *Sally Rand: From Film to Fans* (Bend, OR: Maverick Publications, 1988), 10.

5. Knox, *Sally Rand: From Film to Fans*, 10.

6. Papers of Sally Rand. Chicago History Museum, Box 41, *Chicago Tribune* interview, 1939.

7. Ibid., Box 20, Unknown newspaper interview.

8. Zemeckis, Leslie. *Feuding Fan Dancers* (Berkley, CA: Counterpoint Press, 2018), 60.
9. Ibid., 54.
10. Papers of Sally Rand. Chicago History Museum, Box 44, Interview with Hal Wells.
11. Ibid., Box 23, *Chicago Daily News* interview.
12. Ibid., Box 11, Sally Rand letter to her mother.
13. Ibid., Box 12, Sally Rand letter to a friend.
14. Ibid., Box 13. Letter from Carl Schalet.
15. Ibid.
16. Ibid.
17. Ibid., Box 26, Sally Rand letter to her mother.

CHAPTER 5

1. Papers of Sally Rand. Chicago History Museum, Box 15, Letter from Sally Rand's father.
2. Lowe, Jim. *Barefoot to the Chin* (Tallahassee, FL: Sentry Press, 2018), 98.
3. Papers of Sally Rand. Chicago History Museum, Box 19, Article by Dan Campbell.
4. Zemeckis, Leslie. *Feuding Fan Dancers* (Berkley, CA: Counterpoint Press, 2018), 58.
5. Gloria Swanson in *Sunset Boulevard*, screenplay by Charles Brackett and Billy Wilder.
6. Roberts, Jerry. *The Complete History of Film Criticism* (Santa Monica: Santa Monica Press, 2010), 40.
7. Sherwood, Robert. *Life Magazine* article, 1927.
8. Zemeckis, *Feuding Fan Dancers*, 68.
9. Ibid.
10. Papers of Sally Rand. Chicago History Museum, Box 24, Letter from boyfriend to Sally Rand.
11. Ibid., Box 41, Letter from Sally Rand's mother.
12. Zemeckis, *Feuding Fan Dancers*, 88.
13. Papers of Sally Rand. Chicago History Museum, Box 22, Sally Rand letter to her mother.
14. Ibid., Box 36, Interview with Sally Rand.

CHAPTER 6

1. *New Republic*, New York City, 1931.
2. *New York Times*, September 6, 1932.
3. Ibid., xi.
4. Zemeckis, Leslie. *Feuding Fan Dancers* (Berkley, CA: Counterpoint Press, 2018), 115.
5. Ganz, Cheryl. *The 1933 Chicago World's Fair: A Century of Progress* (Champaign: University of Illinois Press, 2012), 14.
6. Ibid.
7. Ibid., 69.
8. Knox, Sally. *Sally Rand: From Film to Fans* (Bend, OR: Maverick Publications, 1988), 20.

9. Ibid., 21.

10. Ibid.

11. Ibid.

12. Ibid., 22

13. Ibid.

14. Lowe, Jim. *Barefoot to the Chin* (Tallahassee, FL: Sentry Press, 2018), 182.

15. Ibid., 183.

16. Papers of Sally Rand. Chicago History Museum, Box 30, Undated letter.

17. Hazelgrove, William. *Al Capone and the 1933 World's Fair* (Lanham, MD: Rowman and Littlefield, 2017), 71.

18. Ibid., 72

CHAPTER 7

1. Knox, Holly. *Sally Rand: From Film to Fans* (Bend, OR: Maverick Publications, 1985), 35.

2. Ibid.

3. Ibid.

4. Ibid.

5. Ibid., 37.

6. Zemeckis, Leslie. *Behind the Burly Q* (New York: Skyhorse Publishing, 2013), xxii.

7. Ibid., xxiii.

8. Terkel, Studs. *Hard Times: An Oral History of the Great Depression* (New York: Pantheon Books, 1970), 16.

CHAPTER 8

1. Ganz, Cheryl. *The 1933 Chicago World's Fair: A Century of Progress* (Champaign: University of Illinois Press, 2012), 4.

2. Ibid., 1.

3. Brookhouser, Frank. *Our Philadelphia: A Candid and Colorful Portrait of a Great City* (New York: Doubleday, 1957), 117.

CHAPTER 9

1. Terkel, Studs. *Hard Times: An Oral History of the Great Depression* (New York: Pantheon Books, 1970), 171.

2. Papers of Sally Rand. Chicago History Museum, Box 29, Article quote by Benjamin Marshall.

3. Knox, Holly. *Sally Rand: From Fans to Film* (Bend, OR: Maverick, 1988), 23.

4. Terkel, *Hard Times*, 172.

5. Ganz, Cheryl. *The 1933 Chicago World's Fair* (Champaign: University of Illinois Press, 2012), 10.

6. Papers of Sally Rand. Chicago History Museum, Box 45, *Chicago Tribune* article.

7. Ibid.

8. Terkel, *Hard Times*, 172.

9. Ibid.
10. Ganz, *The 1933 Chicago World's Fair*, 10.
11. Terkel, *Hard Times*, 173.
12. Papers of Sally Rand. Chicago History Museum, Box 49, *Chicago Tribune* article.
13. Terkel, *Hard Times*, 173.
14. Papers of Sally Rand. Chicago History Museum, Box 45, *Chicago Tribune* article.
15. Ibid., Box 32, Letter from Sally Rand's father.
16. Shteir, Rachel. *Striptease: The Untold History of the Girlie Show* (Oxford: Oxford University Press, 2004), 150.
17. Zemeckis, Leslie. *Feuding Fan Dancers* (Berkley, CA: Counterpoint Press, 2018), 117.
18. Ibid.
19. Papers of Sally Rand. Chicago History Museum, Box 11, *Chicago Tribune* article.
20. Zemeckis, *Feuding Fan Dancers*, 132.
21. Ibid.
22. Papers of Sally Rand. Chicago History Museum, Box 25, Letter from policewoman.

CHAPTER 10

1. Ganz, Cheryl. *The 1933 Chicago World's Fair: A Century of Progress* (Champaign: University of Illinois Press, 2012), 18.
2. Ibid.
3. Papers of Sally Rand. Chicago History Museum, Box 23, Article by Edgar Hay.
4. Ibid.
5. Knox, Holly. *Sally Rand: From Film to Fans* (Bend, OR: Maverick Publications, 1988), 30.
6. Papers of Sally Rand. Chicago History Museum, Box 23, Article by Edgar Hay.

CHAPTER 11

1. Ganz, Cheryl. *The 1933 Chicago World's Fair: A Century of Progress* (Champaign: University of Illinois Press, 2012), 19.
2. Ibid., 20.
3. Ibid.
4. Ibid., 21.
5. Ibid.
6. Hazelgrove, William. *Al Capone and the 1933 World's Fair* (Lanham, MD: Rowman and Littlefield, 2017), 214.
7. Ganz, *The 1933 Chicago World's Fair: A Century of Progress*, 23
8. Hazelgrove, *Al Capone and the 1933 World's Fair*, 214.
9. Ganz, *The 1933 Chicago World's Fair: A Century of Progress*, 23.
10. Ibid.
11. Ibid., 24.
12. Ibid.
13. Ibid., 27.

14. Papers of Sally Rand. Chicago History Museum, Box 32, Interview with George Burns.

CHAPTER 12

1. Papers of Sally Rand. Chicago History Museum, Box 38, Interview with Sally Rand.
2. Ibid.
3. Ibid., Box 37, *Chicago Tribune* article.
4. Ibid., Box 38, Telegram.
5. Ganz, Cheryl. *The 1933 Chicago World's Fair: A Century of Progress* (Champaign: University of Illinois Press, 2012), 25.
6. Zemeckis, Leslie. *Feuding Fan Dancers* (Berkley, CA: Counterpoint Press, 2018), 148.
7. Ibid.
8. Ganz, *The 1933 Chicago World's Fair: A Century of Progress*, 26.
9. Ibid.
10. Ibid.
11. Papers of Sally Rand. Chicago History Museum, Box 52, *Chicago Tribune* article.
12. Ibid.
13. Ibid.
14. Ganz, *The 1933 Chicago World's Fair: A Century of Progress*, 8.
15. Papers of Sally Rand. Chicago History Museum, Box 24, *Chicago Tribune* article.
16. Ibid.

CHAPTER 13

1. Zemeckis, Leslie. *Feuding Fan Dancers* (Berkley, CA: Counterpoint Press, 2018), 95.
2. Ibid.
3. Ibid.
4. Ibid., 98.
5. Papers of Sally Rand. Chicago History Museum, Box 26, *Chicago Tribune* article.
6. Ibid.

CHAPTER 14

1. Zemeckis, Leslie. *Feuding Fan Dancers* (Berkley, CA: Counterpoint Press, 2018), 181.
2. Papers of Sally Rand. Chicago History Museum, Box 42, Newspaper article.
3. Ibid., Box 42, *Chicago Tribune* article.
4. Zemeckis, *Feuding Fan Dancers*, 142.

CHAPTER 16

1. Papers of Sally Rand. Chicago History Museum, Box 10, Letter from Sally's father.
2. Ibid.
3. Ibid., Box 11, Letter from fellow dancer to Sally's mother.

4. Ibid.

5. Ibid., Box 12, Boston newspaper article.

6. Ibid., Boston newspaper article.

7. Ibid., Box 14, Letter from William Morris Agency.

8. Ibid.

9. Ibid.

10. Ibid., Letter from Sally Rand to her agent.

11. Ibid., Letter from William Morris.

12. Ibid., Letter from Sally Rand to her agent.

13. Ibid., Box 28, Letter to theater manager from Sally Rand.

14. Ibid., Box 30, Letter to Sally Rand's mother.

15. Zemeckis, Leslie. *Feuding Fan Dancers* (Berkley, CA: Counterpoint Press, 2018), 164.

16. Papers of Sally Rand. Chicago History Museum, Box 41, Interview with Earl Wilson.

17. Ibid., Box 42, Letter to a friend.

18. Ibid., Sally Rand letter to her mother

CHAPTER 17

1. Papers of Sally Rand. Chicago History Museum, Box 17, *Chicago Tribune* article.

2. Ibid., Box 18, Letter from a lawyer to Sally Rand.

3. Ibid.

4. Ibid., Box 35, Newspaper article.

5. Ibid., Box 32, Letter from Sally Rand's father.

6. Ibid.

7. Ibid., Box 40, Interview with Karl Malden.

8. Ibid.

9. Ibid., Box 41, Sally Rand letter to her mother.

CHAPTER 18

1. Papers of Sally Rand. Chicago History Museum, Box 18, Letter to Thurkel's parents.

2. Ibid.

3. Ibid., Box 15, Letter from Sally Rand to Turk's sister.

4. Ibid., Box 15, Letter from Sally Rand to her mother.

5. Ibid.

6. Ibid., Box 19, Letter from Sally Rand to Turk.

7. Knox, Holly. *Sally Rand: From Film to Fans* (Bend, OR: Maverick Publications), 61.

8. Papers of Sally Rand. Chicago History Museum, Box 10, Sally Rand letter to a friend.

9. Ibid., Box 10, Newspaper article.

10. Ibid., Box 14, Letter to her mother.

11. Ibid.

12. Ibid., Box 36, *Chicago Tribune* article.
13. Ibid., Box 39, Court proceedings.

CHAPTER 19

1. Papers of Sally Rand. Chicago History Museum, Box 42, Letter from Sally Rand accountant.
2. Ibid.
3. Ibid., Box 42, Letter from attorney.
4. Ibid., Letter from small business.
5. Ibid., Letter from attorney.
6. Ibid., Box 45, Newspaper article.
7. Ibid.
8. Ibid.
9. Ibid., Box 51, Letter from Sally Rand attorney.
10. Ibid.
11. Ibid., Box 52, Newspaper article.
12. Ibid.
13. Ibid., Box 53, Newspaper article by Sally Rand.

CHAPTER 20

1. Papers of Sally Rand. Chicago History Museum, Box 50, Letter to Sally Rand.
2. Ibid., *Billboard Magazine*
3. Ibid., Box 51, Letter to state fair from Sally Rand.
4. Ibid., Box 51, *Daily Mail* article.
5. Ibid.
6. Ibid.
7. Ibid.
8. Ibid., Box 54, Article on Sally's adopted baby.
9. Ibid.
10. Ibid., Box 56, Letter from Sally Rand to her lawyer.
11. Ibid.
12. Ibid., Letter from Sally Rand attorney.
13. Ibid.
14. Ibid.
15. Ibid.
16. Ibid., Box 58, Letter from Sally Rand dancer.
17. Ibid., Box 58, Letter from Sally Rand to a friend.
18. Ibid., Box 10, Prescription from doctor.
19. Ibid.
20. Ibid., Babysitting service flyer.
21. Ibid., Box 9, Poem by Sally Rand.
22. Knox, Holly. *Sally Rand: From Film to Fans* (Bend, OR: Maverick Publications), 69.
23. Ibid.

24. Ibid., 66.
25. Ibid., 67.
26. Papers of Sally Rand. Chicago History Museum, Box 29, Newspaper article.
27. Ibid.
28. Ibid., Box 35, Letter from Sally Rand to Harry Finkelstein.
29. Ibid.
30. Ibid., Letter from Harry Finkelstein to Sally Rand.
31. Ibid., Letter from Sally Rand to Harry Finkelstein.
32. Ibid.
33. Ibid.
34. Ibid.
35. Ibid.
36. Ibid.
37. Ibid.
38. Ibid.
39. Ibid., Harry Finkelstein letter to Sally Rand.
40. Ibid., Box 32, Letter from Sally Rand attorney.
41. Ibid., Box 32, Letter from Sally Rand attorney.
42. Ibid.
43. Ibid., Box 40, Divorce proceedings.
44. Ibid., Box 41, Letter from Sally Rand to a friend.
45. Ibid.
46. Ibid., Box 42, Sally Rand letter to herself.
47. Ibid., Box 10, Letter from William Beck.
48. Ibid.
49. Ibid.
50. Ibid., Box 11, Letter from William Beck to his son.
51. Ibid., Box 12, Letter from Sally Rand's mother.
52. Ibid., Letter from William Beck to Sally.
53. Ibid.
54. Ibid.
55. Ibid., Box 22, Letter from admirer.
56. Ibid., Box 23, Letter from Sally to Sean.
57. Ibid., Box 24, Childcraft pamphlet.
58. Ibid., Box 25, *Chicago Tribune* article.

CHAPTER 21

1. Papers of Sally Rand. Chicago History Museum, Newspaper article.
2. Ibid.
3. Ibid., Article from Oklahoma newspaper.
4. Ibid., Box 28, Newspaper article.
5. Ibid., Box 28, Letter from governor's office.
6. Ibid.
7. Ibid.

8. Ibid., Box 31, Sally Rand letter to a friend.
9. Ibid., Box 32, Lawsuit, State of Kansas.
10. Ibid., Box 32, Newspaper article.
11. Ibid.
12. Ibid., Box 32, Letter to Liquor Board.
13. Ibid.
14. Ibid., Box 32, Newspaper article.
15. Ibid., Box 32, Complaint against Sally Rand.
16. Ibid., Box 32, Kansas City newspaper article.
17. Ibid.
18. Ibid.
19. Ibid.
20. Ibid.
21. Ibid.
22. Knox, Holly. *Sally Rand: From Film to Fans* (Bend, OR: Maverick Publications), 83.
23. Ibid., 84.
24. Ibid.
25. Ibid.
26. Ibid., 85.
27. Ibid.
28. Ibid., Box 39, Pamphlet from Church of Christian Science.
29. Knox, *Sally Rand: From Film to Fans*, 85.
30. Ibid.
31. Papers of Sally Rand. Chicago History Museum, Box 24, Newspaper article.
32. Ibid.
33. Ibid., Box 32, Letter to Sally Rand accountant.
34. Knox, *Sally Rand: From Film to Fans*, 86.
35. Ibid., 87.
36. Ibid.
37. Ibid.
38. Ibid.
39. Ibid.
40. Ibid., 91.
41. Ibid.
42. Ibid., 94.
43. Ibid.
44. Ibid., 76.
45. Ibid., 75.
46. Ibid.
47. Ibid.
48. Ibid., 77.
49. Ibid., 78.
50. Papers of Sally Rand Box 25 Letter from father
51. Papers of Sally Rand Box 25 Letter from mother

Chapter 22

1. Papers of Sally Rand. Chicago History Museum, Box 32, Dallas newspaper article.
2. Ibid.
3. Ibid., Box 23, Letter from Sally Rand accountant.
4. Ibid.
5. Ibid.
6. Ibid.
7. Ibid., Box 29, Deposition from accident.
8. Ibid.
9. Ibid., Box 44, International news service.
10. Ibid., Box 45, Sally Rand letter to IRS.
11. Ibid.
12. Ibid., Box 43, Letter from Sally Rand accountant.
13. Ibid.
14. Ibid., Box 44, New York City newspaper article on movie about Sally Rand.
15. Ibid., Box 45, Newspaper article on Sally Rand wealth.
16. Ibid., Box 46, Bank letter demanding payment.
17. Ibid., Letter demanding payment for storage locker.
18. Ibid., Letter from friend demanding payment.
19. Ibid., Box 47, Letter demanding tax payment.
20. Ibid., Letter from lawyer demanding payment.
21. Ibid., Small business demanding payment.
22. Ibid., Box 48, Letter demanding payment.
23. Ibid.
24. Ibid., AFL letter demanding payment.

Chapter 23

1. Papers of Sally Rand. Chicago History Museum, Box 38, Sally Rand letter to friend.
2. Ibid.
3. Ibid.
4. Ibid., Box 40, Article in LA paper.
5. Ibid., Letter to Fred Lalla from Sally Rand.
6. Ibid., Box 41, Letter from Sally Rand to Fred's parents.
7. Ibid., Newspaper article.
8. Ibid.
9. Ibid., Letter from Fred Lalla to his parents.
10. Ibid., Sally to Fred Lalla's parents.
11. Ibid.
12. Ibid., Box 42, Letter from Lalla to Sally.
13. Ibid.
14. Ibid.
15. Knox, Holly. *Sally Rand: From Film to Fans* (Bend, OR: Maverick Publications), 99.
16. Ibid., Box 45, Newspaper article on writing a book.

17. Ibid.
18. Ibid.
19. Ibid.
20. Ibid.
21. Ibid.
22. Ibid., Box 25, *Chicago Tribune* article.
23. Ibid.
24. Ibid., Box 30, Letter from Sally Rand to Fred Lalla.
25. Ibid., Letter from Sally to a friend.
26. Ibid., Box 34, Sally Rand letter to herself.
27. Ibid., Diary of Fred Lalla.
28. Ibid., Box 45, Interview with Sean Rand.
29. Ibid., Box 46, Affidavit, Fred Lalla divorce.
30. Ibid.
31. Ibid., Box 39, Letter to Sally's mother.
32. Ibid., Box 40, Letter.
33. Ibid., Box 41, Letter from Sally Rand to Fred Lalla.
34. Ibid., Letter to friend from Sally Rand.

CHAPTER 24
1. Wolfe, Tom. *The Right Stuff* (New York: Farrar Straus, 2008), 287.

CHAPTER 25
1. Papers of Sally Rand. Chicago History Museum, Box 20, Newspaper article.
2. Ibid., Box 21, Newspaper article.
3. Ibid., Box 22, Newspaper article.
4. Ibid.
5. Ibid.

CHAPTER 27
1. Papers of Sally Rand. Chicago History Museum, Box 29, Newspaper article.

CHAPTER 28
1. Knox, Holly. *Sally Rand: From Film to Fans* (Bend, OR: Maverick Publications), 120.
2. Zemeckis, Leslie. *Feuding Fan Dancers* (Berkley, CA: Counterpoint Press, 2018), 262.
3. Papers of Sally Rand. Chicago History Museum, Box 56, Newspaper interview.
4. Ganz, Cheryl. *The 1933 Chicago World's Fair: A Century of Progress* (Champaign: University of Illinois Press, 2012), 17.
5. Ibid., 18.
6. Ibid.
7. Ibid., 17.

CHAPTER 29

1. Ibid., 14.
2. Ibid., 11.
3. Ganz, Cheryl. *The 1933 Chicago World's Fair: A Century of Progress* (Champaign: University of Illinois Press, 2012), 26.
4. Ibid.
5. Ibid.

Selected Bibliography

Allman, Barbara, and Shelly O. Haas. *Dance of the Swan: A Story about Anna Pavlova.* Minneapolis, MN: Carolrhoda Books, 2001.

Bergreen, Laurence. *Capone: The Man and the Era.* New York: Simon and Schuster, 1994.

Carlton, Donna. *Looking for Little Egypt.* Bloomington, IN: IDD Books, 1995.

Charyn, Jerome. *Gangsters and Gold Diggers: Old New York, the Jazz Age, and the Birth of Broadway.* New York: Avalon Publishing Group, 2003.

Cotter, Bill. *Chicago's 1933–34 World's Fair: A Century of Progress.* Charleston, SC: Arcadia Publishing, 2015.

Davis, Lee. *Scandals and Follies: The Rise and Fall of the Great Broadway Revue.* New York: Limelight Editions, 2000.

Earle, Marcelle, and Arthur Homme. *Midnight Frolic: A Ziegfeld Girl's True Story.* Twin Oaks Pub. Co., 1999. Fruitcover, FL: Twin Oaks Publishing Company, 1999.

Flemmons, Jerry. *Amon: The Texan Who Played Cowboy for America.* Lubbock: Texas Tech University Press, 1998.

Ganz, Cheryl R. *The 1933 World's Fair: A Century of Progress.* Champaign: University of Illinois Press, 2008.

Hazelgrove, William Elliott. *Al Capone and the 1933 World's Fair. The End of the Gangster Era in Chicago.* Lanham, MD: Rowman and Littlefield, 2017.

Hoefling, Larry J. *Nils Thor Granlund: Show Business Entrepreneur and America's First Radio Star.* Jefferson, NC: McFarland and Company, Inc., 2010.

Husum, F. *Chicago and World's Fair, 1933.* Chicago: Husum F. Publishing Company Inc., 1933.

Jones, Jan. *Billy Rose Presents: Casa Manana.* Fort Worth: Texas Christian University Press, 1999.

Kenney, William Howland. *Chicago Jazz: A Cultural History, 1904–1930.* New York: Oxford University Press, 1993.

Knox, Holly. *Sally Rand: From Film to Fans.* Bend, OR: Maverick Publications, 1988.

Lowe, Jim. *Barefoot to the Chin.* Tallahassee, FL: Sentry Press, 2018.

McDougal, Dennis. *The Last Mogul: Lou Wasserman, MCA, and the Hidden History of Hollywood*. Boston: Da Capo Press, 2001.

Mordden, Ethan. *Ziegfeld: The Man Who Invented Show Business*. New York: St. Martin's Press, 2008.

Papers of Sally Rand. Chicago History Museum, Chicago.

Price, Ryan Lee. *Stories of Old Glendora*. Charleston, SC: History Press, 1912.

Ringley, Tom. *When the Whistle Blows: The Turk Greenough Story*. Greybull, WY: Pronghorn Press, 2008.

Rydell, Robert W. *World of Fairs: The Century-of-Progress Expositions*. Chicago: University of Chicago Press, 1993.

Sengstock, Charles A. *That Toddlin' Town: Chicago's White Dance Bands and Orchestras, 1900–1950*. Champaign: University of Illinois Press, 2004.

Shteir, Rachel. *Striptease: The Untold History of the Girlie Show*. Oxford: Oxford University Press, 2004.

Slide, Anthony. *Silent Players: A Biographical and Autobiographical Study of 100 Silent Film Actors and Actresses*. Lexington: University Press of Kentucky, 2002.

Sothern, Georgia. *Georgia: My Life in Burlesque*. New York: New American Library/Signet, 1972.

Stein, Sarah Abrevaya. *Plumes, Ostrich Feathers, Jews, and a Lost World of Global Commerce*. New Haven, CT: Yale University Press, 2010.

Stencell, A.W. *Girl Show: Into the Canvas of Bump and Grind*. Toronto: ECW Press, 1999.

Terkel, Studs. *Hard Times: An Oral History of the Great Depression*. New York: Pantheon Books, 1970.

Vogel, Michelle. *Olive Thomas: The Life and Death of a Silent Film Beauty*. Jefferson, NC: McFarland and Company, Inc., 2007.

Walker, Stanley. *Mrs. Astor's Horse*. New York: Blue Ribbon Books, Inc., 1935.

Wood, Larry. *Wicked Women of Missouri*. Charleston, SC: History Press, 2016.

Zemeckis, Leslie. *Behind the Burly Q: The Story of Burlesque in America*. New York: Skyhorse Publishing, 2013.

Zemeckis, Leslie. *Feuding Fan Dancers: Faith Bacon, Sally Rand, and the Golden Age of the Showgirl*. Berkeley, CA: Counterpoint Press, 2018.

Ziegfeld, Richard. *The Ziegfeld Touch: The Life and Times of Florence Ziegfeld Jr.* New York: Harry N. Abrams, Inc., 1993.

Index